# A VERY MUTINOUS PEOPLE

# *A Very* Mutinous People

## The Struggle for North Carolina, 1660–1713

NOELEEN MCILVENNA

The University of

North Carolina Press

Chapel Hill

THIS BOOK WAS
PUBLISHED WITH THE
ASSISTANCE OF THE
THORNTON H. BROOKS
FUND OF THE
UNIVERSITY OF NORTH
CAROLINA PRESS.

Designed by Jacquline Johnson
Set in Garamond MT
by Keystone Typesetting, Inc.

The paper in this book meets the guidelines for
permanence and durability of the Committee on
Production Guidelines for Book Longevity of the
Council on Library Resources.

The University of North Carolina Press has been a
member of the Green Press Initiative since 2003.

Part of this book has been reprinted in revised form
from "Escape through the Great Dismal Swamp,"
*Tar Heel Junior Historian* 47, no. 1 (Fall 2007): 27–29,
© North Carolina Museum of History.

Library of Congress Cataloging-in-Publication Data
McIlvenna, Noeleen, 1963–
    A very mutinous people : the struggle for North
Carolina, 1660–1713 / Noeleen McIlvenna.
        p. cm.
    Includes bibliographical references and index.
    ISBN 978-0-8078-3286-8 (cloth: alk. paper)
    1. North Carolina—History—Colonial period, ca.
1600–1775. 2. North Carolina—Social conditions—
17th century. 3. North Carolina—Social
conditions—18th century. 4. Albemarle Sound
(N.C.)—History. 5. Farmers—North Carolina—
History. 6. Community life—North Carolina—
History. 7. Equality—North Carolina—History.
8. Landowners—North Carolina—History.
9. Anglicans—North Carolina—History. 10. Social
conflict—North Carolina—History. I. Title.
    F257.M39 2009
    975.6′102—dc22    2008047141

13 12 11 10 09   5 4 3 2 1

TO SEAN O'CONAILL

# CONTENTS

# ACKNOWLEDGMENTS

This book is dedicated to my first history teacher, Sean O'Conaill, at Loreto Convent High School in Coleraine, Northern Ireland. For three years, Mr. O'Conaill kept me enthralled with the story of the modern world from the Declaration of Independence to Sun Yat-sen. When I was an adolescent about to go off the rails, he pleaded with me to go to university. I owe him more than I can say.

My thanks go to many: to the librarians and archivists at Duke University, Guilford College, and the North Carolina State Archives in Raleigh; to Warren Billings for help locating an important document; to my writing groups at Duke (Deborah Breen, Dominique Bregent-Heald, Derek Chang, Ian Lekus, Chuck McKinney, and Gwenn Miller) and at Wright State University (Erin Flanagan, Lance Greene, Doug Lantry, Peggy Lindsey, and Sarah Twill); to the members of my dissertation committee (Lil Fenn, John Thompson, and Susan Thorne); to the Department of History at Wright State for a leave, allowing me to strip the manuscript down and rebuild; to Peter Wood, for his editing, guidance, and encouragement at moments when my faith was low; and to my readers at the University of North Carolina Press, Alan Gallay and Marjoleine Kars, for their detailed and invaluable critiques.

My parents, Maeve and Hugh, and my many siblings—Bernadette, Rory, Owen, Siobhan, Teresa, Brian, Stephen, Peter, Margot, Una, and Pearse—challenged me to make something of my life.

Tess distracted me, ensuring I enjoyed life through the long process that has culminated in this volume.

My single biggest debt is to Lance Greene, first for his hard work in guiding me through the agony of writing descriptive passages, preparing the maps, and formatting the manuscript for publication, tasks he completed with great generosity of time, energy, and expertise, and second for always being there.

A VERY MUTINOUS PEOPLE

# INTRODUCTION

"Wee will have noe Lords noe Landgraves noe Cassiques we renounce them all."[1] With these words, the earliest settlers of North Carolina declared their complete rejection of any social hierarchy in their colony: aristocrats not welcome. Settlers extended no deference to those who prided themselves on social superiority by means of either blood or land. Enveloped by colonies ruled by ambitious men intent on becoming America's peerage, North Carolina's colonists defected, voting with their feet for their own liberation. They set out to build and defend, with force if necessary, a society of equals. The only safe place to build such a utopian community was in the shadows of the British empire: a remote, swampy, hurricane-prone region where communication with the outside world meant a struggle through boggy terrain, where every household had to fend for itself, and where life did not lend itself to dreams of great prosperity. The settlers carved out an independent society on a dangerous coast with no luxuries save one: the opportunity to answer to no one but themselves. But after years laboring for others without pay, that opportunity felt like opulence.

The mainland colonies along the American Atlantic coast accommodated all kinds of experimental societies in the early seventeenth century: Puritans setting up godly communities in New England, tobacco plantations scattered along the rivers flowing into the Chesapeake, a cosmopolitan, international trade center at New Amsterdam. While most European immigrants came from countries with tightly delineated social classes, supposedly socialized in behaviors demanding deference to those ranked higher, the newcomers often stepped off the gangway and realized that no police system existed to make them conform. Opportunities abounded for those who sought alternatives. Fishermen and farmers desiring a respite from the suffocating administrations of their original colonies could sneak off to any backcountry area if they were willing to deal with Native Americans. Puritans might exile dissenters for questioning authority, but exile did not necessarily spell disaster. Roger Williams's establishment of the Rhode Island colony as a sanctuary for the most radical of those questioning religious authorities allowed further resistance to conformity.[2]

But not all who challenged the status quo confined their questions to matters of religion. While we can never know how many individuals abandoned the European colonies to live among the Indians, small groups set up self-governing communities in places such as Maine and later New Jersey. In Maine, fishermen chose not to replicate Massachusetts-type settlements, preferring more isolated farms, traveling by boat rather than building roads, always seeking to put distance between themselves and Bay Colony officials, who regarded Maine as "a refuge for vicious men."[3] The late seventeenth century saw even more resistance to established governments. After the 1660 Restoration of Charles II, the British captured New Amsterdam, renaming the area New York and New Jersey, proprietary colonies granted to Charles's brother, James, and his aristocratic loyalists. Small groups took advantage of the proprietors' inability to control their possessions and moved away from the center of power. These breakaway factions created politically autonomous communities, jealously—and successfully—guarding their sovereignty.[4]

Such political rather than religious dissent sprang from the English Revolution. In England, the 1649 beheading of King Charles I demystified power and brought in its wake a great deal more questioning of the legitimacy of political authorities. "Oliver's Days," Cromwell's republican regime, touched all those who lived through the period. The Roundheads removed heavy-handed church censorship, releasing a dizzying array of religious and political ideas. If a king could be questioned and found treacherous, then no legitimacy stemmed merely from custom and reverence. If a divine-right king could be decapitated, if the House of Lords could be dissolved, if the Anglican Church lost its position as the sole interpreter of God's word, then all authority lay open to reason. Even the pulpits no longer carried their traditional moral authority. The "Restoration" of another Charles, obviously the decision of the new head of the army, only reinforced the idea that power truly lay in the control of force, not in the mystic anointment of a man in a majestic coronation ritual. No one owed any "natural" deference because of bloodlines and social rank. As English people emigrated to the American mainland, these revolutionary ideas traveled, too.

The Restoration came to the colonies in the shape of the return of William Berkeley to the governorship of Virginia. Politically minded independents who had crossed the Atlantic from England during the Interregnum and now found themselves back under a royal regime refused to accept a life under his rules. Joined by misfits, social outcasts, religious dissidents, and others who disdained hierarchy, such independents flocked to the Great Dismal Swamp and the coastal region of North Carolina, the most inaccessible Atlantic coastline of North America. The colony operated officially as a Restoration colony, owned and supposedly managed by English proprietors. On the ground, however, small farmers who had come of age in a revolutionary era contemplated the possibilities for fulfilling those revolutionary ideals. These farmers sought to forge a society founded on the principle that all men should have a say, a place where none outranked another as a consequence of accident of birth, for they acknowledged "no difference between a Gentleman and a labourer."[5] When the proprietors granted free land in the region, known at the time as Albemarle, they inadvertently provided political possibilities in a hidden, remote area of the globe.

North Carolina's ideals remind us of the principles of 1776, but a century earlier, muddying the narrative of American history and the steady development of liberty. As we read our history books forward through time, the story of an ever broader franchise and an expansion of civil rights to ever more people conjures up a picture of a society on a road—not always a smooth road, certainly, but a road relentlessly progressing toward the fullest freedoms of the fullest number. Yet the road to democracy can twist and turn back on itself. Seventeenth-century settlers, rarely household names like their eighteenth-century counterparts, felt entitled to a government of the people, by the people, for the people. North Carolinians built such a politically free society, only to have it destroyed.

By 1700, both the English monarchy and the American gentry realized that to control their populations, to ensure their customs or rental revenues, and to secure great estates for themselves, they must shut down such havens. The history of the late seventeenth century in the British Atlantic world, largely writ, tells of the attempt to impose the hegemony of the monarchy and gentry using structures of church, courts, and military force—especially the Royal Navy. In London, the newly commissioned Board of Trade, charged with bringing order to colonial administration and curbing piracy, set to work in 1696. Devout Anglican Queen Anne's accession to the throne in 1702 brought joy to conservatives. The Anglican Church, with its theological validation of social hierarchy, would crush dissenters, long suspected of harboring republican sentiments, and underpin the new world order. The message sent to the empire encouraged the development of elite power to counteract the threat of democratic tendencies.

Nowhere was this effort more successful than in the southern colonies. Virginia and South Carolina gentry imposed the Anglican Church and committed themselves to economies founded on a labor system of race slavery. Planters managed the councils and assemblies and courts, writing the slave codes that came to define their societies. But outside their borders lurked dangers, alternatives that threatened their power. Piracy must be stopped. North Carolina's defiant independents must be dealt with.

North Carolina's story allows us the opportunity to examine in fine detail how this transformation of southern society proceeded. Colonial history has seldom shown us exactly how the people on the seventeenth-century frontier reacted to the formation of a powerful landed gentry. Few of the alternative societies left enough records that historians can piece together the step-by-step account of the entrenchment of elite rule and the resistance to it. A detailed narrative of the conflicts in Albemarle illustrates the tangible strategies southern planters adopted to counter resistance and to fortify their wealth and privilege.

Reading between the lines in the papers of those elites, we can tease out the hopes and fears of their poorer neighbors and see how small farmers regarded large planters and their aristocratic pretensions. Planters' values clashed with those of the second generation of North Carolinians, who battled the expansionistic slave society taking shape throughout the South. These North Carolinians fought to preserve the religious toleration that guaranteed political freedoms. They also willingly crossed racial lines to build a coalition for freedom. Albemarle constituted a liminal space—a borderland where identities were porous. The settlers called on Native Americans to come to their aid, appealing to a common cause against a plantation world that sought to use Indian lands to build a society of enormous disparity of wealth and power, rationalized by a theory of racial hierarchy, and sanctioned in the final analysis by brute force.

Lasting fifty years, this is a tale of almost continuous struggle. Although relatively few in number, the settlers were fiercely determined to maintain their political and religious freedoms, thereby drawing our respect and leaving us wondering why eighteenth-century planters get credit for developing philosophies of liberty. More than a century before wealthy Virginia slave owners debated the meaning of liberty, the Dismal Swamp country sheltered the most free society in the European purview. Every time their independence was challenged, the settlers presented arms to protect it. Those "very mutinous people," as one Virginia governor labeled them, and the autonomy they offered jeopardized the development of a slave society by the early eighteenth century.[6]

# PROLOGUE

"Olivers days come again." So an Anglican missionary disparagingly described society in North Carolina in 1711, comparing his surroundings to England during the reign of Oliver Cromwell, when monarchy, aristocracy, and the established church had been pushed from power and the removal of censorship allowed radical ideas to circulate. The missionary disdained such freedoms, preferring "order" as he saw it—rule by "natural" leaders such as the gentry and the church. Instead he found himself governed by Quakers, representatives freely elected by the people and firmly devoted to the maintenance of an egalitarian community.[1]

The Carolinas are known as Restoration colonies, founded as a result of Charles II's return to England in 1660. Charles bestowed the Carolinas on the men who orchestrated his accession to the throne. But although born of the Restoration, the colonies were really shaped by the previous twenty years, a period of civil war and revolution during which Charles's father had been executed and censorship had been ended and during which the British people witnessed the birth of radical ideas about power and politics and about who exactly constituted "the people." An understanding of the English Revolution is crucial to understanding the formative years of the North Carolina colony, for the politics of the people from top to bottom had been formed in the crucible of "Oliver's Days." The mixture of politics, religion, economics, and military experience suffused the thinking of all who had come of age in the twenty years prior to 1660. The future colonists of North Carolina had been exposed to all these ideas.

The second Stuart king, Charles I, succeeded to the throne of England, Scotland, and Ireland in 1625. By 1640, his political and religious policies had alienated many of the gentry. Charles's appointee as archbishop of Canterbury, William Laud, pursued Arminian reforms, restoring altars, stained glass windows, ornate vestments, and rituals to the Church of England. While some horrified Puritans fled to Massachusetts in response, most remained in England, their resentments building year by year.

Exacerbating these religious grievances, the king's collection of taxes —called ship money—coupled with his monopolies on soap and salt to provoke bitterness. Designed to keep Charles independent of Parliament, these fiscal policies worked through the 1630s. Tight censorship prevented public and sometimes even private airings of opposition.

In 1637, the introduction of a new Arminian prayer book into the liturgy roused a strong resistance movement in Scotland, leading to mass signing of a national covenant. The covenant constituted both a religious and a nationalist statement, proclaiming that all signees committed themselves to Presbyterianism and to the independence of the Scottish Parliament. Charles wanted to crush this rebellion against his authority and called up a new Parliament in London that he hoped would supply the funds to raise an army against Scotland.

Instead of voting money for the king, the 1640 Parliament, seething with long-standing grievances, imprisoned the king's ministers and bishops and then turned to constitutional matters. Parliament declared that it could not be dissolved except by its own consent, a major limitation of royal power. Pushing the king and the House of Commons even further apart was the news of the 1641 Irish Rebellion, a serious uprising interpreted in England and Scotland as one part of an international papist plot, with Archbishop Laud as a leading conspirator. Charles reacted by charging leading Parliamentarians with treason. They escaped, but many people at all levels of English society believed that the king had set his mind on absolutism. Charles left London for safety and to organize his Cavalier army. The Parliamentarians, or Roundheads, raised their own. Hostilities began in the fall of 1642.[2]

Early battles went the way of the royalists, so the Parliamentarians reorganized their army in 1644. This New Model Army would take shape under the principle of a "career open to the talents": the most able soldiers would be promoted to the officer corps. Under the command of Oliver Cromwell, the new army turned the tide of the war the following year and crushed the royalists' military force.

The idea that promotion depended on merit rather than class rank was a revolutionary doctrine in a nation of monarchy and aristocracy, and although Cromwell had never meant the concept to go beyond the army and his immediate military needs, the spread of ideas could not be controlled. The revolutionary premise gained momentum from simultaneous religious and political developments. Censorship ended in 1641, and pamphleteering erupted on an astonishing scale. Radical ideas about a wide distribution of power and the franchise and about religious toleration circulated at unprecedented levels. An array of religious sects sprang to life, zealously challenging clerical control of faith and practice, the imposition of tithes for a state church, and the elaborate system of patronage that allowed the ruling class to select the clergy. Cromwell's support of freedom of conscience, although it did not extend to Catholicism, furthered the proliferation of religious dissent and the questioning of all types of authority. As the leading historian of the period writes, "The deference and decencies of all social order seemed to be crumbling."[3]

Radical thought found its epicenter in the New Model Army. The soldiers had witnessed the success of a meritocracy, proving that intelligence and competence were not the exclusive possessions of the landed gentry. In April 1647, as a reaction to arrears in pay, the rank and file chose representatives, called agitators, from each regiment and formed the General Council. Their demands went far beyond military grievances. They wanted what they felt they had fought for. The most radical among them, known as the Levellers, developed a program demanding that the franchise be extended, that parliamentary seats be more equitably distributed, and that "all titles, by Prerogative, Priviledge, Pattent, Succession, Peerage, Birth or otherwise to sit and act in the Assembly of Parliament, contrary to, and without the free choice and Election of the People, be utterly abrogated, nuld and made voide."[4] They rejected an established church and its attendant tithes. They argued against the enclosures of the common lands of each town, asking that those lands be

"laid open again to the free and common use and benefit of the poore."[5]
They wanted legal reforms, too—laws written in English and freedom
from imprisonment for debt. Their opponents claimed, "They have cast
all the mysteries and secrets of government . . . before the vulgar. . . .
They have made the people thereby so curious and so arrogant that they
will never find humility enough to submit to a civil rule."[6] A special
meeting of the General Council was held in Putney in November 1647,
where famous debates took place that constituted an important moment
in the history of democratic theory.

In late 1648, the army moved against Parliament, believed to be too
conciliatory toward the king. The members of Parliament allowed to
remain voted to try Charles on charges of treason. He was executed in
January 1649, and the monarchy and House of Lords were abolished,
creating a republic. The Levellers, although not unhappy with the new
commonwealth, resented the means (military force and an unrepresen-
tative Parliament) by which it had been achieved and published pam-
phlets stating their argument. Cromwell saw that they now threatened his
power and moved against them. The Leveller leadership, civilian and
military, was arrested. When some regiments mutinied, Cromwell ordered their suppression. He and his major generals seized control of
the commonwealth and ruled England through the 1650s. The Leveller
movement suffered defeat, but its ideas did not.

With the army and the political structure firmly under his control,
Cromwell maintained a policy of toleration toward many religious sects
in which radicalism found a new home. Ranters believed that Christ lived
in every man, and some carried that idea further to claim they were
therefore incapable of sin. Ranters tended to be fond of carousing, but
one prominent Ranter, Abiezer Coppe, calling God "that mighty Leveller," argued that the greatest sins lay in "not letting the oppressed go free,
the not healing every yoke and the not dealing of bread to the hungry."[7]
Another, Lawrence Clarkson, held forth against the state clergy and their
tithes: "It is more commendable to take a purse by the highway than
compel any of the parish to maintain such that seek their ruin, whose
doctrine is poisonable to their consciences."[8] A new group that emerged
in the early 1650s, the Society of Friends, commonly referred to as the
Quakers, attracted many Ranters. Headed by James Nayler, who had

served in a radical regiment, this church's theology recognized little authority and no centralized control of religious practice. Their early devotees interrupted Episcopal services, and Nayler was brought before Parliament on charges of blasphemy. John Lilburne, a principal leader of the Levellers, converted to Quakerism in 1656. Quakers would play a leading political role in early North Carolina; their belief system reveals much about that community's ideals.

That the House of Commons accorded so much of its time to hear Nayler's case indicates how badly the Quakers frightened the powerful. Just a few years later, Quakers also faced prosecution in Virginia and Massachusetts. What danger did these people pose to English society and to England's American colonies? A contemporary politician labeled Quakers "all Levellers, against magistracy and property."[9] Their speech and dress constituted an affront to secular authority and perhaps even sedition. Quakers understood that language was imbued with layers of meaning that custom had somewhat disguised. The use of the personal pronouns "thee" and "thou" signaled a refusal to recognize class rankings. They would not refer to themselves as "humble servants" or accord anyone else titles of superiority such as "your excellency." They refused to dress to reflect their wealth or lack thereof. Likewise, they refused to participate in social manners of deference, such as tipping one's hat to one's social or economic betters, that only reaffirmed inequality.

Quaker theology went beyond anything previously seen since the breakdown of censorship, for they even posited a leveling of the patriarchal order. The English Revolution had offered women a window of opportunity for involvement in the political sphere. The social upheaval of the war, coupled with the questioning of all authority that accompanied the overthrow of monarchy, led women into the streets, where they organized, petitioned, and even preached. The more radical the group, the more likely women were to play a public role. One historian who examines the experiences of women in England through the seventeenth century notes that "women were particularly visible within the popular movement which might have established a wider political democracy, among those people 'commonly though unjustly styled Levellers.'"[10] While the Interregnum saw an outpouring of prophesy, pamphleteering, and preaching by women attached or aligned with many different sects, the Quakers were "the most receptive to the spiritual authority of women." The most thorough and recent study of the early Quakers claims that "there was complete equality as regards the ministry at least in theory, between men and women, and there are no early records of men being preferred to women."[11]

Oliver Cromwell died in 1658; his son, Richard, took over as head of the commonwealth but could not command the loyalties of his father. The power vacuum led to a reawakening of the sects. Their search for freedom from authority stretched far beyond what the Puritans had set out to do to the monarchy. One historian calls 1659 the summer of the "'Quaker terror.' . . . The saints of the 1640s had been overtaken on the road to the new Jerusalem by the Quakers."[12]

From 1653 on, England's upper ranks gradually reunified, as those Roundheads and Cavaliers who had assumed opposing sides during the Civil War on religious grounds now realized that their commonalities in terms of property ownership outweighed their differences. The concept of liberty, of a free Parliament, had sprung far out of their control and, as Lawrence Stone tells us, now constituted "too dangerous a spirit to be allowed abroad. The problem was how to use it in order to transfer control from the King and his personal advisors to men of property, without also sharing this liberty with the middling sort of people."[13] George Monck, Duke of Albemarle, and Anthony Ashley Cooper (later known briefly as Lord Ashley and then as the Earl of Shaftesbury) conspired with their old Cavalier enemies, such as Edward Hyde, Earl of Clarendon, to bring back the monarchy and the House of Lords.[14] Even the Anglican Church would be reestablished as a safeguard against the spread of meritocracy and the danger that such ideas posed to their property. Charles I had explained, "People are governed by the pulpit more than the sword in time of peace."[15] These men were to be rewarded for their efforts with more property than they could measure.

Monck, at the head of an army he had purged of both royalists and "fanatics," partnered with Shaftesbury and switched sides. In negotiations with the dead king's son, Charles, exiled with his close adviser, Hyde, at Breda in Holland, Shaftesbury and Monck asked Charles to sign an agreement protecting land settlements of the commonwealth and guaranteeing some measure of religious toleration. Both Monck and

Shaftesbury were pragmatists. No great friends of the Anglican Church, they sought order rather than conformity. Charles signed the deal in April 1660, and he returned to England and the throne a few weeks later. The restored state infrastructure suppressed the radical ideas of the revolution during the 1660s.

America apparently also belonged to the English throne to dispose of as the monarch wished. In 1663, three years after the Restoration, Charles II carved up his portion of the globe to thank his faithful supporters. He issued a charter for the area from the coast of the Carolinas to the Pacific Ocean to eight well-connected "lords proprietors": Hyde; Monck; Shaftesbury; William Lord Craven; John Lord Berkeley; his brother, Sir William Berkeley, the governor of Virginia; Sir George Carteret; and Sir John Colleton. Occupied with political events and their estates in England, among these proprietors only William Berkeley had any plans for spending time anywhere near his new endowment, and he imagined that he could control it safely from Jamestown.

The plan was that the immense acreage would serve as a lucrative and potentially perpetual source of income for the lords of colonization. Quitrents from settlers, profit from commodities such as tobacco, and of course gains from the sale of humans and their labor would flow home to the coffers in London. Four of the proprietors belonged to the Royal Adventurers to Africa, and two others already owned or had investments in Caribbean plantations.[16] John Locke, Shaftesbury's close associate and his coauthor of the feudal Fundamental Constitutions, which would be the proprietors' blueprint for governing the new colony, also had investments in the slave trade.[17]

The lords proprietors laid their plans for Carolina from afar. Ironically, the Crown's favorites, rewarded for restoring order to the realm, would establish a colony filled with people inspired by the Quakers and Levellers the ruling elite had suppressed.

*Part One* ◄◄

# The First Generation

That the foundation narrative of one of the original thirteen colonies is so poorly known may seem strange. Two old histories of the proprietary period exist, the first written by Francis Hawks in 1858 and the second penned by Samuel Ashe in 1908.[1] Hawks's history is a quirky collection of documents and stories, organized in a rather idiosyncratic manner. Ashe's work covers the basic chronology but is short on detail and marred by inevitable errors given the lack of sources employed at the time. Both works have faded from view. Most recent studies skip quickly past the early period of settlement. The latest textbook of colonial North Carolina, for example, devotes far more space to the eighteenth century than to the earliest decades of the colony.[2] While studies of colonial South Carolina proliferate, its northern neighbor lies neglected.[3]

Good reasons underlie the dearth of information. As all historians of the seventeenth-century Atlantic world know, sources do not threaten to overwhelm the archives. We must attempt to put together a jigsaw puzzle with most of the pieces missing, while those that have survived for three hundred years have differential preservation. No completed picture guides the solution. What has made the task even more arduous for historians of North Carolina is the nature of its society in the seventeenth century. The early European settlers were not the kind of people who liked to keep records.[4]

The treacherous coastline of the Outer Banks, the eerie, inhospitable terrain of the Great Dismal Swamp, and the saga of an Elizabethan colony forever lost offered reasons enough to discourage English settlement of the region south of Virginia for the first half of the seventeenth century. Yet such a place held special appeal for certain people. North Carolina's first permanent transatlantic inhabitants sought to escape the reach of their masters and governors. They came because of the swamp, not despite it. Imbued with notions of equality and deferential to none, the settlers founded a society on revolutionary principles. To maintain it required secrecy. No one would publish a pamphlet advertising Carolina as a sanctuary for runaways from indentured servitude. Any paperwork might lead to detection by former masters or by debt collectors, perhaps even by tax or tithe collectors. Only land deeds merited the risk of a paper trail. Therefore, almost the entire record base gives the perspective of those who opposed this society. From their papers we must squeeze out the actions and the attitudes embedded in those actions of those closer to the bottom of the social ladder. The volume of documentation does not reflect the importance of these farmers' role in colonial history. The sanctuary of North Carolina seriously threatened the control of slave and servant so essential to Virginia planter hegemony.

North Carolina's story fits none of the familiar models of colonial American history. Protestant dissenters came to seek freedom, but this was no City on a Hill. Ex-servants and sailors made it their home, but no port city bustled with politics and commerce. That no city or town of any kind existed for most of the period provides one clue to understanding the society. The lack of a town eased concealing one's presence from any government inspector, collector, or law enforcement officer whom the proprietors might appoint. It also signifies that the settlers felt no need to fortify themselves against Indians.

The settlers wished to be left alone, but when external authorities tried to seize control and impose taxation, the first generation of settlers, servants, debtors, and dissenters along the rivers flowing into Albemarle Sound continued to wage the English Revolution against the king, lords, and church.

ONE ◄◄►

# ESCAPE TO THE SWAMP,
# 1660–1663

America's southern colonies held forth all kinds of promises to seventeenth-century Europeans: fast money for the younger sons of the aristocracy, religious freedom for the persecuted devout, and escape from the rigors of poverty for the landless. But by 1650, Virginia was a place of possibility only for the already well connected. An aristocracy of rising tobacco planters had emerged, and while the climate and terrain may have looked exotic to an impoverished new arrival from England, the social, economic, and political structures would have felt very familiar. In the Chesapeake, members of the servant class were horribly exploited for their labor, and when their terms of indenture expired, they discovered that all the good fertile bottomland already lay in the hands of the rich few. Those elite families began to turn their attentions to the labor potential of enslaved Africans, increasing their wealth and power over society. Servants and small farmers held little hope of improving their lot.

But to the south, where the Virginians had no political control, lay an area of opportunity. The area was not easily accessible: a huge swamp, already known as the Great Dismal, barred the way. Of course, the planters were developing a sense of entitlement to arable land, and they eventually showed interest in acquiring real estate to the south. The lack of a navigable harbor deterred their settlement, for planters needed a way to ship their staple crops to transatlantic markets. For those with nothing

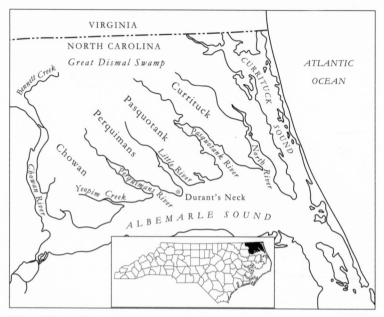

Map 1. Albemarle, 1663–1695

*Source*: Adapted from Maurice A. Mook, "Algonkian Ethnohistory of Carolina Sound," *Journal of the Washington Academy of Sciences* 34, no. 6 (June 1944): 183.

to lose, however, Carolina offered some prospects. In the early 1660s, some seeking an escape from the strictures of hierarchy ventured into the unknown for the chance at a life unbounded by plantation precepts—a "career open to the talents."

While unknown Carolina appealed to the vastly different desires of Virginia's rich, poor, and enslaved, for some people, Carolina was not a dream but a reality. Native Americans, mostly Iroquoian-speaking Tuscarora but also members of many smaller Algonkian-language groups hostile to the Tuscarora, dwelled along the Carolina coast.[1] By 1660, they were already familiar with Europeans and Africans, although no large-scale settlements from other continents had been attempted in the region. In the sixteenth century, slaves brought by the Spanish and by Francis Drake to the coast of present-day North Carolina were abandoned to an unknown fate.[2] Raleigh's "Lost Colony" of Roanoke had disappeared by 1590; survivors may have married into or otherwise joined the local population. Traders, both European and Indian, from along the eastern seaboard would also have informed the native North Carolinians about the newcomers and their ways of life. Thus, these Indians had not been entirely protected from the devastation wrought by the diseases carried across the Atlantic by the earliest European and African visitors. Smallpox and measles epidemics followed the traders and took the lives of at least 50 percent of the Native Americans who came into contact with the diseases.[3]

Most Coastal Plain Indians lived in small villages of perhaps ten households, where the women tended to two small crops of maize, beans, and squash each year, supplementing them seasonally with nuts and berries, while the men hunted and fished in their bountiful surroundings. Hunters, mostly out in the fall and early winter, observed a certain respect for their prey as fellow inhabitants whose spirits must be acknowledged. Indians on the Outer Banks enjoyed oysters and other shellfish, while those further inland used traps and trotlines each spring to catch the spawning sturgeon and herring.[4]

The mighty Tuscarora, at least eight thousand strong, whose towns and villages lay along the rivers to the south and west of Albemarle, were moving out of self-sufficiency and building strong commercial links with Virginia planters. The trade in pelts and deerskins allowed the Tuscarora to establish their predominance over the region's smaller Algonkian groups and therefore to view the Europeans as valuable newcomers rather than as a menace as long as the settlements stayed out of Tuscarora hunting grounds.[5] The burgeoning fur trade also led to centralization of political authority as some village headmen emerged as organizers of the huge, multivillage, winter hunting drives and presided over business negotiations with the Virginians.[6] Not yet entangled in the web of the slave trade, the Indians of northern Carolina stood on that verge and would soon experience its trauma.[7]

⊰⊹⊱

Between 1590 and 1663, circumstances beyond the Spanish presence in Florida stopped official English attempts to acquire native lands in the Carolina region. The lack of a good harbor deterred adventurers. The Outer Banks, the sandbar islands along the coastline, prevented large vessels from docking along the mainland, and the inlets constantly shifted in size and location, rendering mapmaking difficult and offering no confidence to ship captains. An early surveyor from the 1660s noted that "Capt. Whitties vessel this winter at her coming in found fifteene feete water, yet her going out she had but eleaven feete." The poor captain "struck twice or thrice notwithstanding they had beatoned the Chanell and went out in the best of it, at full sea."[8]

The Great Dismal Swamp, south of Virginia, further discouraged potential settlers. It measured twenty-two hundred square miles, constituting a barricade to easy passage for anyone traveling by horse or on foot from Virginia to Carolina. Travelers suffered through a wretched and dreadfully slow, damp, and dreary journey. Even after nearly fifty years of European settlement, the routes through the swamp were not clear. Two of Virginia's leading gentlemen slogged their way around the area in 1711, trying to establish the border between the two colonies. Their journal gives us a taste of the long and miserable trek through the wetlands: "In this 6 mile we Crosst several miring branches in which we were all terribly bedaubed . . . Having almost spent the day in this toilsome tho short Journey." Three days later, they "were well soused in a myery meadow by the way of which we crossed severall." At certain points they resorted to canoe travel, disembarking two miles from their intended destination and taking a long detour, "there being no firm land nearer." Another two days into their trip, they recorded that they had "mist our way being wrong directed, and rid 11 mile almost to a myery swamp, almost impassible." Finding no one available to help them, the two wandering planters, one already suffering from a fever, led their horses "3 mile through a terrible myery Pocoson to a verry great marsh to the River side." Finally arriving at their lodgings for that night, they reported, "to comfort us we soon found that this little house which was well filled was full of the Itch." Unaccustomed to such hardships, the gentlemen surrendered their plans, "there being no passage through the Dismall."[9]

Their admission of defeat is certainly understandable. Sprawling bald cypress and tupelo gum forests grew in standing water and saturated soils. The giant bald cypress trees measured more than 5 feet in diameter and 120 feet high. Mosquitoes and other biting flies loved the stagnant water and rotting vegetation, but worse awaited the sojourner. Lurking in the dark habitat, poisonous species of cottonmouth moccasins, copperheads, and canebrake rattlesnakes threatened all travelers. Bobcats preyed on human interlopers, and howling wolves terrified the uninitiated. The stench overpowered the senses.[10]

The Dismal Swamp comprised a mixed set of terrains, most of them difficult to navigate. Pocosins, or bays, housed evergreen shrub bogs. These waterlogged soils, capable of sustaining only low-growing shrubs, lay relatively open. However, plant life included a variety of briers and dense stands of cane, all exceedingly difficult to penetrate. Somewhat drier soils in the swamp gave birth to large Atlantic white cedar forests, yet even these soils remained wet enough to impede travel. One of the few welcome geographic features for the traveler in the swamp was the hammock. Slightly elevated landforms that contained several species of oak as well as beech and tulip poplar, hammocks were navigable even on horseback. But these small natural features were scattered only randomly throughout the swamp. While travel on foot or horseback was exceedingly difficult, sustained travel on water proved almost impossible: although the vast majority of the swamp stayed saturated year-round, almost no waterways were navigable. Thus, all swamp travelers shared the Virginians' frustrations.[11]

Gentlemen might be reluctant to dismount and dredge their way through the swamp, but others willingly took the challenge. For those who wished to escape the rigors of indentured servitude and slavery in plantation Virginia, the Dismal Swamp was more of a beacon than a barrier. The tobacco boom in Virginia created a massive demand for labor but did not lead to better working conditions for those who toiled in the Chesapeake. The numbers of servants, mostly young single men, crossing the Atlantic under indenture peaked during the Interregnum period. Long, hard days in the humid tobacco fields came as a physical shock to the English, used to the cool summers of home. Masters had license to whip their servants, contracts were freely bought and sold, and the courts furnished little recourse for injustice—the planters controlled the legal system. Those schooled in Cromwell's Leveller Army did not take what they felt to be a violation of their rights lying down. Two separate groups of Virginia servants unsuccessfully plotted rebellion in the early 1660s, one in York County, the other in Gloucester. "Several mutinous and rebellious *Oliverian* Soldiers" led the Gloucester insurrection.[12] The York rebellion was also believed to be headed by ex-Cromwell men.[13]

Not only was servitude brutal, but little hope of reward accompanied the end of one's term. No automatic grant of land awaited Virginia's ex-servants, and the land grab by the larger planters in the first half of the seventeenth century had left limited opportunities for the newly freed to sustain themselves. By the 1660s, "landownership for poor whites had become a dubious possibility."[14] Enough of those still indentured freed themselves by escaping that Virginia passed a 1660 law that sought to break the bonds between servants and slaves who ran away together. English servants who ran off "in company with any negroes" were to have their terms of indenture extended not just to make up for their own lost work time but also to compensate owners for the loss of the labor of their slaves, who were already bound for life.[15] For a few brave or desperate souls, therefore, Carolina presented a strong temptation.

Another group joined the runaways escaping bondage and those seeking free land. Quakers in America, like those in England, had come under attack in the early 1660s. The Quakers were viewed as politically dangerous in America as well as England, not only by Cavalier aristocrats such as Virginia's governor, William Berkeley, but also by Puritans, who were prepared to kill Quakers rather than risk having their ideas spread through Massachusetts. Persecution in Maryland and Virginia was as intense as colonial officials could muster, given the difficulties of policing in rural areas. The Virginia Assembly passed the Act for Suppressing the Quakers in 1660, and in August of that year, Berkeley scolded the sheriff of Lower Norfolk County, the area of Virginia bordering on Carolina, for failing to enforce the measure more rigorously: "I hear with sorrow that you are very remiss in your office, in not stopping the frequent meetings of this most pestilent sect of the quakers. . . . I do charge you . . . not to suffer any more of their meetings."[16] The sheriffs subsequently became a great deal more vigilant, and Quakers were punished for meetings in 1661 and 1662, with fines of two hundred pounds of tobacco levied on each attendee caught. Governor Berkeley remained concerned that Lower Norfolk County was not clean of Quakers in 1663, and he appointed extra county commissioners to help in the task: "Especially to provide that the abominated seed of the Quakers spread not in your county which to prevent I think fit to add these four to the Commission. . . . Once more I beseech you gent: to have an Exact care of this Pestilent sect of the Quakers."[17] The prosecutions continued, but so did the meetings, with thirty-four people caught on November 12, 1663. The fines more than doubled with a second conviction, and the court banished third-timers. The county court commissioners also added an extra fine of fifty pounds of tobacco against recalcitrant felons for failure to attend public worship at the Anglican Church. At least one of the repeat offenders from Lower Norfolk County was living in Albemarle by the 1690s.[18]

The first European recorded as settling in the area was Nathaniel Batts, a fur trader who carried on a trade with the Yeopim Indians. In keeping with the words of explorer John Lawson—"The Indian traders are those which travel and abide amongst the Indians for a long space of time; sometimes for a Year, two, or three. These men have commonly their Indian Wives, whereby they soon learn the Indian Tongue, keep a Friendship with the Savages"—Batts married an Indian woman.[19]

A few old deeds recording the purchase of land from the kings of the Yeopim have survived. Batts and George Durant, perhaps partners in the early exploration of the area, bought land in 1660 and 1661.[20] Rev. Thomas Bray, a colonial missionary for the Society of the Propagation of the Gospel, described the region as "peopled with English, intermixt with the native Indians to a great extent."[21] The native population may well have needed friendly newcomers with disease immunities to join their devastated villages.

Batts was undoubtedly rough around the edges, and he certainly left Virginia in disgrace, abandoning a wife there. But having purchased his land from the natives and maintained a trade with them since the 1650s, he set a precedent for fair dealing and friendly intercourse. With Batts as the unofficial governor, the earliest settlers followed his lead in their contacts and relationships with their Indian neighbors. Quaker leader George Fox, on a missionary trip to the Albemarle region in the 1670s, sensed no signs of acrimony between the native inhabitants and the English-speaking newcomers. He found a colonial society where Indians and settlers lived close to one another and indeed were willing to worship together (or at least shared a curiosity about Fox). In fact, no communication troubles at all seemed to exist.[22]

Durant, the colony's future leader, came of age in England during the revolution, emigrating to Virginia in the late 1650s. When Berkeley returned to power, Durant remained in Virginia only long enough to marry the smart, self-assured Ann Marwood before setting off to explore the Albemarle area, where he witnessed Batts's land purchase in 1660. Durant, like Batts, willingly recognized Indian rights. (Later generations of Yeopim kings bore the name Durant.) The land along Albemarle Sound appealed to his disenchantment with government and his desire for autonomy.[23]

In small craft, people disillusioned with life in Virginia followed Batts and Durant to Carolina. They wended their way down the creeks and streams to the peninsulas poking into Albemarle Sound. They found a wilderness, certainly, but a hospitable wilderness. Aside from the occasional hurricane, the climate was gentle. Short winters led to long warm springs, hot summers eased by coastal breezes, and beautiful autumns. The soils, although poorly drained in parts, were enriched enough by the area's floodwaters to deliver high crop yields. The oak, cedar, and pine forests teemed with deer, turkey, and bear, while the rivers delighted the European newcomers with their quantities of beaver, bass, trout, bluefish, and sturgeon. The fish in turn attracted legions of wildfowl. Those who settled on the islands of the Outer Banks added shellfish and whale meat to their diet. Northern Carolina's Coastal Plain offered all the ingredients for a sufficient life for any English man or woman who could clear some acreage for corn, vegetables, and tobacco.[24]

And settlers would not necessarily be limited to tobacco farming. The Outer Banks remain known as the Graveyard of the Atlantic, and Lawson later claimed that those living closest to the coast harvested washed-up whales and counted on occasional hurricanes "for the Benefit of Wrecks, which sometimes fall in upon that Shoar." Coastal residents considered wrecking, scavenging, smuggling, and piracy legitimate endeavors.[25] The most western precinct of Albemarle, known as Currituck, sheltered some of the poorest people, perhaps those too nervous to claim headrights for fear that registering their names would lead authorities to their doors—if they had them. One visitor to the area described his lodgings as "a wretched open old house.... [I]t kept the Dew from us but had it rained we should have been well souzed." Nonetheless, even here they feasted on "verry large good fatt oysters and much fish."[26]

An Anglican missionary to Albemarle painted a picture of a community of skilled ex-servants, the men serving as their own "carpenters Joiners Wheelwrights Coopers Butchers Tanners Shoemakers Tallow Chandlers waterman & what not," while the women were "Soap makers Starch makers Dyes &c . . . over and above all the common occupations of both sexes." "All seem to live by their own hands of their own produce," he went on.[27] Settlers worked hard when they had to, but they worked for themselves. Escape from servitude and obligation was the chief reason for taking up residence in the area. Although tobacco might be the only source of cash, vital for the purchase of rum, subsistence-level farming readily provided enough Indian corn for many people, and plenty of fish and game surrounded their farms. Livestock required little care, making for an "easy Way of living in that plentiful Country," according to one traveler in the area.[28] Access to markets would have been difficult for those so inclined. The lack of a good port on the coast, combined with the arduousness of travel northward through or around the swamp, made transportation costs prohibitive.

It was, of course, a land of hurricanes; an enormous one hit in 1667.[29] Earthfast buildings developed as the period's most common architectural form in the region. Settlers stuck wooden posts deep into the ground without construction of any foundation, covered that frame with wattle and daub, and then thatched the roof. Quickly constructed and easily destroyed by storm or fire, the buildings were deliberately impermanent. It made little sense to devote energy and resources to housing, with violent storms expected every few years and no cash to pay masons.[30] Surrounding the house, a typical two-hundred-acre mostly wooded farm probably had between a dozen and twenty acres cleared for crops—corn and wheat in addition to tobacco—and a small vegetable garden for beans and peas.[31] The newcomers scattered themselves some distance from each other, avoiding the contagions of disease that had so plagued the Virginia settlements. They kept large dogs to protect their livestock against the wolves in the woods around them.[32] Northern Carolina seems to have offered an often lonely lifestyle, but farmers occasionally rowed their boats across the rivers to help each other harvest and to enjoy some merrymaking.[33] For most settlers, life in Albemarle, however hard, obviously trounced what they had left behind in William Berkeley's Virginia.

≺⊹

Even before Charles II had been officially restored to the throne of England, Berkeley regained control of Virginia. Most of the lessons of the Interregnum were lost on Berkeley. Comfortably ensconced in the Cavalier colony for the 1650s, he had trouble accepting that all forms of "natural" or divine authority had been questioned and found wanting. Governor Berkeley's genteel birth and his time at court bequeathed him a status superior to that of any other man in the American colonies, and even the biggest planters in Virginia deferred to his rank. His grand home, Green Spring House, reflected his social standing and projected his attitude toward social hierarchy. Berkeley had a working relationship with the great planters; together they created a society "in which," according to his biographer, "the mighty were at liberty to fathom the intricacies of authority in ways that singularly benefited themselves . . . at the expense of the overwhelming number of settlers who were slaves, indentured servants, and lesser planters."[34]

Of the group of proprietors of Carolina in 1663, Berkeley ranked lowest, having less direct personal connection with Charles II and carrying no serious weight in the corridors of Parliament. But he was the only original proprietor ever to see the shore of America.[35] Edward Hyde and George Monck, the most powerful of the proprietors, too occupied with events at court and in the royal armed forces to show the slightest interest in their grant, hoped perhaps that income would flow without effort. The experiences of both king and courtiers during the Interregnum and their preoccupations elsewhere following the Restoration provided the foundation for the strange March 1663 document known as the Carolina Charter.

While ex-Levellers plotted servant insurrections in Cavalier Virginia and Berkeley hunted Quakers, Charles II was incorporating a very different tone into parts of his charter for the Carolinas. Eager to encourage settlement, the monarch allowed that Carolina inhabitants might feel that they "cannot in their private opinions conform to the public exercise of religion according to the liturgy forms and ceremonies of the Church of England or take or subscribe the oaths and articles made and established in that behalf." The king felt that dissenters in Carolina, "by reason of the remote distances of those places," would not threaten a "breach of the unity and uniformity established in this nation." He therefore granted permission in writing to the proprietors "to give and grant unto such person and persons inhabiting and being within the said Province or any part thereof who really in their judgements and for conscience sake cannot or shall not conform to the said liturgy and ceremonies and take and subscribe the oaths and articles aforesaid."[36]

We can only try to guess why such a tolerant society was set up—the "oaths" are a direct reference to Quakers who refused to take them—but a clue lies in the words "the remote distances of those places." One lesson from the Civil War (which was well learned by Monck and Shaftesbury, who had stayed in Britain for the entire Interregnum) taught that dissenters refused to return peacefully to the Anglican fold. In light of the desire to disperse troublemakers to the margins of the empire and the quest for profit, the charter makes sense: both grantor and grantees hoped to rid England of Quakers and to make money on the deal. Berkeley likely had little input on the text, because even if the charter helped draw leveling types out of Virginia, Carolina would have been a little too close for comfort. But to persecuted Quakers in Lower Norfolk County, freedom of conscience a few miles away must have been a magnet.

Before the charter, locals called their region Roanoke (not to be confused with Raleigh's lost colony or the island of that name). In honor of Monck, the proprietors renamed the huge saltwater inlet south of the Dismal Swamp Albemarle Sound and dubbed the fertile area on its northern shore Albemarle. However, as the Quakers knew well, words bore extra meaning. If the renaming meant to inspire awe at the magnitude of proprietary power, it failed. The settlers already abiding in Albemarle were well aware of their remoteness and used it to their full advantage. In fact, the original draft of the charter did not include most of the Albemarle settlement, for the grant marked the border with Virginia in the middle of Albemarle Sound. A second charter in 1665 fixed the border at its current location of 36°, 30'.[37]

By late August 1663, the proprietors had drawn up a declaration to woo potential settlers to Carolina. They promised representative government for more prosperous landowners, "the major part of the freeholders," and "in ample manner as the undertakers shall desire, freedom and liberty of conscience in all religious or spiritual things." For the first five years, as an added incentive to settlement, they offered lucrative land grants. Land was to be held in freehold, with a quitrent of a half penny per acre owed to the absentee landlords.[38]

Although the proprietors tried to exert rights to the area, settlers in the region recognized that Indian claims superseded those of English lords. A parcel of land granted to George Catchmany by Governor Berkeley overlapped with the tract Durant had purchased from the Yeopim king, and in 1663, Catchmany signed it over to Durant, thereby acknowledging Yeopim sovereignty.[39] This action directly disobeyed the orders of the proprietors, who acknowledged that some settlers had purchased land from natives but directed that any new grants replaced those deeds, although new settlers should reimburse the old for whatever they had paid the Indians.[40]

The area between Virginia and Florida also had its attractions for others around the Atlantic world. Second-generation New Englanders, their towns filling up, were looking around for new land, preferably with a longer growing season and less rocky soil than the region settled by their parents. Moreover, the Restoration and the fear of what it might mean for religious toleration offered another motivation. In response to these pressures, New Englanders had already formed a group called the Adventurers about Cape Fayre. Agents in England were appointed to try to persuade the king to grant them a charter. Early in 1663, before news of the proprietary charter had reached Massachusetts, a group set off to establish a new settlement around the Cape Fear River (near the present-day border of North and South Carolina). They returned home within two months, with little explanation other than that a local man had given them some information, possibly of the proprietary charter. Their representatives in London negotiated with the proprietors about a colony in Carolina, but these efforts came to naught.[41]

The only white settlers in Carolina in the early 1660s, therefore, were those few hundred who had deserted the British empire and waded their way through the Dismal Swamp from Virginia to take up farming on the isolated lands along the creeks and Albemarle Sound. Events in England suddenly placed them back under the rule of the lords of empire. Nevertheless, when it came to building the framework of the new colony, these small farmers of a revolutionary generation had carried to Carolina some ideas of their own.

# TWO

# BUILDING THE SANCTUARY,
## 1664–1673

The English lords who were awarded Carolina explored a range of ideas about how to enjoy their land grant. Some of those in England looked to the enormously profitable Caribbean islands as a model for colonization and encouraged planters from Barbados to seek fresh lands in Carolina. But only one proprietor, Virginia governor William Berkeley, had any real opportunity to impose his will on Albemarle, for he had the authority to appoint a governor and council for the region. His choices reflected his personal colonial experience, leading him to select men he trusted to fashion a colony in Virginia's image rather than that of the sugar colonies. Even Berkeley never fully devoted his attention to Carolina.

Numerous runaways had departed Virginia before the charter appeared, seeking new lives outside the British empire. They must have been dismayed to learn that they again lived in an English colony, but the settlers were nothing if not politically astute. They quickly realized that a piece of paper called a royal charter had no teeth without an army to enforce it. With a row of barrier islands as well as the Atlantic Ocean between them and the men in power, they could ignore any commands that did not serve their purposes. They left few records, yet a clear picture emerges through the journal of a Quaker missionary: the formative years of the colony saw the development of a society based on the needs and wishes of small farmers and former servants rather than on those of the great men of empire.

No profit could be made by the proprietors without settlers filling the vast region, paying quitrents, buying slaves from the African Company, and perhaps even discovering valuable minerals, from which the proprietors would retain a portion of any profits. Negotiations to settle Carolina began with a company on Barbados. William Yeamans, the Barbadians' representative in London, worked out a set of "concessions" with the proprietors. One small group moved into the Cape Fear region in the spring of 1664, calling the area Clarendon County. Clarendon proved an unhappy and short-lived settlement. Supplies were destroyed by storms at sea, while war with the Dutch, the Great Plague, and the Great Fire of London over the next two years completely held the attention of the proprietors in England, leaving pleas for help unanswered.[1] Unlike the early settlers of Albemarle, who had recognized from the beginning their dependence on Indian neighbors and had behaved accordingly toward them, the Clarendon settlement attempted to sell Indian children into slavery. Violent hostilities broke out quickly. By October 1667, no European remained on the Cape Fear River.[2]

The 1665 Concessions and Agreement negotiated by the Barbadians mark the proprietors' first attempt to set out the rules of government and the arrangements for the dispersal of lands. They envisioned three counties for Carolina: Albemarle, near Virginia; Clarendon, on the Cape Fear River; and Port Royal, in the southern region. Although the residents of Albemarle had played no part in the negotiations, the Concessions became the governing constitution for their community until 1669 and, with small modifications, also formed the basis for the proprietors' other colony in New Jersey. Guaranteeing liberty of conscience and representative government, this document also designated the conditions of land grants to settlers. Those who had arrived before 1665 would get headrights of eighty acres for the head of household, with eighty more for a wife and the same for any male servant able to bear arms.[3] In addition, "weaker" servants—females, children, and slaves aged over fourteen— would bring their masters forty acres, but the children of the settling family received nothing. Christian servants received forty acres when released from their indentures.

The Concessions placed a premium on haste. For those who arrived during 1665, the grants fell from the earlier eighty and forty acres to sixty and thirty acres, respectively; for settlers arriving in 1667, the allotments dropped to forty and twenty acres. Quitrents were set at half a penny per acre per year, twice Virginia's current rate. After 1667, land would presumably only be available through purchase. To discourage land speculation, the Concessions required that landowners retain one servant for every hundred acres above that granted to a married couple; those who did not do so risked forfeiting their land.[4]

When the Concessions reached Albemarle in the spring of 1665, the authors appeared out of touch with the going rates for land in the American colonies, and the Concessions suggested the impossible task of laying out towns to encourage an unnecessary security against Indians. The people of Albemarle thus did not greet the instructions warmly. Since Albemarle's residents, unlike those of Clarendon County, survived without the goodwill and practical assistance of the proprietors, they could afford to contest the proprietors' plan. Their initial assembly immediately sent a petition to protest the land distribution regulations. Thomas Woodward, the new surveyor of Albemarle, dispatched a letter in June, making clear their disagreement, albeit in a respectful and submissive tone. Woodward, appointed by Berkeley and no Leveller, personally wished for more rich men and a little more of a pecking order in Albemarle: "Besides to have some men of greater possessions in land then others will conduce more to the well being and good government of the place than any levelling parity. . . . It is my opinion (which I submit to better judgements) that it will for some time conduce more to your Lordships' profit to permit men to take up what tracts of land they please at an easie rate, than to stint them to small proportions at a great rent." Woodward hoped that bigger headrights would produce more of the social hierarchy he found so sadly lacking in Albemarle. Forced to represent the settlers, he asked for larger grants and lower quitrents for everyone.[5]

No proper response came for several years. John Colleton wrote back in September 1665, explaining, "We partners are now divided into several counties, by reason of the sickness. . . . [T]he great plague in and about London keeps us asunder." Without the consent of all the partners, he could offer only an informal opinion, but he did not sympathize with the residents of Carolina. Unlike Berkeley, Colleton had obviously envisaged a Barbados-type colony and was not happy to hear the farmers of Albemarle compare themselves to the farmers of Virginia. "The way of the Virginia settlement is pernicious to the planters, of little good or advantage to the king or his people, pray therefore think of the Barbados industry, their way and manner of living, working and contriving, they work the year throughout, the Virginians as I am informed but half the year."[6] His advice went unheeded; Albemarle's ex-servants had no desire to replicate the extreme and horrific inequities of Barbadian society.

In 1664, Berkeley chose William Drummond to serve as the first governor of Albemarle. Though the decision seemed minor at the time, it had momentous consequences. Originally from Scotland, Drummond, a Virginia lawyer with servants, must have appeared to Berkeley something akin to a natural leader: a man with a vested interest in the status quo. But Berkeley misread Drummond. Drummond was a former indentured servant who had plotted to escape from his master with his fellow servants, suffering a savage lashing and having extra time added onto his indenture. He empathized with the settlers who had moved south to Carolina, the "abundance of people that are weary of Sir Williams Government," as he reported to a friend in 1666.[7]

This first governor set the tone, creating a model that several generations of North Carolinians believed succeeding governors should follow. Drummond served only three years, and few of his decisions survive in the official colonial records, but folklore holds that he invited every man in the region to the first meeting of the Albemarle Assembly in February 1665, a gathering held under an oak tree on a knoll overlooking Hall's Creek in Pasquotank.[8] No barrage of complaints occurred during his term of office, a telling difference from the tenures of most future governors not chosen by the settlers. Most telling of all, ten years after Drummond finished his term in Albemarle, Berkeley executed the former governor for his part in Bacon's Rebellion. Drummond's radicalization may well have grown during the time he spent with the Carolinians.

One main issue affecting the settlers concerned the transportation of tobacco. The main crop of Virginia, tobacco was the cash crop most of the first Albemarle immigrants knew best. It served as the region's chief medium of exchange, so everyone needed to grow a little. Those who owned larger tracts and had brought slaves or servants or even had large numbers of children could attempt to harvest sizable crops. However, the price of tobacco spiraled downward during the 1660s and 1670s, creating great unrest in the Chesapeake Bay colonies. The large Virginia and Maryland tobacco economies entered a state of impending crisis, as indentured servants, now surviving their terms in unprecedented numbers, bought land wherever they could and set themselves up as tobacco farmers.[9] According to the large planters, the resulting tobacco glut necessitated curtailing production to push prices higher, since the bigger, more established planters could more readily cope with short-term losses in income than could the yeomen. In an attempt at cooperation, the three colonies organized a July 1666 conference in James City. Representatives from Albemarle (Drummond and Woodward), Virginia, and Maryland met to sign a treaty agreeing to "a totall cessation from sowing, setting, planting, or any waies tending any tobacco in any the three Colonies abovesaid, or any part of them in the yeare 1667."[10] Leaders in each colony, especially Berkeley, hoped that this action would not only drive prices higher but also encourage greater diversification by the farmers and produce a more balanced economy. The strategy never received a chance to work, however. Lord Baltimore, proprietor of Maryland, vetoed the deal because he declined to accept the cut it would have brought in his personal income.[11]

If there could be no agreement, then there must be tariffs. By 1672, the Virginians had imposed a tax on tobacco from Albemarle shipped through Virginia's ports. Incensed farmers sought help in two places: England and New England. While pleading to the proprietors for relief, they also found traders from the northernmost colonies who could navigate small coastal fishing boats past the area's barrier islands, men willing to take tobacco and other produce from Albemarle Sound to Boston without concern for any duty owed to the mother country. Within the decade, this commitment to nonpayment of taxes—to either Virginia or Charles II—led to armed rebellion.

In the original 1663 instructions to Berkeley, the other proprietors had given the representative assembly the power to write its own laws, "which laws shall be transmitted to us within one year after publication, there to receive our ratification but to be in force until by us denied."[12] With a friendly governor and the proprietors almost incommunicado as a consequence of the plague and the 1666 Great Fire, the inhabitants were free to establish whatever rules they wanted. With liberty of conscience guaranteed and no attempt under way to establish a church that would demand tithes, little could bother the settlers. Their only "tax," the quitrent, remained a concern, however. By English standards of landownership and taxation, this sum amounted to a pittance, and the settlers had up to five years to pay, yet the quitrent still galled them.[13] Beyond the money, quitrents implied a loyalty to the lord to whom it was paid.[14] The Carolinians refused to pay, and the proprietors had no means of enforcement. An old saying from England's first colony—"England's emergency is Ireland's opportunity"—applied to the independent-minded early settlers in northern Carolina. They understood that a new era had begun. They had to live within the framework of a proprietary colony, but they could subvert the system to make it work for them instead of for their absentee landlords.[15] Perhaps not every newcomer was pleased with the developments; Woodward certainly longed for a colony closer to the Virginian style. Small farmers, however, outnumbered such men in the broad franchise.

The lords had been out of touch for almost three years when they finally responded to the petition from Albemarle's first assembly asking for more lenient land laws. The various colonies' competition for settlers gave those in America more leverage than a tenant farmer in England could expect from his local aristocrat, and in May 1668, the proprietors issued the Great Deed of Grant, allowing Carolinians to "hold their lands of us the Lords Proprietors upon the same terms and conditions that the Inhabitants of Virginia hold theirs."[16] This change reduced the quitrent by half and eliminated ownership of servants as a condition for landholding. The settlers had won their demands and for decades to come held the Great Deed more binding than any other issuance from London. The proprietors, so optimistic at the outset that the area would fill up fast, discovered their initial expectations unmet. In a further concession, they changed the rules again in 1670 and granted sixty acres (plus fifty for each servant) to anyone who settled by 1672.[17]

From Virginia, Berkeley attempted to restore his version of normality in 1667. He dismissed Drummond and appointed a new, less popular, governor, Samuel Stephens. Sometime in 1669, the Albemarle Assembly dispatched to London its first legislation to be ratified by the proprietors, but the laws went into effect while the colony awaited a response. These laws caused great consternation for Governor Stephens and his haughty wife, Frances (who at other times married two different southern colonial governors). Stephens, a grandson of Abraham Peirsey of Flowerdew Hundred plantation in Virginia, enjoyed his status as Berkeley's protégé. Their families interacted so closely that Berkeley married Frances Stephens within months of her husband's death. Perhaps the aristocratic Stephens, horrified by egalitarian, Quaker-like laws, had felt secure that the proprietors would not ratify them. He may have tried to prevent their enforcement in the interim. Certainly "there were great factions fomented against him. . . . [S]ome were so insolent as to draw their swords against him" during his time in Carolina.[18] His death prevented him from having to suffer the pain of enforcing the radical acts.

The legislation in question offers striking evidence that North Carolina stood among the most liberal societies in the British Atlantic. The first measure, "An Act Prohibiting Sueing of Any Person within 5 Years," made Albemarle a safe haven for all debtors: "Noe person living in this County shall on any pretence whatsoever receive any letter of Atturney Bill or account to recover any debt within the time above mentioned of a Debtor living here with out the said Debtor freely consent to it." The law applied not only to debts back in England but also to those from anywhere "without the County," including, therefore, the other colonies and among them Virginia.[19]

The second measure, "An Act Concerning Marriages," acknowledged that "there is noe minister as yet in this County" and went on to render civil wedding ceremonies legal. In a decade of settlement, no formal religious services had taken place in the region, a common occurrence throughout the Chesapeake and southern colonies in the seventeenth century as a consequence of the general lack of ministers.[20] In North Carolina, civil marriages continued for several generations.[21]

"An Act against Ingrocers" addressed the problem of "engrossing," or cornering the market in an essential product. It decreed that "any person whatsoever within this County that shall . . . presume to engrose any quantity of goods from any adventurer to sell and retaile againe at unreasonable rates to the Inhabitants" would face the stiff penalty of ten thousand pounds of tobacco. The act established a moral economy, forbidding speculators from taking advantage of the isolation of the new colony to drive up the price of a commodity by monopoly.[22]

"An Act What Land Men Shall Hould in One Devidend" set a maximum of 660 acres for any landowner. Before ratifying this act, the proprietors exempted from this measure both themselves and the new hereditary nobility they planned to nominate, but that clause proved irrelevant, as the lords never established any successful plantations in North Carolina. Instead, they gave their approval to a society of relatively small farmers. The act legally prevented the formation of huge plantations such as those taking shape in Virginia.[23]

These acts passed during a time whose economy most often has been described as nascent capitalism, born of Calvinist doctrines on discipline. Yet here a politically astute community carefully created an alternative to the colonial models of both Virginia and Massachusetts. The Carolinians attempted to set up a moral economy that did not require a church structure but rather was based on a humanist, secular morality that refused to enforce a particular religious faith—or the need for any faith—among its subscribers. Understanding clearly the lessons learned from the defeat of the Levellers, northern Carolina's Assembly legislated an upper limit for landholdings in this free land. Political independence was crucially linked to economic independence. The freedom to have a voice in one's own governance must be protected by as wide a distribution of land as possible and thus the widest franchise the settlers could conceive.

The Albemarle Assembly sent the acts to London for ratification in 1669. In April of that year, the proprietors met in Whitehall. With Hyde in exile and both Colleton and Monck now dead, Shaftesbury came to the fore as the man most powerful and most interested in Carolina. The settlements in Albemarle occupied a tiny portion of the Carolina grant. Shaftesbury wanted to sponsor a new settlement in the southern region of the land grant (the area to become known as Charles Town) and had been working on that project with his secretary, John Locke. Shaftesbury persuaded his fellow proprietors to risk the start-up costs of launching a fresh settlement, arguing that if the colony were led by experienced planters from Barbados, the returns would be worthwhile. Each proprietor except for Virginia's Berkeley signed on and invested five hundred pounds. Three ships, outfitted in England, were to stop in Ireland to pick up extra servants before crossing the Atlantic. They intended to drop anchor far to the south of the Cape Fear River in the area known as Port Royal. The plans moved ahead quickly. In the summer of 1669, Joseph West, the captain of the expedition, gathered supplies and personnel. The proprietors ratified the Albemarle Acts but devoted a great deal more attention to a new constitution.[24]

This new document being considered by the lords blatantly contradicted the spirit of the Albemarle Acts, but the paradox is easily explained. The constitution was being drawn up for a brand-new colony and would only by default apply to the citizens of Albemarle also. The Fundamental Constitutions for the new colony of Carolina, penned at least in part by no less a theorist than Locke, constituted an imaginative attempt by Locke and Shaftesbury to set up a hereditary feudal system with aristocrats called landgraves and cassiques. Locke, forbidden to use English titles, chose an Indian word meaning "chiefs," perhaps believing that doing so would somehow make an ancient European power structure fit the New World. Whatever the names, the explicit hierarchy sought to provide "for the better government of the said place" and to establish "the interest of the Lords Proprietors with equality, and without confusion; . . . and that we may avoid erecting a numerous democracy."[25]

This preamble led to a lengthy and detailed description of how the colony should be organized into seigniories and baronies, overseen by these hereditary nobles and their descendants. An elaborate court system consisted of eight separate tribunals, each presided over by one of the proprietors. To assure rapid settlement, freedom of religion was confirmed specifically for "Jews, Heathens and other dissenters from the purity of the Christian religion." The proprietors hoped that by peaceful contact and the exemplary behavior of Christian neighbors, the non-Christian "natives of that place" would be converted. But there would not be freedom from religion, for atheists lost their civil rights. The proprietors provided for the eventual establishment of the Anglican Church. Slaves had freedom of religion, too, but the constitution explicitly stated that professing Christian beliefs would not protect them from slave status, as "every freeman of Carolina shall have absolute power and authority over his negro slave of what opinion or religion soever."[26]

Further instructions for the governor and Council of Albemarle acknowledged that the Constitution "was principally intended for Port Royall which we have sent to plant this yeare and is designed the Chiefe seat of our Province."[27] The proprietors understood that it would not be feasible in Albemarle "to putt it fully in practise by reason of the want of Landgraves and Cassiques and a sufficient number of people." Nevertheless, they called for an immediate election there and the formation of a council to figure out how to implement as much of the constitution as possible.[28]

The contradictions are readily apparent. Locke's theories of possessive individualism—men of property should control government, while the landless (the majority) would be kept obedient by threats from the pulpit suggesting divine retribution—suffused his Fundamental Constitutions.[29] North Carolina's leveling types, however, put these theories into a new context. Their quest for landownership was also a quest for participation in civil society. The constitutions enfranchised anyone owning fifty acres—less than the amount awarded to each settler and even to servants at the end of their indentures. In effect, therefore, all early male settlers would receive the right to vote within their lifetimes. And in Albemarle, the pulpit held no control, for there would be no pulpit for another thirty years. Those few who cared to attend worship would do so in meetinghouses.

The constitution was an irrelevant document for the northern portion of Carolina. It was never put into service, no one could police it, and no "natural" deference existed among the settlers that would render them obedient to the word of a faraway lord. The Fundamental Constitutions, rarely even referred to by the settlers, are useful to us only as an indication of what powerful Englishmen at the end of the English Civil War considered the proper manner to run a New World colony. Concerned with avoiding the errors of England's recent past, they allowed freedom of religious practice as long as all persons knew their social place, a rank determined by one's landholdings. Yet the lords failed to see the contradiction when they also ratified the Albemarle Assembly's legislation: the act prohibiting huge landholdings would soon "erect a numerous democracy." Meanwhile, the proprietors, led by Shaftesbury, turned their attention almost exclusively to the other section of their grant, the area around the Ashley and Cooper Rivers, where they had a capital investment. The residents of Albemarle would continue to govern themselves.[30]

Albemarle's Council and its governor formed the executive branch of government. Berkeley appointed the original council members, but as the system developed, the other proprietors directly deputized men as their personal representatives on this council. Peter Carteret, a kinsman of proprietor Sir George Carteret, was the first such deputy, appointed in 1664.[31] After Stephens's death, Peter Carteret rose to the position of governor. By 1670, the proprietors began sending blank deputations to the governor, who could then fill the council with whomever he thought worthy and presumably friendly.[32]

The 1670 council, composed of local men led by John Jenkins and John Harvey who had some property but lacked allegiance to the proprietors, took seriously their positions as representatives of their fellow settlers. It was their duty to enact the Fundamental Constitutions, a second draft of which they received in October 1670. But the councillors dragged their feet, claiming disingenuously that they lacked sufficient competence and understanding. Writing to the proprietors in May 1671, the council members pleaded that given "such meane Capacityes as wee are endowed with," they could not comprehend "thinges ... Exhibited in Such Unaccustomed termes." They understood well enough, however, to protest any changes to the way they had organized landholdings and the political process. First, they found no way to comply with the Fundamental Constitutions' accompanying instructions that land should be laid out in 10,000- or 12,000-acre squares, "without prejudice to those already seated." Second, the quitrents demanded in the constitution counteracted the Great Deed of Grant of 1668. Beyond those complaints, the council members wanted the act that provided for a maximum of 660 acres per holding to be amended so that those who had purchased larger lots from the Indians before the charter—leading men such as Nathaniel Batts and George Durant, plus Jenkins and Harvey—could retain their property. The council's letter also stressed that "the people" would not take kindly to a clause "restraininge persones chosen by the people from a freedom of propossall" in the assembly. It is not clear to which clause they were referring in this instance, but it seems that in Albemarle, settlers believed that the constitution empowered only council members, not other elected representatives, to propose legislation.[33]

These objections, wrapped in language of humility and devotion and presented as if the humble settlers of Albemarle depended on the "Lord-shipps wisdome and morall prudence" to guide them, were firm protests nonetheless. Receiving no reply by April 1672, the Albemarle Council dispatched Peter Carteret to the mother country, thus ridding themselves of the only English gentleman in their midst.[34] The proprietors listened to Carteret's pleas and in November 1673 endorsed laws to ease the settlers' discontent. The lords allowed that current settlers had rights to their land, even those pre-charter settlers who had purchased their hold-ings from Indians or had grants from Virginia.[35] Again, the settlers had won their demands. With Carteret gone, Jenkins filled the position of governor.

≺≁

The three ships dispatched by the proprietors from the English coast in August 1669 to settle the new colony in the southern regions of Carolina had less than smooth sailing. The Irish seemed rather ungrateful for the opportunity to serve Englishmen; storms wrecked one of the ships in Barbados and another in the Bahamas and blew the third off course. A fourth ship, rented to replace the first, also lost its way. The Spanish captured one ship captain and some of his passengers. Not until May 1670 did the final group reach Carolina's Ashley River. In Barbados, the emigrants had picked up a surveyor willing to try his hand in the new colony, a young man named John Culpeper.[36]

The lords proprietors must have been greatly dismayed at the mis-adventures of their small fleet, but not all was lost. The wrecking of the ship *Port Royal* in the Bahamas led directly to the addition of those islands to the proprietors' private empire. The tiny colony of settlers there had been set up by William Sayle in 1648 specifically as a place for religious radicals from Bermuda. The execution of the king the following year so shocked the Bermudian elite that they deported radicals, political and religious, to the Bahamas whether or not they desired to move.[37] Two Bermudian planter-entrepreneurs were more interested in an orderly government for the Bahamas, where they owned a plantation. The planters met the shipwrecked passengers on their way to Carolina in January 1670 and learned of the proprietors' charter. In February, they wrote to Shaftesbury asking him to take out a "Patent for New Providence and the rest of the Bahama Islands that the poor people may have protection there and be governed according to his Majestys' Laws." Before the end of the year, he had indeed secured a charter for the Bahamas for the Carolina proprietors. Added to the charter for New Jersey granted to some of the same proprietors in 1664, these huge new territories spread the attention of the men of empire very thin. They remained focused on the new settlement, and Shaftesbury maintained a flow of correspondence with the men from Barbados he had appointed to fill offices in southern Carolina. In December 1671, young Culpeper was commissioned as surveyor-general for that new province.[38] Meanwhile, the Bahamas enjoyed a period of salutary neglect, and Quakers, ex-slaves, and pirates built a community free from government and protected from planters by dangerous coastal terrain.[39] In New Jersey, too, settlers both Quaker and Puritan governed themselves, ignoring whatever orders from England they found not to their liking.[40]

--

By 1673, Albemarle society deviated radically from that foreseen in the Fundamental Constitutions. Newcomers to Albemarle did not find living conditions easy. Peter Carteret, who had come straight from England, had had particular troubles adjusting his expectations and learning to cope with the climate, the mosquitoes, and the Atlantic storms. The proprietors wanted Carteret to set up a vineyard on their personal lands in Carolina, but as he reported in his unhappy account of 1665, the effort "produced litle by reason that wee were all Sick all the Sumer that wee could nott tend it & the Servants Soe weake the fall and Spring that they could doe litle worke."[41] Those who had come from Virginia were, of course, more seasoned to the conditions and held less ambitious ideas. They wanted independence more than they wanted huge profits and sumptuous lifestyles.

In the Chesapeake colonies, as the tobacco economy faltered, a class war brewed between large plantation owners on one hand and small tobacco farmers and landless laborers and servants on the other. But in

Albemarle, the existence of leveling politics among the settlers produced a more united front. First, there were no plantations on the scale of the Virginia Tidewater.[42] Earlier numbers are hard to come by, but as late as 1721, the end of the proprietary period, when Carolina's population was two generations removed from the English Revolution, most households still could not claim even two tithables. Unlike their neighbors in the colonies bordering on the north and south, North Carolinians saw no huge gap between rich and poor; so few of the excessively wealthy planters common to South Carolina and Virginia lived in Albemarle that the region resembled "a poor Virginia precinct."[43] The numbers from the 1660s would have been even more reflective of a society of runaways, escapees from slavery and servitude, from debt, from a "restored" aristocratic governor, and from religious persecution.

During the summer of 1672, two visitors from England's Society of Friends landed in Maryland. George Fox went north at first, while William Edmondson turned south to Virginia. He then made the treacherous journey through the Great Dismal Swamp to preach in Carolina. Fox followed him to Albemarle, arriving in November. The journals of these two missionaries provide the best description of life in the Albemarle region during these years.

As Edmondson recalled, the journey between Virginia and Carolina was awful. The isolation and boggy terrain of the Dismal Swamp bewildered even the locals at times, "it being all wilderness and no English inhabitants or pathways, but some marked trees to guide people. . . . [W]e were sorely foiled in swamps and rivers, and one of the two who were with me for a guide, was at a stand to know which way the place lay we were to go to." They eventually came to the house of a couple named Phelps, already Quakers. Eager to assess the situation for himself, Edmondson called a meeting the same day, even before his wet clothing had dried out. He reported a well-attended gathering, "but they had little or no religion, for they came and sat down in the meeting smoking their pipes." Albemarle officeholders arrived, including "a justice of the peace, and his wife who received the truth with gladness." This pair offered to host the next meeting on the following day, although their home stood "about three miles off, on the other side of the water."[44] Though Edmondson's account of Albemarle is brief, it illustrates a community that lived on the water and traveled by boat more than by horse. Nevertheless, the settlers had already evolved a relatively speedy system of communication, for word of the Quaker's arrival traveled fast. There had been no organized religion to date.

Fox's journal tells us much more about the people of Albemarle, both their lifestyle and their political attitudes. In November, having spent some time among the Quakers of Lower Norfolk County in Virginia, Fox made his way through Albemarle's woods, creeks, and bogs in search of settlers. "And the next day we passed all the day, and saw neither house nor man through the woods, and swamps, and many cruel bogs and watery places, that we were wet to the knees most of us, and at the night we took up our lodging in the woods and made us a fire, all of us being weakly horsed. . . . And the next day we passed through the woods, and over many bogs and swamps, and at the night we came to Bonner's Creek, and there we lay. And the woman of the house lent us a mat, and we lay on it by the fireside and this was the first house in Carolina."[45]

Fox and his friends left their horses at this house in the western district of Albemarle, called Chowan, and for the next eighteen days traveled through the region only by boat or on foot. They came by canoe to the home of Batts, described by Fox as "formerly Governor of Roanoke," which obviously still functioned as a meeting place for the surrounding settlers. Fox considered Batts a "rude and desperate man" but acknowledged that he "hath a great command over the country, especially over the Indians." For his part, Batts had heard of Fox—particularly of his power to heal—and had already "spread it up and down among the people in the country."[46]

Not only Batts but also the council members encouraged the denizens to follow the Quaker. One friendly local loaned the missionary a larger boat, for he was getting soaked in his original canoe, "and in that boat from thence we came to the governor's house." The draft of the borrowed boat proved too deep for the shallow waters, and Fox had to wade quite some way to reach the home of Governor Jenkins, "who with his wife received us lovingly." They too hosted a meeting, a lively one, for an atheistic doctor in the audience challenged Fox. According to Fox's account, he managed to persuade the rest of the attendees of the Light by calling on an Indian in attendance. The Indian agreed that he felt guilt when he lied or treated others poorly, rendering the skeptical doctor "ashamed in the sight of the governor and the people." The next day, Jenkins walked two miles through the woods with Fox, while the boat was brought around to an easier dock.[47]

After a meeting at the home of Joseph Scott, "one of their burgesses," Fox called another meeting at the home of Henry Phelps on the Perquimans River. The Phelps family had already served as Edmondson's host, and news of another gathering with a different preacher spread quickly. The attendees included the secretary of the colony, "which formerly had been convinced." Fox then went to an Indian village just a couple of miles from the Phelps home and spent a day preaching. There too, he felt warmly received: "Their young king and others of their chief men were very loving."[48]

In his memoir, Fox recalled traveling several miles between houses in the area, always by boat. Visiting late in the year, the weather often made his journeys unpleasant. Returning from the Indian community, he stopped, but not without difficulty: "And after the meeting we passed away to the secretary's house, ten miles by water, and we were very wet, it being much rain, and in a rotten boat very dangerous. The water being shallow we could not get the boat to the shore, and the secretary's wife came in a canoe, barefooted and barelegged, to get us to land out of our boat, and so we stayed at their house all that night. And the next day in the morning, our boat was sunk."[49]

Women in Albemarle could not indulge in the finer social graces and were not controlled by them. A later visitor prefaced his observations regarding another female resident to indicate her local reputation was that of "a very civil woman" who "shews nothing of ruggedness or Immodesty." He then described how "she will carry a gunn in the woods and kill deer, turkeys . . . shoot doun wild cattle, catch and tye hoggs, knock down beeves [slaughter cattle] with an ax." The fine lady could "perform the most manfull Exercises as well as most men in those parts."[50]

Fox and his companions wended their way by canoe back to the Batts residence. They slept on a mat by the fire, as they had on most of their overnight stays. Within a short distance lived Hugh Smithwick, who hosted another Quaker meeting the following day with an audience of both settlers and Indians. From there, Fox rowed back to the Virginia border region and picked up his horse, "having spent a matter of eighteen days in the north of Carolina."[51]

A year later, in a letter to Virginian Friends, Fox mentioned a meeting that had been pending when he left Carolina: "If you go over again to Carolina, you may enquire of captain Batts, the old governor, with whom I left a paper to be read to the emperor and his thirty kings under him of the Tusrowres, who were to come to treat for peace with the people of Carolina."[52]

Peace reigned between the people of Albemarle and the Tuscarora for the next forty years. The imbalance of power between an "emperor" with thirty lesser leaders and Captain Batts representing the few hundred European settlers meant that the Tuscarora negotiated from a position of strength. Developments in the colony over the next generation indicate that Batts guaranteed boundaries to English settlement under this 1672 treaty: the regions west of the Chowan River and south of Albemarle Sound would remain Indian country, protected from English encroachment. As long as they honored these terms, the early settlers never had to deal with the levels of Indian hostility that their neighbors to the north and south aroused.[53]

That Jenkins and other officeholders welcomed Fox and helped him through deep woods and high water highlights an important contrast between northern Carolina and Virginia. Not long before these events, Virginia's governor had persecuted Quakers and called them a "pestilent sect." But in Albemarle—whether or not Fox won a great number of religious converts—political leaders showed leveler tendencies. They appeared open to a church that believed that tithes were wrong, that women might teach the Gospel as ably as men, and that social deference to others had no place in the eyes of God.

As with other Quaker communities in the late seventeenth century, Albemarle's was remarkably literate despite its remoteness. The settlers built no public schools, but a study of the period 1661–95 in Perquimans County found that 30 percent of the women and almost 70 percent of the men were literate. The Society of Friends demanded that its adherents teach not only their own children but all those of the community to read so that they could read Scripture for themselves rather than accept the interpretation of a priest or minister.[54]

-+-

The 1660s were the foundational era for North Carolina. Those who came through the Dismal Swamp to take up farming in the bottomlands along the creeks off Albemarle Sound made deliberate decisions about the society they were creating. Many historians have concluded that the region attracted the lawless, the heathen, the impoverished, and the uncultured, a reasonably accurate description. However, most later observers have assumed or concluded that this situation constituted some kind of historical accident brought on by geography or incompetent governance. Others have blamed a small minority of renegades who supposedly worked against the wishes of most settlers, who, it is again assumed, wanted nothing more than to be rich Virginia planters.[55] In actuality, the opposite held for most of the Virginians who came south. Filled with egalitarian ideas from the Interregnum and politically shrewd enough to understand that powerful forces would be arrayed against them after the Restoration, a majority of Albemarle's people endeavored to establish their colony as a legal alternative to their neighbors' world. Nor did they seek to create a City on a Hill, like the first settlers of Massachusetts; attention, in their experience, brought only repression. There was no need for aggression against Indian neighbors when friendly relationships better served their interests. So most settlers set up small farms, employing neither servants nor slaves, and took concrete political measures to ensure a tight rein on those who would have it otherwise, as some of course did. Thomas Woodward, for example, sought to impose a government by wealthy men, supported and justified by a hierarchical church. But he and his ilk never could achieve numerical superiority, and the broad franchise prevented their ascendancy for fifty years. They would not stop trying.

# THREE

# CULPEPER'S REBELLION, 1673–1680

The Albemarle community faced its first major trial in the 1670s. When the British empire decided to cash in on its colonies by passing the Navigation Acts, almost all the colonies on the American seaboard ignored them and set up elaborate smuggling operations. Nowhere was better equipped to do so than northern Carolina, where the remote and rugged geography stymied imperial law enforcement. Yet even there, men who spied a chance to enrich themselves through government sinecures attempted to establish customs collection. One such man, Thomas Miller, moved to Albemarle in 1673. Another 1673 arrival, John Culpeper, joined the community, too, and ultimately became Miller's nemesis.

What followed comprised a long and often dramatic story, on one level concerning tobacco and taxation, on another, the tensions between king and proprietors. The situation demanded that the backwoods settlers marshal political organizers, community solidarity, and political sophistication on an imperial level and that they commit themselves to using force if necessary against those who threatened their sanctuary. Their resistance would be tried at the empire's highest levels of power as their opponents warned that word of the Albemarle sanctuary would spread to all the oppressed of the mainland colonies. The warning went unheeded, and the episode known as Culpeper's Rebellion, although much less famous than Bacon's Rebellion to the north, secured for the people of Albemarle their right to govern themselves, at least in the short term.[1]

A full understanding of the course of events in this swampy colonial backwater requires recognizing that the story's protagonists lived on the periphery of an Atlantic world.[2] Moving around the ocean, people and their goods and ideas circulated not merely between the mother country and each colony but among the mainland colonies, the Caribbean islands, and Africa. In an effort to control this world, England's first Navigation Act, passed in 1651, prohibited the use of foreign vessels in the transportation of any import or export among England, Ireland, and the colonies. But no means to enforce the act existed, so the law had no teeth. No customs officials were appointed. One of Charles II's first decisions was to affirm the Navigation Act in 1660, and his administration, with Carolina proprietor Shaftesbury as chancellor of the exchequer (and later president of the Council of Trade and Plantations), moved toward better enforcement. Another provision of this measure specified that certain "enumerated" commodities, including sugar and tobacco, must pass through an English port before being sold abroad. The Staple Act of 1663 required "all goods produced or manufactured in Europe and destined for the Plantations to be carried first to England in 'lawful' ships, and there unloaded, before being carried thence in English-owned and manned ships."[3]

A further piece of mercantilist legislation, however, fell hardest on tobacco producers in Virginia, Maryland, and Albemarle. The 1673 Plantation Duty Act demanded the payment of English duties on the intercolonial trade, so that southern tobacco producers had to pay a customs duty of a penny a pound even when selling to New England or to the English colonies in the Caribbean. The act also called for the appointment of colonial customs officers who would answer directly to England, not to the colonial governors. Royal customs officials ultimately became among the most hated men in the colonies.[4]

One of the proprietors disapprovingly described the state of the tobacco trade in North Carolina during the 1670s: "The illness of the harbours was the cause that this Northern part of Carolina had no other vent for their Comodityes but either by Virginia where they paid dutyes to the Government or to New England who were the onely immediate Traders with them; And Ventur'd in, in small Vessells & had soe manadg'd their affayres that they brought their goods att very lowe rates, eate out & ruin'd the place, defrauded the King of his Customes."[5]

Virginia, on whose ports the people of Albemarle depended, had also imposed a tax on Carolina tobacco. The grievances Peter Carteret brought to the proprietors in 1672 included "the Injury Sustained by Us by Constraint of Entreyes and Clearing in Virginia and paying 2[s.] per hogshed thought shippt for England by Us being Owners."[6] With the additional duty from the 1673 act, the tobacco farmers of Albemarle were doubly taxed. It seemed essential that they get tax relief from England or find some extralegal means to export their produce.

For a remedy, they looked to the small trading boats of Massachusetts, capable of navigating the shallower waters of northern Carolina. A well-developed trade already moved between New England and the Chesapeake.[7] A willingness to evade duties enabled "about half dozen traders" of New England to secure a monopoly over the Albemarle tobacco output, which the settlers happily granted.[8] John Jenkins and other members of the council fully cooperated with the smuggling operation.[9] This type of illegal trade was not limited to northern Carolina. Throughout the mainland colonies, merchants and farmers allied with sailors from around the globe to find imaginative ways to circumvent the Navigation Acts. Boston led the way, and Albemarle happily followed.[10]

Further south, the new settlers on the Ashley River did not face the same problems, for they had easy access to a good harbor, but they had problems of their own. The leadership group was composed mostly of merchants, not experienced farmers, and by the winter of 1672, their council, because of the "extream wants of provisions this year," rationed food. By the following summer, some people had had enough. John Culpeper, the surveyor from Barbados and a member of the assembly, along with two members of the council, organized a protest among the settlers. They failed to displace Governor Joseph West. Justice was not tender in southern Carolina (runaways and thieves faced the death penalty), so the conspirators fled in June 1673. Their estates forfeited, they never returned to the Ashley River area. Culpeper headed north to

Albemarle. Already the region's characterization as a shelter for dissidents was known, and his migration only added to that reputation. Forever disenchanted with imperious leadership, he soon befriended George Durant and John Jenkins.[11]

Thomas Miller, an Irish apothecary, also had recently settled in Albemarle. Unlike most of the settlers, Miller willingly paid his tariffs and thought disparagingly of his fellow Carolinians. In March 1673, he hired Robert Riscoe, master of the brigantine *Good Hope of Albemarle*, to ship his tobacco to England. But trouble ensued. The leaky boat ran aground on shoals, and Riscoe abandoned the idea of crossing the Atlantic. He docked the crippled vessel in Newport, Rhode Island, a month later. Miller sued Riscoe in a Newport court for breach of contract and for the loss of and damage to his tobacco. Miller claimed that the vessel had been leaky before it left Albemarle and that the leaks had not resulted from the accidents that occurred during the journey. Riscoe argued that the treacherous shallows of the northern Carolina coast, combined with violent storms, had caused the leakage and therefore that he could not be held responsible for any damage. The court found in favor of Riscoe and ordered Miller to pay his court costs. The furious Miller refused and skipped town. Believing that the Newport court had not given him a fair trial, he appealed the case to the county court in Boston the following month, but he lost there, too.[12]

Miller never forgave what he felt was a conspiracy of Carolinians and New Englanders to cheat him of his rightful money. Returning to Albemarle in the fall of 1673, he set out to change the way that colony conducted business. He teamed up with Thomas Eastchurch, another unpopular newcomer with a score to settle with his neighbors. Eastchurch, appointed surveyor-general of Albemarle in 1671, was in Virginia when he claimed that "severall persons at Albemarle pretending that I am indebted to them have Atacked and otherwise made spoyle of my estate."[13]

Miller and Eastchurch decided to take advantage of the colony's unusual constitutional position. Jenkins's term as governor expired in 1674. The proprietors, concerned with matters at home and in their other global enterprises, did not bother to appoint another, feeding rumors that they had sold the Albemarle region outright to Virginia's Berkeley.

These rumors were not without foundation, for Berkeley had neither signed on nor provided funds for the settlement in southern Carolina. In March 1672, the other proprietors in England had considered a deal whereby Berkeley would get the Albemarle region and surrender his rights to the rest of Carolina. The contract never went into effect, but for several years, it was widely believed.[14]

The story that Berkeley might become Albemarle's sole proprietor sounded dreadful to the majority of the settlers in the swamp. Berkeley persecuted Quakers, which was bad enough, but he had also levied taxes and fees on Virginia's small farmers with great abandon. Marriage licenses cost 200 pounds of tobacco, and tavern owners had to pay an annual fee of 350 pounds of tobacco. Moreover, the governor demanded frequent "gifts" from his key political supporters and insisted on salary increases from the House of Burgesses (the representative assembly). Virginians also lavishly supported their representatives through poll taxes and paid fees to officeholders such as sheriffs. The colony's larger planters held these governmental positions at every level and backed Berkeley in the interest of their own pockets. Finally, Virginians had to pay tithes to an established Anglican church. The taxpayers bore these burdens at the same time that tobacco prices slumped and the Navigation Acts enriched the king at their expense.[15] Most citizens of Albemarle had no desire to join this political system.

A few felt differently, for they perceived in the rumor of Berkeley's sole proprietorship of northern Carolina an opportunity to occupy lucrative offices. Eastchurch became speaker of the Assembly after elections held in 1675 and arrested and imprisoned Jenkins, claiming authority in the power vacuum created by the proprietors' silence. Acting as a de facto governor, Eastchurch set up a council and court. Most outrageously of all, he and his friends decided to enforce the Navigation Acts and began to collect the tobacco tax. Eastchurch had no constitutional basis for his actions and, despite some support from others calling themselves the "Loyal party" (meaning loyal to the proprietors), his behavior enraged most of the local inhabitants. They had left Virginia for the Dismal Swamp to escape the burden of arbitrary government and would not submit deferentially. After learning what had become of Jenkins, another community leader, John Willoughby, beat a man sent to arrest him.

Willoughby declared that the older settlers still formed "the Court of Courts and Jury of Juries," and he set off for safety in Virginia.[16]

That winter, in meetings organized by Durant and Culpeper in homes up and down the rivers of Albemarle, they planned to strike back. Jenkins's wife, Joanna, too, played a major role in the organization. In the early months of 1676, the rebels attacked the prison and freed Jenkins. With the new title "generalissime," Jenkins again took control of the reins of government, and Eastchurch fled to England to protest to the proprietors. Miller, part of the Eastchurch faction, also became a prominent target.[17]

Culpeper recounted a story of treasonable talk by Miller, and the settlers decided to pursue the matter. According to Durant, Culpeper, and other witnesses, Miller had been sounding off about the royal family the previous summer. After news reached Carolina that the Duke of York had died, Miller allegedly responded by wishing "that som of the rest would not bee long after him." Durant laid a trap by discussing loyalty to the king, declaring that he would be willing to fight and die for any cause Charles would espouse. According to his accusers, Miller fell into Durant's snare, calling Durant a fool and saying, "There was noe righteous dealing among the Cavaleares for the King had his hand in a whores plackett."[18] Miller might well have felt safe in saying such things in the company of Levellers.[19] Still believing that Berkeley might be the sole authority of their region, the Albemarle leadership imprisoned Miller on charges of treason and blasphemy, accusations they felt would be particularly galling to Berkeley, and sent Miller to face trial in Virginia in May 1676.[20]

Berkeley had much bigger problems on his hands. Small farmers in Virginia, bearing the weight of his heavy taxation, had grown restless under his administration. Nathaniel Bacon, scion of a prominent Roundhead family during the Civil War, was organizing a force, ostensibly to attack Indians on the Virginia frontier but also to launch a direct challenge to the governor and his corrupt burgesses. Bacon's supporters included William Drummond, Carolina's first governor. Culpeper, presumably accompanying Miller to his Virginia trial, met with Drummond in Jamestown in early June to pledge the support of the Albemarle settlers, so familiar with Berkeley's exploitative regime. Culpeper promised a safe house in Carolina for those who might need it. "If wee cannot prevaile by our armes at least to make our conditions for peace or obtaine the priviledge to elect our owne Governors wee may retire to Roanoke," declared Bacon. With "Carolina" as their watchword, his rebel force drove Berkeley and his cronies briefly out of government and burned Jamestown that September. After Bacon's death in October 1676, the defeat of the rebellion, and the execution of Drummond, the surviving Virginia rebels headed to Albemarle.[21]

His case quickly dismissed by Berkeley, Miller immediately departed to join Eastchurch in London, where they pursued their claim of jurisdiction over Albemarle. The proprietors had some trouble figuring out exactly what had happened in the northern section of their colony over the previous year or two, but as they admitted, they did not want to put themselves out very much over a region that generated no profit.[22]

At a meeting in the fall, presented only with Eastchurch and Miller's version of events, the proprietors decided to appoint Eastchurch as the new governor and send with him a new set of instructions. Their letter, addressed to the Albemarle Assembly, firmly denied the rumors about Berkeley's ownership of Albemarle. It declared that the proprietors would never part with the area, though they also admitted that they had ignored the northern branch of their colony. They excused their actions by arguing that the settlers had not tried to build links with the Ashley River settlement: "The Rivers of Phampleco and Newse should have bin before this welplanted and a way and Intercource by Land should have bine discovered between you and our Plantation on Ashley River, and the neglect of these two has bine the Cause that heitherto wee have had noe more Reguard for you." Miller and Eastchurch blamed everything that displeased the proprietors on the old settlers and made it clear that the traders from New England had entered into a conspiracy with Durant, Jenkins, and others to cheat people like themselves, for Miller had not forgotten his bitter experiences with Riscoe and the Boston court. The proprietors demanded that the assembly investigate and report on how to avoid this connived dependency on the New England boats by sending "an exact account of how many foot there is at Low water in your severall Inlets, what safety there is when a shipp is in and where she may doe best to unlade or take in Commodities for this has bine soe concealed and uncertainely reported here as if some persons amongst you had joyn'd with some of New England to engross that poore trade you have and Keep you still under hatches." The proprietors did not understand that the illegal commerce between Albemarle and New England did not benefit the few but the many, for it meant evasion of the Navigation Acts. Despite the feelings of Miller and Eastchurch, most of Albemarle's small farmers did not agree with the proprietors' assessment that the New England monopoly brought them "a certaine Beggery." Paying royal taxes would more likely cause such financial ruin.[23]

In any case, the settlers would not have to concern themselves with the proprietors' instructions for at least eight months, for the disgruntled apothecary did not return to Albemarle until the following summer. Those in Albemarle had been consumed with the rebellion against the Virginia governor, for they still suspected that Berkeley was their sole proprietor. Bacon's fight had put them in a difficult position, however, for he at first declared war only on Indians. The settlers in Albemarle had no fight with their Indian neighbors and no desire to see that peaceful relationship upset. But they allied with Bacon against Berkeley and his planter elite during the summer and fall of 1676, and his belligerent excursions forced Virginian Indian groups into the wilderness of the swamp, where they met all white men with hostility. Quaker missionary William Edmondson described the situation as "perilous travelling, for the Indians were not yet subdued, but did mischief and murdered several; the place they haunted much was in that wilderness betwixt Virginia and Carolina, scarce any durst travel that way unarmed."[24]

The Quaker pacifist philosophy helped keep skirmishes to a minimum and mend relations with the natives over the course of the winter and spring. Life returned to normal for a few months in Albemarle. But Miller soon returned. He and Eastchurch left England in the summer of 1677 with the proprietors' letter and instructions, including the appointment of Eastchurch as governor. The latter, however, got distracted on the voyage, finding a quicker and easier way to make money than extracting taxes and fees from American settlers. He met a wealthy widow on the Caribbean island of Nevis, where his ship had stopped. No sooner had Eastchurch encountered this "woman that was a considerable fortune" than he "took hold of the oppertunity marryed her and dispatched away Mr Miller for Carolina." Miller previously had been appointed customs collector, and Eastchurch now deputized him to fill the role of governor as well. He landed in July.[25]

Since most of the locals already despised Miller, they jeered and threatened him when he returned and insisted that His Majesty's customs would not be collected. But one lesson had been learned during the English Civil War and reinforced recently by Virginia's Berkeley: retribution could be harsh for those found guilty of treason. The law's tentacles might reach even into remote regions, so the settlers held back from their stated desire to "run their knife" through Miller. Miller understood that he must secure the force of law behind him and to that end immediately called a meeting of the assembly to legitimize his authority by publishing his commissions.[26] It was the last meeting of the assembly for many months: having secured his status as temporary governor, Miller refused to allow any further gathering of representatives that might attempt to curtail him.[27]

Flushed with power, Miller stamped his authority all over Albemarle, appointing friends as deputy collectors in Chowan precinct to the west and Currituck to the east. He empowered Timothy Biggs and Henry Hudson not only to collect the customs duties on tobacco as it shipped out of these areas but also to seize any items considered illegally imported European goods smuggled in by New England traders.

None of these actions would garner Miller any popular support, and he had little to lose. He could now obtain revenge on his neighbors for packing him off to Virginia for a treason trial the previous year. Going after his former enemies and employing a "pipeing guard" to enforce his commands, he imposed a large fine (two hundred pounds) on Willoughby, who had slighted Eastchurch the year before. Valentine Bird, the previous customs collector, received a fine of five hundred pounds for his lax enforcement of the Navigation Acts. By December, Miller had collected more than one thousand pounds in bonds. In the same busy period, he had also gathered additional fees for himself.[28]

In the fall, Culpeper, an experienced leader of public protest (one proprietor later described how Culpeper had "fled from South Carolina where he was in danger of hanging for . . . indeavouring to sett the poore people to plunder the rich") quietly began organizing the settlers.[29] The council members, now forbidden to meet officially, kept in touch, trying to figure out how to deal with Miller and restore their version of order. They held most meetings in Pasquotank precinct, just across the Little River from Durant's Neck, since Durant was abroad selling his tobacco. The objectives included not merely ridding themselves of this particularly odious customs collector and governor but also reestablishing their own government, with its broad franchise and freely elected Parliament, and installing a friendly person in the post of collector of His Majesty's customs.

Given the Atlantic political realities, this effort would require both armed rebellion in Albemarle and delicate diplomacy in London. As usual, the rebels kept an eye on developments around them, with the situation in Virginia especially relevant. Governor Berkeley had crushed Bacon's Rebellion, but the repression had been so absurdly brutal that London had intervened. The king ordered Berkeley to London to explain the violent episode and his vindictive response, and he had died there. Virginians currently found themselves caught up in a wrangle for power between the king's replacement governor, trying to pacify the colony by listening to the grievances of former rebels, and the local magnates, still bent on plundering rebel estates.[30]

The Carolinians believed that under such circumstances, they might meet with some sympathy in London if they presented their case in just the right fashion. To do so meant taking into account the tension between the monarch and their proprietors. That relations between the king and the Carolina proprietors had deteriorated is an understatement, for Shaftesbury sat in the Tower of London. In the seventeen years since the Restoration, Charles II had slowly but surely revealed that he harbored similar views to those of his father regarding the proper powers of king and Parliament. This king refused to accept limitations on royal prerogatives, let alone parliamentary control. The current Parliament, elected at the time of the Restoration, still included enough supporters of Charles—the Court party—to force Shaftesbury into opposition. His efforts to dissolve the so-called Cavalier Parliament in the hope that fresh elections would bring his "County party" back to power had landed him in the Tower.[31]

In formulating their response to Miller, the organizers in Albemarle had to consider all these political realities. The king certainly would want his customs money, but he had proven himself receptive to accusations of corruption against governors. The proprietors, conversely, gained nothing from customs revenues but benefited only from quitrents. They wished merely not to be bothered very much by the northern residents now that the lords had diverted their attention to the potentially more profitable Charles Town area and to politics at home. If the Albemarle rebels could take these two factors into account, they might be able to justify a revolt against Miller.

While Culpeper, the old council, and some of the New England men took leadership roles in planning the overthrow of the hated governor, they had a broad base of support. Nothing rankled their opponents more than "their industrious labor to be popular." The entire community was welcomed to join the planned revolt and did so in droves. They formed a remarkable alliance among the colonial population, for an alleged one-third of their group was composed of "Indians, Negros and women."[32] Throughout the fall, they laid the groundwork.

Durant returned from England on December 1, 1677. He arrived on the ship of a Boston trader and captain, Zachary Gillam, carrying a heavy cargo of munitions. Late that night, Miller came on board to collect his duties. Gillam refused to pay. Miller drew his gun and tried to arrest Durant but was assailed by Gillam's crew and tied up. Valentine Bird and William Crawford went on board immediately to bring Durant up to date on Miller's actions during Durant's absence and to finalize the strategy for an attack. They released Miller temporarily while they developed their plans. Durant knew that they had to be well coordinated, for some of Miller's supporters surely would try to get to Virginia to raise a militia. Durant pointed out that they needed to protect themselves legally by destroying any official papers authorizing Miller or recording his accounts of customs collected. The group spent two days figuring out logistics. They decided that they would disperse throughout the small colony in several armed groups, each composed of at least thirty men. Gillam had plenty of extra cutlasses on board, should they be needed. His boat would serve as headquarters for the immediate future, with Crawford's house as the insurrection's land base.[33]

On December 3, a party of men armed with muskets and swords

advanced on the home of Timothy Biggs, Miller's deputy customs collector. They broke open locked chests and located the papers appointing Miller collector and deputizing him as acting governor. After the raiders departed for Crawford's house with these crucial documents, Biggs contacted Miller and John Nixon, magistrate during Miller's term in office and a loyal supporter. They immediately came to Biggs's house, only to fall into a well-laid trap. Bird, at the head of another armed group, seized all three men and brought the prisoners to Crawford's house. A messenger took news of the capture to the men aboard Gillam's boat. With the chief officers of government locked up, Culpeper, on board ship, conferred with Durant and penned a revolutionary declaration.[34]

"The Remonstrance of the Inhabitants of Paspatancke to All the Rest of the County of Albemarle" called all the residents of Albemarle to arms. It asked them to join forces with the rebels not only to protect their right to government by the people but also to secure their much-needed supplies from the New England trade. It began, "First the occasion of their secureinge the Records & imprisoning the President is, that thereby the Countrey may have a free parlement." Miller's refusal to call the assembly constituted the primary issue, repeated again in the next sentence: "In the first place (omitting many hainous matters) hee denied a free election of an Assembly." Like the more famous declaration of a century later, it also spelled out economic grievances, charging that Miller "hath positively cheated the Countrey of one hundred and thirty thousand pounds of Tobacco."[35]

Culpeper then appealed to the public's need for duty-free goods, explaining that "Captain Gillam is come amongst us with three times the goods hee brought last yeare." But faced with port duties, Gillam would have "gone directly out of the Countrey" if he had not been "earnestly perswaded by some" to remain. The last grievance detailed how Miller "went aboard with a brace of pistolls and presenting one of them cockt to Mr. Geo. Durants breast & with his other hand arrested him as a Traytour." Word of Durant's arrest would have enormous shock value to the settlers. Culpeper's remonstrance pleaded that immediate action was crucial to avoid financial ruin at the hands of Miller, for "many other Injuries, mischiefes, and grievances hee hath brought upon us, that thereby an inevitable ruein is comeing (unlesse prevented) which wee are now about to doe and hope & expect that you will joyne with us therein." The remonstrance bore the signatures of thirty men of Albemarle.[36]

Culpeper dispatched the declaration to the other three counties of Albemarle. Durant's neighbor, Samuel Pricklove, brought it to his home territory of Perquimans, and Richard Foster went east to Currituck, while Culpeper headed west to Chowan to round up support. Miller's sheriff in Perquimans arrested Pricklove, but neighbors came to his aid, and the sheriff, too, was put under armed guard. Foster seized another of Miller's deputies, Henry Hudson, and called a meeting to choose delegates for a new assembly. The citizens of Currituck held clear ideas on the topic of representation, and they excitedly declared an overthrow of the Fundamental Constitutions: "Wee will have noe Lords noe Landgraves noe Cassiques we renounce them all." Foster, a well-educated man with some understanding of the constitutional niceties of the situation, calmed the members of the crowd and reminded them to stay within defensible limits. Having chosen representatives, the Currituck meeting issued instructions. The single-most-important issue would be the elimination of any collection of customs duties. Miller should be tried for his corruption, and the seized tobacco should be returned. With these guidelines, the delegation set off for Durant's house, carrying Hudson as a prisoner.[37]

Culpeper called on the residents of Chowan precinct, west of Pasquotank, to join the rebellion. After describing for them the arrest of Miller and his associates, he returned to the center of activities. Despite the efforts of the Chowan sheriff to raise "Posse Comitatis," all five Chowan representatives from the old assembly agreed with Culpeper's argument that Miller had overturned their government. A few days later, an armed guard of local settlers brought Chowan's sheriff to Crawford's house. Once all prisoners and their papers had been secured, Albemarle's government returned to its normal site, Durant's home, where he held court two weeks after his return from England. The prisoners came in boats across the Little River, with Gillam firing his ship's guns in celebration as the flotilla went by. Foster and the men of Currituck brought Hudson.[38]

With representatives from all four precincts meeting at Durant's house, they elected a new assembly. While the leading men of Albemarle

—Jenkins, Crawford, James Blount, Patrick White, Foster, and Bird— were appointed as council and court, the eighteen burgesses included the five previously elected from Chowan and a wide cross-section of the population, including, to the disgust of Miller and Hudson, a young drummer. Culpeper would fill the position of collector of customs and Durant that of attorney general.[39]

The new government immediately resurrected the old charges of treason and blasphemy against Miller. A New England trader served as the foreman of a grand jury. But just as the indictment was given and another jury impaneled for the trial, a messenger appeared. Friends of Miller had escaped to Virginia during the fortnight's rounding up of his allies. Eastchurch had finally arrived from the Caribbean and become aware of the developments in Albemarle. He drew up a proclamation asserting his authority and sent it ahead by this messenger, bringing an abrupt halt to the proceedings.[40]

Eastchurch's proclamation tested the Albemarle settlers' commitment to the society they had created in the swamp. The stakes were high. They could fight for a free assembly, but they had seen what had happened to those such as their old friend Drummond in Virginia. Many followers of Bacon now lived among the Carolinians, having had to abandon their homes and farms. Would the gain be worth the risk? It would mean the right to make their own laws and set their own taxes, but these were not yet accepted "rights" in the Atlantic world. The gathered settlers from the four corners of Albemarle discussed their options. They decided to fight.

Keeping Eastchurch out of Albemarle, along with any militia he might muster in Virginia, was imperative. To protect their assembly, the settlers made a commitment to the use of force. The gathering selected a band of men to go to the Virginia border and use armed resistance to prevent Eastchurch's progress. The rest of Albemarle should be armed and ready.[41]

Hoping that diplomacy would preclude the need for force, the Albemarle group dispatched a letter on December 27 to Herbert Jeffreys, acting governor of Virginia. Signed by Foster, Crawford, Bird, Blount, and Thomas Cullen in the name of the "almost Unanimous Inhabitants," the letter pleaded with Jeffreys to ignore those friends of Miller who had fled north. They were merely "Mislead persons (though A Small Number) who live amongst us (yett are not of Us)." The rebels admitted that they had arrested Miller and listed the charges against him. They dismissed Eastchurch's "Proclamation sent from Nansemond," which seemed to support Miller, declaring, "as if [Eastchurch's] Court were at Nansemond" and questioning why he had not come to Albemarle in person. Still, they wanted him to come alone, not accompanied by armed Virginians.[42]

They held their breath, wondering what Eastchurch could do. Not much, it turned out, for the appointed governor had fallen ill. He died in February, just five weeks after his arrival in Virginia. Virginian authorities seemed reluctant to take on a rebel force in the swamp, despite Governor Jeffreys's contempt for their "Despiseing all Authority but Their Owne."[43] When word of Eastchurch's death reached Albemarle, the settlers relaxed. The first meeting of the new assembly convened at Governor Jenkins's house.

The prisoners had been kept under armed guard on Durant's property, but a more permanent jail had to be arranged. The settlers constructed a ten-foot-square log house on Pasquotank riverside property, and there Miller undoubtedly seethed for almost two years, away from his deputies and associates. The men who had volunteered as soldiers on the Virginia border received the customs tobacco taken from Miller as reward. Life returned to normal for a few weeks, with the New England men free to come and go, trading goods from Europe and Massachusetts for the tobacco from Albemarle without any payment of customs duties.[44]

They relaxed too soon. Biggs escaped around the end of January 1678. He fled first to Virginia and from there to England; arriving in April, he went immediately to speak to the proprietors. The Albemarle Council met and decided to dispatch emissaries across the Atlantic to argue the council's case. Durant and Willoughby, appointed as agents of the council and assembly, left hastily to intercept Biggs or to plead the corruption of Miller, whichever proved necessary.[45]

The proprietors ordered Biggs to draw up an affidavit describing how events had unfolded in Albemarle. He presented it in person to the Duke of Albemarle and to the Earl of Danby, the lord treasurer (the current favorite of the king and the man chiefly responsible for Shaftesbury's imprisonment). The duke told Biggs to ready a copy for the King's Council. Acting on his own initiative, Biggs also prepared some proposals for the proprietors, implying that they bore some responsibility for the rebellion and calling on them to take a more active role in their colony. He pointed out that in contrast to their investments in the southern parts of Carolina, "you have not beene out as yet any thing upon that County in the province called Albemarle" and claimed that "had your Lordships smiles & assistance but a tenth part of what your Southern parts have had It would have beene a Flourishing Settlement." Biggs made it clear that the rebellion was not a mere factional fight between Albemarle planters. The lords' neglect greatly discouraged "Men of Estates" from settling in northern Carolina.[46]

Biggs pointed out the potential for profit from Albemarle should the proprietors take a firmer hand in its management. But the immediate crisis demanded that the rebellion be crushed as rapidly as possible, before the rebels could strengthen their forces. Biggs recommended "a Vessell with 8 or 10 Guns & full power to beat up for Volunteers in Virginia to suppresse them."[47]

An added level of threat lay in this rebellion, one with far-reaching consequences for all of British North America. Biggs warned the proprietors that "not onely his Majesty's Customes are unpayd and your Lordships interests lye at stake by the great Injury it will be to the neighbouring Governments as New England, New Yorke, Maryland & Virginia by servants, Slaves & Debtors flying thither which will in continuance of time make them so stronge."[48] Albemarle already provided a home for runaways of many types, and this rebellion might make it a stronghold that would attract even more.

Another Albemarle resident whose name is now unknown later wrote a document supporting Biggs's argument. The social composition of the rebel force most frightened those with planter aspirations. The geography of the region already made northern Carolina a haven for the disenchanted. Their political control of the colony might create an alternative society that would undermine the powerful and wealthy in the New World. The writer made plain that the rebellion did not reflect a spontaneous reaction to any one particular grievance. It "was not accidentall . . . but rather the effect of a more mature or deliberate contrivance." As Biggs had already pointed out, the authorities should not shirk from considering the potential ramifications: "If they be not suddenly subdued hundreds of idle debters, theeves, negros, Indians and English servants will fly into them & from thence make Inroads and dayly Incursions, whence great mischief may follow which may better be foreseene and prevented than after remedied, for considering the vast coast and wild woods of the backside of Virginia they may come from Maryland & the Wilderness between Virginia and Albemarle extending one hundred miles without one Inhabitant they may and some already do go into them in defiance of all the care the governor and Magistrates there take for prevention."[49]

The warnings fell on deaf ears. Biggs did not understand, at least at first, the English political situation in which he was operating. The last thing the proprietors wanted was royal attention to their mismanagement of their charter colonies. First, Charles II and Danby did not need any further ammunition against Shaftesbury personally, although they had recently released him from the Tower.[50] Second, the increasingly precarious situation of all proprietary charters would be further shaken by these revelations that the proprietors had proved incapable of enforcing the collection of His Majesty's customs. Therefore, from the proprietors' perspective, the more quickly they covered up the issue, the better. Shortly thereafter, Biggs was greatly surprised to receive a command to drop the matter entirely.[51]

Durant and Willoughby had arrived in London. They, too, had an audience with the proprietors and gave their version of the story. They fully admitted arresting and imprisoning Miller but claimed complete loyalty to the lords. This was a rebellion not against all authority, Durant argued convincingly, but merely against an unlawful and corrupt governor. The proprietors, not terribly concerned with who was running Albemarle or with customs collection, happily listened. Enmeshed in intrigue to bring about the contraction of royal power, they sought an easy explanation. Their solution to the situation lay in a new man, Seth Sothell, who had joined their ranks. Sothell had purchased the Clarendon share of the proprietary and offered to go live in Albemarle and serve as governor.

Durant and Willoughby "promised the utmost submission" to Sothell, both as governor and in his other role as customs collector. And so the proprietors silenced Biggs.[52]

Durant and Willoughby sailed home in the summer of 1678. Sothell, too, headed for Albemarle that fall, but the harsh reality of Atlantic piracy interfered. Turkish pirates seized Sothell's ship and carried him as a prisoner to Algiers. When the news of his capture reached England, Biggs pleaded that he be allowed to replace Sothell at least in the royal position as customs collector. Anxious to keep Biggs from drawing attention to the situation, the proprietors agreed (although they had no authority to appoint anyone to royal posts such as collector of customs), and Biggs set off for Albemarle with papers confirming his appointment as comptroller and surveyor-general of His Majesty's customs.[53]

Biggs returned to Carolina in early February 1679. If he thought his papers would guarantee him respect and compliance, he was very much mistaken. After summoning him to appear at Durant's house with his papers, the council members indicated that they had no intention of allowing him to proceed with enforcement of the Navigation Acts. Biggs defiantly posted his appointment on the court door, but Culpeper removed it, replacing it with an emphatic declaration of his own authority. Culpeper addressed his bill "to all the inhabitants or any that may arrive in the County of Albemarle," and "to the intent that noe person whatsoever may be deluded or run into danger by meanes of the said proclamation," he threatened that "whoever shall enter or clear with [Biggs] thinking they have done their duty therein he or they may be hereby informed that I will make seizure of them & bring them to tryall according to Act of Parliament."[54]

Individuals who recognized Biggs as a customs official would find themselves in serious trouble with the Albemarle Assembly. According to an associate of Biggs, he and his family and friends slept with loaded guns by their beds for some time thereafter.[55]

With Sothell unavailable, the proprietors again were forced to deal with the issue of Albemarle. They wrote to their colony in early February, appointing John Harvey as temporary governor and sending another copy of the Fundamental Constitutions and some instructions. The proprietors pleaded neither for Miller's release nor for any restoration of a vigorous collection of customs duties but merely asked that law and order prevail. They stated that they were not prepared to "use force to reduce the seditious to reason" and assured settlers that "the good and welfare of all the Inhabitants of our province" remained "what wee most desire and not the taking away any mans life and Estate."[56] The new governor, Harvey, a longtime resident of Albemarle, had steered as neutral a course as possible through the violent stage of the rebellion. But he never actively opposed it and worked well alongside Jenkins, Durant, and the other rebels until his death the following year. The Albemarle rebellion's goals seemed to have been secured. Yet the rebels' elation was soon dashed.

The council had retried Miller on the old charges of blasphemy, found him guilty, and put him back in prison.[57] Biggs struggled to help Miller by drawing up affidavits during that summer, but to no avail. In September, he collected one from some friends among the practicing Quakers, who made it clear that they—even those who had served as elected representatives to the Albemarle Assembly—had played no part in the violent events of December 1677. Biggs told them their statement would be presented to the proprietors.[58] Unprepared to give up his struggle against the rebels and with the help of Miller's ex-deputy, Henry Hudson, and others, Biggs planned a counterattack. In November 1679, they sprang Miller from jail.

Miller quickly made his way to Virginia, despite being "followed by hue & cry," and he and Hudson took passage to England on the boat of a trader.[59] They reached London in December. Culpeper and Gillam were in England, too, preparing to return to Carolina, when the king's Privy Council served an arrest warrant on them on December 19. Biggs's experience taught Miller that he needed to go over the heads of the proprietors, so he went straight to royal authorities. The Privy Council, impressed by Miller's account, ordered a search of all sloops in the Downs bound for Virginia and placed both Culpeper and Gillam in custody. Culpeper was the only person from Albemarle available to face charges; thus, the rebellion has borne his name ever since. Although he was one of the chief organizers, no single person led this popular revolt.[60]

Miller's actions brought the rebellion to the attention of the highest levels of imperial authority. The Privy Council turned the matter over to the Treasury, which then asked the Board of Customs to investigate. It seemed to the royal government that the real issue lay not in the interpretation of who constituted the rightful government of some wilderness colony but rather in the serious matter of the loss of customs money owed to the Crown. The empire had imposed the Navigation Acts to bring important revenues to London, and royal officials would not take lightly any avoidance of that taxation on principle, whatever the sums in question. According to Miller's account, the sum totaled £1,242, "eight shillings and one penny sterling" in cash, plus 817 hogshead of tobacco.[61] The Customs Board's report supported Miller wholeheartedly and called for the prosecution of Culpeper and Gillam. Two weeks later, the council delegated the matter to the Committee of Trade and Foreign Plantations, with the stipulation that the lords proprietors of Carolina must attend a meeting of that committee and furnish a report about the "breach of Peace in that Government with an authentick Copy of their Charter."[62] In a brief to the king, the council reported that Culpeper made no denial of the facts presented but begged for pardon or at least to be tried in Carolina. However, the memo also made clear that the customs commissioners did not want him released until he had delivered the money he owed.[63]

On February 8, the Committee of Trade and Plantations held its first hearing at Whitehall. Culpeper, Miller, Hudson, and two witnesses friendly to Miller ( John Taylor and Solomon Summers) attended, as did three proprietors (Shaftesbury, Peter Colleton, and the Earl of Craven). Shaftesbury took the floor first and promised that he and his colleagues would soon deliver a copy of their charter and a complete account of the rebellion. He made clear immediately that although Culpeper, Durant, and Gillam had certainly rebelled, Miller had to some extent provoked his own overthrow. Next, a royal customs commissioner produced Miller's account of the customs money seized by Culpeper. Culpeper pleaded that he represented a lawful assembly "and that the people of Carolina agreed upon him as their Collector." On this he based his defense, endeavoring to make the issue a broader question of rightful authority in Carolina. The proprietors, of course, wanted to avoid this question lest it draw attention to their inability to control their chartered property. Even after Hudson, Summers, and Taylor had testified against

Culpeper with dramatic accounts of the December 1677 violence, the proprietors claimed that Albemarle was "now quieted" and that the missing customs money should be collected personally from Culpeper and "not the whole Country by a Tax to bee laid on them."[64]

This solution proved acceptable to the committee, much to the dismay of Miller and his friends. They learned, much as Biggs had eighteen months earlier, that the proprietors did not sympathize with their case. After Gillam's trial was scheduled for the following week, the hearing broke up. The next day, Colleton wrote the proprietors' official account of the rebellion. According to Colleton, Miller, "as Governor he did many extravagant things, making strange limitations for the choice of the Parliament gitting power in his hands of laying fynes, which tis to be feared he neither did nor meant to use moderately."[65]

Gillam had his hearing before the committee on February 19, with Shaftesbury and a representative of the customs commissioners in attendance. Despite the sworn affidavits of Miller and his friends, Gillam protested his innocence, claiming to be nothing but a trader who paid customs duties in England, sold weapons to the Carolinians only "for their defence Against the Heathen," attended Miller's trial for treason only as a convenient way to meet many customers at a central location, and had always given out alcohol as a friendly gesture toward customers, adding, "Mr Miller had his sheare of it."[66] The committee apparently had little faith in Miller's testimony, for they set Gillam free. They called for the proprietors and the commissioners to meet to settle the rules for customs collection in Carolina.[67] At an April meeting, the proprietors agreed to set up commissions of inquiry to investigate both the lost duties and the compensation owed to Miller.[68]

Culpeper finally came to trial for treason in a Westminster court in the late spring of 1680. He had languished in Newgate jail for five months. He was charged with "plotting with all his powers, intending to arouse and wage war against the King in Carolina." Culpeper pleaded not guilty and was acquitted.[69] The trial transcript contains little further information, but Miller claimed later that Shaftesbury "unexpectedly appeared at the Tryall as a witness for the Defendant." The proprietor testified that Miller's regime did not constitute a legal government "and that therefore the taking of Armes & acting against them could not amount to Treason." He went on to explain that the assembly elected by the rebels met lawfully under the Fundamental Constitutions, "the people having a right to choose them at two years end." Shaftesbury thus secured Culpeper's freedom.[70]

Shaftesbury had his reasons. The southern part of the colony, which he referred to as "my Darling," finally turned a profit. His Indian trading company was getting under way. Albemarle might be a thorn in his side, but the charter included all of Carolina, and Shaftesbury did not want any negative attention to threaten proprietary government in general and its place in Carolina in particular. Better to portray Miller as the guilty party than to admit that almost the entire Albemarle population had slipped out of his control.[71]

Miller was aghast. First Gillam and then Culpeper had been released. The proprietors apparently had declined to do anything to help Miller. The commissions of inquiry they had promised had not materialized. At the same time, back in Albemarle, Biggs was still trying to collect the customs, perhaps assuming that Miller's escape and Culpeper's arrest would soon result in the overthrow of the rebellion. He enlisted former rebel Samuel Pricklove as his deputy. In early February 1680, coincident with the hearings in London, Biggs dispatched Pricklove to board two New England vessels docked in Albemarle. Instead, Pricklove was seized and kept prisoner for several weeks. Biggs then petitioned Charles II for relief, arguing that the proprietors were doing nothing about the rebel government or its defiance of the Navigation Acts. Biggs asked the king to provide a boat, well manned and gunned, and to order the Virginia government to help restore a legal government in Albemarle.[72] Virginia was not prepared to take military action, although the current governor there, Thomas, Lord Culpeper (no relation to the rebel John Culpeper) understood the threat of a free Albemarle and disparaged it: "Carolina (I meane the North part of it) alwayes was and is the sinke of America, the Refuge of our Renagadoes."[73]

Pricklove had his trial on March 27, but it hardly went as Biggs had hoped. Pricklove's attempt to enforce the Navigation Acts aggrieved his accusers, and he was convicted and given a severe sentence: "Ordered that Samuel Pricklove stand in the pillory three hours, and loose his right ear, and be banished this county for ever, and to live in prison without bayle in yrons, or otherwise, until hee shall bee shipped for his transport, and their aboard kept in yrons, till at his place he be landed with costs and fees." Pricklove was one of the very earliest settlers of Albemarle, so his sentence imparted a clear message that the assembly would show no mercy to anyone unwilling to recognize its authority.[74]

Despite defeat in England and Carolina, Miller would not yield, but he failed to understand the complex, delicate intricacies of power relationships in English politics. Following up on Biggs's action, Miller appealed to the king in June and again a week later in July. With Culpeper no longer the focus of his wrath, Miller pointedly accused the proprietors of supporting the rebellion, claiming that "their Lordships seeme rather to countenance the present settlement of things under the Rebells." Miller also declared them guilty of collusion in the noncollection of customs.[75]

This time the lords proprietors themselves stood on trial. The matter again came before the Committee for Trade and Plantations, and the entire process was reopened. Biggs sent fresh evidence of the latest developments, including the arrest of Pricklove, along with original documents from his 1678 attempt to get justice from the proprietors. He specifically referred to their command that he let the matter drop.[76] A petition from a few Albemarle settlers (a small minority of the population, who bewailed the fact that "the whole Country is now overswaied by the said Rabble") also accused the proprietors of collusion with the rebels.[77] Durant, Albemarle's new attorney general, sent copies of the depositions from Miller's trials for treason and blasphemy, quoting Miller vilifying the sacraments, Cavaliers, monarchy in general, and Charles II in particular. Durant explained that Miller had escaped from custody, naming Biggs and Hudson, among others, as accessories to the escape.[78]

The committee called for a hearing in mid-August 1680 with all parties to be in attendance. But bigger issues were afoot in England. The king's health sank. Shaftesbury directed all his attention to ensure the removal of the king's "Popish" brother, James, from the line of succession. To hear that Miller had named Shaftesbury in his petitions and charged him with customs evasion must have enraged the earl. Colleton, pleading ill health, got an extension of the Miller case. Miller stewed until November 20.[79]

When at last the hearing was held, Miller learned that he had taken on one of the most powerful men in the early British empire. The proprietors forcefully responded. Whereas in earlier hearings, they had not condoned the rebellion and had criticized both Culpeper and Miller, now they turned full bore against the man who had dared challenge them head-on. According to their account, "Mr Thomas Miller without any legall authority gott possession of the government of the County of Albemarle in Carolina in the yeare 1677 . . . doeing many illegall and arbitrary things and drinking often to excess and putting the people in generall by his threats and actions in great dread of their lives and estates." They accused Biggs of trying to disturb the peaceful collection of customs. The proprietors claimed that they had found yet another governor, Captain Henry Wilkinson, for Carolina. They concluded their report by indicating that Miller would never receive a position of any authority in Albemarle.[80]

The committee was hardly likely to consider the testimonies of unknown provincials with the same weight it would accord a peer of the realm who recently had served as lord president of the Privy Council. They accepted Shaftesbury's explanation but made the proprietors promise to use their influence in Carolina to ensure some compensation for Miller's losses in the affair. Shaftesbury and his fellow proprietors promised easily, for they had long since accepted that they had very little influence on the people of Albemarle.[81]

Thomas Miller had never grasped the political realities of the Atlantic world. His opponents in Albemarle, conversely, had learned those lessons through experiences in the English Civil War and Virginia. They understood the advantages of living in a backwater. Their location, not conducive to large-scale trade, would not induce powerful interests to expend much trouble to bring it under control. They understood that English lords and particularly Shaftesbury did not often stand on principle, having watched them change sides and reinstate a monarchy they had overthrown. They understood that when confronting power, maintaining the delusion required them to go through the motions of deference, but there was no need to truly acquiesce to those with little reason or will to back up their desires with force.

Those at the bottom of society learn these lessons well; their survival often depends on figuring out how delicately to manipulate those at the top. Culpeper's Rebellion might be better named the Albemarle Revolution, for it was a grassroots, democratic movement against imperial authority in all its forms. They fought to preserve their right to representation and against both imperial taxation and the corruption of imperial officials on the ground, like the American Revolution of a century later.

Unlike that revolution, the people of Albemarle united across race, gender, and class lines. The allegation that Indians, free blacks, and women composed one-third of the active rebel force surely exaggerated, but these numbers cannot be dismissed out of hand. Although specifics on the activities of these groups are scant, some documents contain tantalizing references that place unexpected people in the role of decision maker. The wives of Jenkins and Patrick White were mentioned by name in affidavits as coconspirators. Durant's wife, Anne, a leading figure in the community, held power of attorney for her husband when he traveled abroad. The rebels were characterized as "rabble" by Miller, Hudson, and other opposing witnesses. They willingly let a lowly drummer boy serve as an assembly member. Opponents described Willoughby as "alwaies imperious amongst his equals, courteous to his inferiours . . . stubborne and disobedient to superiors."[82] This willingness to give a voice to all members of the community not only sets Albemarle apart from the colonies to its north and south but also set it up as a target for traditional authorities in the Atlantic world. It would certainly be a beacon to the silenced from other places, those "hundreds of idle debters, theeves, Negroes, Indians and English servants" who might seek refuge from oppressive masters in neighboring colonies.

# FOUR

# THE RISE AND FALL
# OF SETH SOTHELL,
# 1681–1695

The people of Albemarle did not long enjoy the fruits of their successful rebellion. Thomas Miller was not the only man seeking opportunities for power and profit in the New World. As Albemarle's population grew, the colony attracted not just runaways but those looking to leap social strata in bounds unthinkable in England. The northern section of Carolina had not previously attracted great numbers of such socially ambitious types, for the geography did not lend itself easily to either plantation agriculture or merchant shipping. Too many other regions along the Atlantic coast and in the Caribbean offered room to flourish. However, as times got tougher in these regions, opportunists spread out to new places in search of fast money. In the 1680s, Seth Sothell launched a fresh attempt to wrest control of the colony from the majority of the inhabitants. Finally ransomed from the Turkish pirates in 1681, he brought to Carolina a determination to make up for three lost years of income and found allies willing to help him build a new order.

Sothell, at once both more politically experienced and more ruthless than Miller, knew how to construct a powerful regime, and the Albemarle community reeled in his wake. Yet when the moment presented itself to overthrow him, they grabbed it, for the tradition of representative government had taken root. The locals who aided Sothell, however, stayed after his departure, forever seduced by his vision of an aristocratic society with themselves in the role of grandee.

≺≺

Shaftesbury, forced into exile in 1682, died in Holland a few months later. Albemarle's reluctant defender was gone, and Generalissime John Jenkins, the local leader, had died in December 1681. Governor since 1670, Jenkins had helped George Fox, been imprisoned and rescued during Eastchurch's brief coup in 1674, and served as parliamentary leader. Although accusations that Jenkins was a mere puppet of George Durant may have been exaggerated, the two men were certainly close allies. Durant or some friend of his likely assumed the mantle of leadership in Albemarle.[1]

The proprietors had tried to dispatch an interim governor, Henry Wilkinson, after John Culpeper's trial, but Wilkinson was caught up in the fight between the king and Shaftesbury and was imprisoned for debt before he could sail. The instructions the proprietors had designed for him to bring to Albemarle repeated their futile desire for the construction of a town and a council house in an effort to have more centralized control in the hands of their representative. Another generation would pass before these desires would reach fruition, for the farmers of Albemarle had no wish either for central power or to pay the taxes necessary to fund the construction.[2]

In any case, Seth Sothell was freed from his pirate captivity by the fall of 1681, and he arrived to take over the reins of government the following year. Sothell, unlike any previous governor, was a proprietor, having acquired Clarendon's share in the colony. Sothell and the residents of Albemarle may consequently have believed that his authority surpassed that of any previous governor. He certainly behaved as though he possessed sole authority. Sothell acted as a semidictator over Albemarle during the next few years, buying off a few local men to help him enforce his new regime.

He quickly aroused the wrath of Durant. Albemarle's seat of government had always been Durant's centrally located home. In an effort to break Durant's power, Sothell moved court hearings out to Chowan, the most western precinct of Albemarle. A later missionary to the colony sketched Chowan as "the largest and thinnest seated. . . . [T]here are, I think no Quakers or any other dissenters in this parish: the people indeed are ignorant, there being few that can read, and fewer write."[3] Such a small population could more readily be controlled than that of Perquimans and Pasquotank. Sothell formed an alliance with assembly representatives from Chowan by appointing James Blount and Anthony Slocum as lords proprietors' deputies and other Chowan men as justices.[4] Sothell's first recorded action in Carolina was to charge Durant at that court with "an Infammous Libell he writt" against the new governor. Sothell imprisoned Durant until he agreed to sign a bond of one hundred pounds sterling, an almost impossible amount of currency for him to produce. Sothell also coerced a power of attorney warrant from Durant.[5] The battle lines were drawn. Within a year, Thomas Miller Jr., the son of the old nemesis of the Albemarle Assembly, sat comfortably in the Sothell camp.[6]

Like so many Englishmen with a little capital, Sothell intended to use the colonial experience to build his personal wealth and attendant power at a rate impossible in the mother country. With the price of tobacco so low, the fastest way to do so was to acquire land in great quantities for the purpose of speculation. Such a plan clashed head-on with Albemarle values. To date, the community had generally been a place for small farmers resistant to large plantations and the power that accrued to individuals with enormous holdings. But Sothell set out to grant himself much beyond the 12,000 acres to which he was entitled as a proprietor. In November 1684, he awarded himself between 28,000 and 36,000 acres, with only one grain of corn as annual quitrent for each 12,000 acres. Sothell realized that he needed to build an alliance with others to support his leadership and therefore rewarded several of the councillors who signed off on his huge land grants with extra land for themselves. Anthony Slocum and his family received 1,200 acres, William Wilkison was granted 900 acres, and Blount got an extra 660 acres in exchange for his signature. All these grants were for lands in Chowan precinct. In neighboring Perquimans precinct, Francis Toms acquired 578 acres, while the Scott family received 990 acres. Slocum and Blount had been active players in Culpeper's Rebellion, but the bribes offered by Sothell proved too hard to resist. All these men, along with Miller, served as councillors and justices during Sothell's stint as governor.[7] Miller was awarded half of

William Billing's farm in an action of debt in July 1684, an abnormally harsh decision for the Albemarle justice system.[8] Other Chowan residents, including William Duckenfield, Thomas Pollock, and Henderson Walker, worked for Sothell in various positions over the next seven years. Alexander Lillington, the sheriff and sometime justice for Sothell's regime, lived in Perquimans, but his daughters subsequently married into the Chowan clique.

Their perversion of the land grant system did not happen without public protest, of course, but as justices, Sothell's new friends could retaliate against opposition. In 1684, both Miller and Toms brought charges of "opprobious Language" against some residents who had apparently spoken out publicly against the turn of events. The two justices could hardly expect an unfriendly verdict, and they imposed heavy fines on the defendants. Billing, already forced to surrender so much property to Miller, was charged the following year with "upbraiding the said Wilkison with Bribery." Both Wilkison and Miller served on the court that sentenced Billing to "be brought to the Whipping post." A woman at the same hearing faced charges of "speaking severall scandelous words against the Right honorable Seth Sothell Esqr." The court released her when her husband vouched for her future good behavior. These sentences curtailed public outcry. A definite shift in power had occurred.[9]

The proprietors back in England heard inklings that all was not well in Albemarle. Timothy Biggs, always concerned with law and order by the book, felt as troubled by the new regime as he had been by the rebellion. He went to England in early 1685 to protest "severall injurys done him" and to complain that he could not get a fair trial in Albemarle. The proprietors wrote to Sothell in February, wanting to know who was serving in governmental offices, for Sothell had told them nothing. They also mentioned other accusations of corruption. The colonial secretary had apparently written to complain that Sothell "would not permit him to Injoy the perquisites of his office but that you took them to your selfe." They also made a firm if belated statement on land grants: "Wee Require that you do not deviate from those rules wee have by our Instructions sett for the granting of land, for wee shall not allow of it." Perhaps Biggs had brought attention to the generous tracts Sothell had given his new friends from Chowan. The proprietors admonished Sothell and demanded answers. The governor apparently returned to England to respond in person, for there is no mention of him in any colonial records for more than a year.[10]

The only relief in sight came in the person of John Archdale. An English Quaker, Archdale had purchased Lord John Berkeley's proprietorship in 1678 and could be expected to hold a more receptive attitude to the leveling philosophy of Albemarle settlers. Archdale came to Albemarle shortly after Sothell and served as interim governor during Sothell's absence.[11] Court hearings moved back to Durant's home, and Durant took the opportunity to combat Sothell's maneuvers. In October 1685, Durant filed a "Protest" to "revoake and make null all former powers and warrants of Attorney whatsoever by me grannted to any person . . . warneing him or them to desist." He hoped this action would nullify the papers Sothell had forced him to sign under duress.[12]

Durant had some legal expertise and had served as attorney general of Albemarle in the 1670s. He and his wife, Ann, often worked as lawyers for clients in the Albemarle courts. But when the justices were corrupt political appointees, he could do little. By the summer of 1686, Archdale had returned to England, and Sothell was back as governor. Despite Durant's protest and revocation of the power of attorney he had assigned to Sothell, the court, presided over by the governor, recognized it. The justices ordered Durant to pay Sothell the one hundred pounds bond. With little sterling in circulation, Durant could not, and Sothell seized Durant's entire estate. Although Governor Sothell already possessed title to thirty thousand acres, he apparently remained unsatisfied.[13]

The next three years proved a bleak time for the farmers of Albemarle. Having rendered Durant homeless and made public protest pointless, Sothell continued on a reign of terror. He used the courts to seize farms, cattle, and property (including a slave in one case) from other residents. With serious charges dropped in return for bribes, innocent men were imprisoned or given heavy fines. His loyalists reaped their rewards, too, with Wilkison collecting fines and debts at court hearings over which he presided as justice.[14]

Life grew even harder for those at the bottom of colonial society who had believed they had found a safe haven in Albemarle. During Sothell's term as governor, female servants who had illegitimate children had extra time added onto their terms of indenture, while young men were brought to court to have their age "judged" and time of indenture specified, with six years usually added on.[15] In most of these cases, members of Sothell's inner circle owned the indenture of the particular servants. Alexander Lillington's servant, William, was estimated to be "of the age of Fifteene yeares" and ordered to serve Lillington "till he arrive to the age of Two and twenty yeares." Lillington sat as a justice on the day this decision was handed down.[16] Likewise, Henderson Walker, a Chowan resident of major ambition who was married to Lillington's daughter, brought Robert Evens to court, where the verdict read, "The court Judges him to serve for Six yeares and one Month from this day."[17] Slaves were declared dangerous, and one was hanged for murder.[18] Wives could no longer leave their husbands: in one case, the court "ordered that she forthwith goe Along with her husband where he shall Order her to live in the County upon paine of Twenty Lashes."[19] Punishments became physically brutal; the court decreed the construction of stocks in 1687.[20] No such cases were recorded before Sothell's time.

Durant continued to fight the court corruption. He refused to be silenced by the new regime, challenging Sothell and the sheriff head-on in the courts in late 1687 and even contesting Sothell's right to be a judge.[21] Durant obviously retained a strong base of support among the local population, and he often represented his neighbors in actions against justices and their friends. While he remained relatively personally secure, he made little progress against the administration.[22]

The developments in northern Carolina were not particular to that colony. The concentration of power in the hands of a corrupt few followed a trend evident throughout the British empire in the late 1680s, a trend many observers have seen as emanating from the throne. King James II followed his brother in centralizing royal power, both in England and in the American colonies. Charles had revoked the Massachusetts charter in 1684. James created the new Dominion of New England, placing Massachusetts, Plymouth, New Hampshire, Rhode Island, and Connecticut under a single imperial governor and dismissing all locally elected assemblies. By 1686, he was moving against New York, New Jersey, Delaware, and Maryland. The king added New York and New Jersey to the dominion by 1688, and the Carolina proprietors corresponded about their concerns that the Crown might next appropriate their charter.[23]

In the north, Sir Edmund Andros, appointed the royal governor-general over the new dominion, quickly asserted total authority. Grievances against him included that "*The Greatest Rigour and Severity was too often used towards the soberest sort of people*, when any thing could be found or pretended against them, their humble submissions were little regarded, and *inexorable persecutions ordered against them*."[24] All of the same charges could be laid at the feet of Sothell, who may well have received encouragement from James, if not directly then by example, to conduct government in a similar manner.[25]

James attacked the southern colonies in another fashion as well. The already troubled tobacco economy was hit with new taxation to free James from financial dependence on Parliament. He more than doubled the customs duties on tobacco in 1685. Maryland and Virginia were stricken, but the new levies broke the backs of Albemarle's small farmers. Sothell was unlikely to turn a blind eye to their smuggling, for he and his allies could amass fees through their government offices, such as customs collection. Not surprisingly, then, the Albemarle farmers formed new friendships with more aggressive types of customs evaders—pirates.

Piracy was not new in the southern Atlantic; it had been a state-sponsored endeavor earlier in the century. However, the period from 1685 onward is considered its golden age, as the Navigation Acts foisted ever-heavier duties and the tighter attempts at enforcement made piracy more attractive. Charles Town in southern Carolina welcomed lawless seamen with their cargoes of luxury goods, free of duties. Albemarle's Outer Banks and small inlets provided safe places to hide from the Royal Navy. Such an illegal trade was naturally averse to documentation and thus can be studied more from accusations and denials than from firm evidence. James's administration brought particular attention to the pirate traffic, dependent as he was on income from colonial trade. One early 1684 report to the Committee for Trade and Plantations accused Carolina of "harbouring and encouraging" pirates; the Earl of Craven, now head of the proprietors, denied the allegations. According to Craven, only one pirate, Jacob Hall, had ever been allowed to come and go through Charles Town, and he had received such permission only because he had a commission from the French. The only other pirate to touch the shore, Craven said, had been arrested and executed with his accomplices. Craven's claims were absurd, for Charles Town's leading men warmly received pirates and traded supplies for items captured on the seas. And Craven had so little correspondence with Albemarle that he could not even begin to address events in that region.[26]

The people of Albemarle had both economic and political motives for their friendly relationships with buccaneers. Throughout their short history of settlement, their fortunes had been tightly linked with those of the Boston traders who had helped the Carolinians avoid paying customs, and Thomas Miller's attempts to collect royal duties had triggered the rebellion. Small farmers dependent on small crop yields had little margin of profit and could least afford the burden of customs. They must have been grateful, too, for any hard currency the pirates brought to Albemarle's economy. Moreover, Albemarle had always stood as a place of refuge for those most hard-pressed by state regulation from either England or Virginia. Few people were more hard-pressed than sailors—precisely the reason so many of them turned to piracy. Marcus Rediker documents how "the pirate ship was democratic in an undemocratic age." Political sympathies for pirates would have meant that the people of Albemarle would have encountered no moral or ethical dilemmas in dealing with men and women prepared to steal from rich merchants or royal coffers.[27]

While the proprietors in England, frightened by the threat of the loss of their charters, did their best to combat piracy, they could not do much. In 1686, they dispatched Peter Colleton's younger brother, Joseph, to serve as governor of southern Carolina, ordering him to quash the pirate trade. Colleton made progress, but in so doing he antagonized most of the powerful men of Charles Town, who enjoyed the fruits of that trade. Conversely, Sothell in Albemarle exploited the situation for his personal enrichment. He accused legal merchants of piracy, locked them up without trial, and seized all their property. No records indicate that he made any moves against actual pirates; given his later record, he almost certainly encouraged them when such pursuits suited his pecuniary interests.[28]

By 1688, Anglo-American colonists all along the eastern seaboard were suffering deeply from James's reign. Their assemblies had been destroyed, replaced by arbitrary governors who ruled with iron fists. Taxation soared, while extralegal trade was crushed. The one potential gain from a Catholic king for the homeland subjects lay in the area of religious toleration: perhaps dissenters might get some relief. The colonies, however, had already provided safe havens for English dissenters. The Anglican Andros in the north even requisitioned a Puritan church for the use of his parish. Meanwhile, French Huguenots fled to many colonies (including Carolina) as refugees after the 1685 revocation of the Edict of Nantes. Their horrific tales of Louis's persecution put fear of Catholic kings into Protestant hearts.[29]

The English themselves were far from happy with James, but the elites were prepared to acquiesce in what they hoped would be a short reign, for the dangers of a civil war had not been forgotten. However, in June 1688, James's wife, Queen Mary, gave birth to a son, meaning that the English throne could permanently become Catholic. Within weeks, powerful politicians and a bishop wrote to William of Orange, husband of James's elder daughter, Mary, a Protestant, inviting him to England to restrain James. His army landed on the English shore on November 5.

The Glorious Revolution is revered in English history as the nonviolent overthrow of a despotic king in favor of a constitutional monarch. It certainly restored some power to Parliament, but this was a body elected by 4 percent of the population (and not in secret ballots, but under the eyes of landlords), hardly a representative institution. Unlike the midcentury Interregnum, no great ideas surfaced, no political participation by a wide cross-section of society ensued. Elites quietly and quickly engineered the "revolution" to ensure greater political power for themselves, without any extension of that power to those who might seek a more egalitarian distribution of taxation, land, or wealth.

However, across the Atlantic, news of the change of majesties led to political participation by a very wide cross-section of the population. In Massachusetts, New York, and Maryland, popular uprisings followed word of William and Mary's acceptance of the throne. When Boston received confirmation of the new monarchs in April, men were "running for their arms," while "the country people came armed into the town in the afternoon, in such rage and heat, that it made us all tremble to think what would follow." Andros, his officials, and the companies of soldiers under his command were forced to surrender. While the "principal Gentlemen" of Boston welcomed the overthrow of Andros, they felt the need "to appear, that by their Authority among the People the unhappy Tumults might be a little regulated." Like their counterparts in England, the Boston elites wanted regime change without class tension.[30]

In New York, a combination of the city militia and the farmers of surrounding counties proved enough to drive out Andros's deputy governor the following month, despite his attempts to hide the news of the Glorious Revolution. With the dominion government forced into exile, Connecticut and Rhode Island immediately returned to their traditional governments. Maryland then followed the pattern set by its northern neighbors. In St. Mary's City, the Protestant Association had been formed in the spring of 1689. It seized control of the government in July and called for elections to a representative assembly in August.[31]

As the rebellions moved south along the seaboard over the course of the year, Albemarle acted next. Empowered by the news from the northern colonies, citizens moved against Sothell and imprisoned him. They planned to send him to England to face trial; uncertain about how a new administration would treat him, Sothell begged to be tried before the Albemarle Assembly in hopes that his friends who represented Chowan could soften the sentence. Indeed, given the magnitude of his alleged crimes, Sothell got off lightly, being commanded only to leave Albemarle for a year and prevented from again serving in its government. To justify their coup, the leaders of the rebellion sent the proprietors a long list of charges against Sothell, including the seizure of Durant's estate and those of other residents. They informed the lords that among his "misdemeanors and other opressions," Sothell had "seiz'd upon two persons . . . pretending they were Pyratts" and "kept these persons in hard durance without bringing or pretending to bring them to tryall." They also charged that Sothell had accepted bribes to withdraw "accusations . . . for felony and treason."[32] Sothell headed to southern Carolina, where his position as proprietor would again allow him to play the role of governor and he could find another clique of corrupt local planters to work with him.[33]

Unlike the rebellion against Miller in 1677, the events of the fall of 1689 are shrouded in mystery. That Sothell's overthrow should follow the uprisings against oppressive governors along the eastern seaboard would suggest another grassroots movement in the Boston–New York pattern. But such a movement would seem likely to have brought a harsher sentence on Sothell's head and retribution against those men of Chowan who had aided and abetted him. Instead, they were not charged with anything, and for some time after Sothell's dismissal from the colony, they continued to wield some power.

The grievances cited offer some clues. Topping the list was a complaint regarding the undue arrest of Thomas Pollock, a Scottish merchant who had settled in the Chowan region in 1683. Coming from Scotland, with its tradition of intensely hierarchical social and economic stratification, Pollock carried to Albemarle a philosophy of class entitlement quite out of touch with the views of his Quaker neighbors. Virtually all landed property in Scotland lay in the hands of the gentry, while their tenants had almost no rights under the law. In his late twenties and an educated lawyer and merchant with planter aspirations, Pollock realized that the quickest way to achieve his ambition to become a gentleman was to seek his estate in America. Most of his peers went to New Jersey, but Pollock made his way south.[34] Once in Albemarle, Pollock quickly recognized that he and Sothell shared a worldview of landed proprietors in absolute control, and the Scotsman joined the Chowan clique.

By the summer of 1686, he served with his neighbors as a justice in the court that authorized the seizure of Durant's property, and he continued as a justice for at least two more years. However, as Sothell's corruption grew to that of a tyrant, even the governor's friends were no longer immune to his wrath. Pollock was appointed executor of the will of one of the men accused of piracy who died in the Albemarle jail. Sothell wanted the deceased man's property and thus would not allow Pollock to prove the will in court. This corruption was apparently more than Pollock could tolerate, and he decided to go to England to protest, but Sothell had him imprisoned without trial.[35]

After learning of the Glorious Revolution and the rebellions against the northern governors, the Albemarle settlers must have responded in ways similar to their fellow colonials. As in Boston, leading gentlemen with a lot to lose in a popular uprising may have managed to control the process. Pollock could certainly have presented himself as an aggrieved party and therefore in communion with his neighbors. With his knowledge of the law, he could have helped manage the proceedings, directing the people's wrath only at Sothell and not at the governor's various Chowan friends so that they—and Pollock—might escape punishment for their participation in the regime.

Few of the 1677 rebellion leaders remained to lead this one. Jenkins, Valentine Bird, and John Willoughby were dead, and if alive, Richard Foster would have been a very elderly man. William Crawford had moved to Virginia during the 1680s. The Chowan men, such as Blount, had been corrupted. That left only Durant and Culpeper, and Durant's loss of his estate and home curtailed his ability to organize. In 1688, Culpeper married a Quaker woman; if she was a pacifist Quaker, Culpeper may have settled down and played no part in the 1689 upheavals. No further references to him prior to his death in the early 1690s have survived. A leadership vacuum existed in Albemarle, and into it briefly stepped Pollock.[36]

Yet the Levellers among the Albemarle community could not be totally fooled by Pollock's new status as victim. During some "meetings and merriments," they "Cast forth sundry opprobious words" not only against Sothell but also about other government officials. Late in 1689, the Chowan clique and other leading gentlemen passed an act, supposedly for "the better Establishing of Unity & tranquility amongst the inhabitants here." It became illegal to "revile, utter publish declare or cast forth any opprobious language against any person concerning the late Transactions of this County whereby to cause animosities and disaffection amongst any of the Inhabitants of this County." The residents bided their time. Pollock stepped out of the limelight, and during the 1690s, at least some of the Chowan men received their comeuppance.[37]

The news of Sothell's overthrow reached England by early December. The accusations of injustice against him appear to have been corroborated to some extent, and the lords responded by immediately suspending Sothell and appointing Phillip Ludwell in his place. A Virginian married to William Berkeley's widow, Ludwell had been petitioning the proprietors to obtain rights to a plantation in Albemarle as his wife's inheritance from Berkeley. As the new governor, he would certainly be able to secure that land, an extra incentive needed to accept the job as governor of what Virginians saw as "a very mutinous people."[38] Ludwell played a major role in Virginia politics as a leader of the council. A decade earlier, he had been very involved in crushing Bacon's Rebellion, whose participants he had described as "a Rabble of the basest sort of People." So although he must have been delighted to get a new and high government office, a lucrative position in his home colony, he had no desire to live among such people in a swamp. He intended to rule by decree from the comforts of his Virginia plantation. Absentee governors were not unknown in the colonies; several of Virginia's governors had spent only brief stints in the colony after being appointed to that post.[39]

Ludwell's position in Albemarle was not immediately secure, even with the eviction of Sothell, in part because of the actions of John Gibbs, a major landowner with properties in both Pasquotank and Currituck Counties. Although he had been granted some of the land and awarded the title "cacique" in 1682 by the proprietors, to one of whom he was related, he had never played any role in the political life of the colony before this juncture. However, after hearing of Sothell's overthrow, Gibbs felt that his title automatically made him the governor under the Fundamental Constitutions. For the last few months of 1689, while Sothell sat in the Albemarle jail, at least some settlers acknowledged Gibbs's authority. Then word came of Ludwell's appointment in early 1690.[40]

Ludwell appointed Thomas Jarvis as deputy governor, for Ludwell did not plan to travel to northern Carolina for quite some time. In June, an enraged Gibbs published a declaration calling Ludwell a "Rascal, imposter and Usurper" and threatening to fight any man "as long as my Eyelidds shall wagg." He threatened reprisals against any persons who chose to obey the Virginian, declaring that they would do so "att their utmost perill."[41] One month later, he attempted to carry out this threat. At the head of "15 or 17 men in Armes," Gibbs marched into the county court at Pasquotank and seized some of the officials, carrying them first to his home in that county and a few days later to his Currituck farm. The Albemarle Council wrote to Ludwell, explaining, "Your honors Presents here would bee very necessay if you would plase to permitt it to us with all the speed Imagable for to settle this place in peace."[42]

But Ludwell had no intention of making the uncomfortable journey south through the muggy Dismal Swamp region in July. Instead, he asked

Virginia's lieutenant governor, Francis Nicholson, to intervene, exaggerating the number of Gibbs's men from seventeen to eighty, perhaps the better to provoke a reaction from the Virginia authorities.[43] The haughty Nicholson ordered both Ludwell and Gibbs to England, where the proprietors could sort the issue out so "that little Province will be settled." Virginians had happily ignored the 1677 rebellion, but Nicholson willingly intervened now because of the volatile times engendered by the Glorious Revolution. He was the only colonial governor to survive the upheavals. He knew how infectious popular action could be: as he wrote to the Committee for Trade and Plantations in August 1690, "Att present both to the Southward & Northward of us are in disorder & I fear here is in this Country a great many idle & poor people that would be ready to follow their neighbours if they be suffered to continue in theire loose way." Like elites all along the eastern seaboard, Nicholson acutely understood the threat to his power and wealth posed by disaffected people at the lower end of the social ladder.[44]

The proprietors confirmed Ludwell's governorship, and Gibbs stepped aside, but no evidence suggests that Ludwell set foot in Albemarle before 1694. In late 1691, the proprietors widened his authority by appointing him governor of the entire colony of Carolina, making him responsible for cleaning up Sothell's mess. Sothell had again tried to use his power to enrich himself in the southern region, so Ludwell had his hands full trying to sort out the claims of injustice there. He therefore left the northern region to its own management.

The proprietors made two significant changes in their instructions to Ludwell in 1691. They affirmed their rights under the charter to "publish lawes for the better government of the said Province by and with the advice and consent and aprobation of the freemen of the said Province or their delegates." They gave voting rights to all of the colony's freemen, not merely freeholders. Whether or not the English lords were conscious of the repercussions of their decision, they had just granted something very close to universal white male suffrage in Carolina. As freeholders of more than fifty acres already had the franchise, and most adult males had received that much land for settling in Albemarle, the 1691 change may not have greatly expanded the voting rolls. But adult sons could now vote when of age, whether or not their parents had enough land to give them their own farms. Servants were not officially free, but indentured servitude was a dying institution. The settlers would guard the extended franchise as a right, just as they had fought in 1677 for the right to hold their biennial assembly without a writ from the governor. From this point on, only slaves were excluded from voting.[45]

The other major change in Albemarle's constitution—for this development marked the official end of the Fundamental Constitutions—was the formation of an official bicameral legislature. The assembly of elected delegates of the freemen became known as the House of Burgesses, while the governor and the lords' deputies served as an upper house.[46]

As the settlers gradually realized that Ludwell was going to leave them to their own devices, the newly expanded electorate exercised its power. Jarvis continued as deputy governor until his death in 1694. He had settled in Albemarle in the early 1660s and served on the council in 1672. He had also cooperated with Sothell, and he continued to work with some of the Chowan men. However, Jarvis represented a compromise between the old settlers and the Sothell regime, settling the resentments caused by the ex-governor's regime. Sothell's toppling by the Albemarle people served notice that corruption would no longer be tolerated. During Jarvis's term, authority progressively moved from those who had collaborated with Sothell back to the residents of Perquimans and Pasquotank precincts, and by 1693, the justice system was restored. No court records indicate any corruption, and some of the worst offenders, such as Miller, did not fill public positions. Minor court decisions also went against former justices.[47]

Some land issues remained unresolved. Sothell died, and the Albemarle courts spent much time in the mid-1690s trying to sort out the many and complicated claims against his estate. The settlers' experiences under his administration led them to desire an official recording of their real estate, for which they might or might not ever have held a patent (the contemporary term for deeds or titles). As a result of decades of squatting, ownership of land was sometimes unclear.[48] In November 1693, Ludwell finally issued an order to put the land questions to rest. He confirmed that all lands were to be held under the terms of the Great Deed of Grant of 1668, setting quitrents at a farthing an acre. He gave notice that everyone who proved their headright claims could have their lands surveyed and a patent issued by the assembly. At council meetings held at least twice a month from March 1694 until January 1, 1695, more than one hundred households proved their rights, and the council ordered the necessary surveys and issued the patents under the terms of the 1668 agreement. Those who had difficulty proving their headright claims, either because of the time that had elapsed or because they had merely squatted on the land, still had a chance to secure title to their land. Patrick Henley petitioned to have the farm on which he and his family had lived for the previous twenty years escheated to him, "yor petitioner and his predecessors having paid Quitt Rents ever Since it was first Seated by yor Peticonrs predecessors . . . having lived possessed and built upon it for almost twenty yeares without any molestation."[49] The original grantee had long since left Albemarle. Residents who claimed that they had moved back and forth to Virginia several times occasionally expected—and received—fifty acres for each move, as in the case of one man who had "Imported himself four times into this Governmt."[50] Abuses of the headright system were common throughout the southern colonies, although in Virginia and South Carolina, such incidents usually benefited the planter class.[51]

Jarvis died by March 1694 and was replaced as deputy governor by Thomas Harvey. Like Jarvis, Harvey was well suited to maintaining peace between opposing political forces. He had married Generalissime Jenkins's widow, Joanna, one of the planners of the 1677 rebellion. At the same time, Ludwell made a fresh attempt to bring Albemarle politics back into the normal Virginia planter's frame of reference: power in the hands of the large landowners. Governors in proprietary colonies had some leverage through their control of council, or upper house, positions. Each proprietor in England had the right to appoint a personal deputy as a representative on the council, but because few of the proprietors knew anyone in Albemarle, they sent blank deputations to the governor. Ludwell hoped to use these blank deputations to circumvent the democratic input allowed by the broad franchise. He filled these positions on the council with men of estates, including some of Sothell's old friends from Chowan.[52]

One indication that Ludwell's attempt to empower the Chowan planters had failed lay in the prosecution of William Wilkison. A crony of

Sothell, "Colonel" Wilkison owned more slaves than almost anyone else in Albemarle.[53] The council removed Wilkison from his many offices in Chowan precinct in September 1694 and requested that his proprietary deputation be given to Daniel Akehurst, a Pasquotank Quaker: "There being noe deputy in Pascotank precinct[, this] will be a considerbly satisfaction to the Inhabitants."[54] In November, the court decided that Wilkison must "give good and sufficient surety for his good abearing" toward the king, the proprietors, and the "inhabitants of this County" for a year and a day. Wilkison posted a £150 bond.[55] Even this action did not satisfy everyone. The exact charges against him have not survived, but the electorate moved against him. The assembly impeached Wilkison for "divers Crimes and offences," arresting both him and his wife in March 1695.[56] The people thus sent a message to the entire council that they retained a great deal of power and were prepared to use it against the corrupt. Wilkison refused to accept his fate passively. In November, he and a fellow Chowan resident, Henderson Walker, returned to court, offering "sundry affronts" to the justices. They forbade the two men from serving as attorneys for other residents of Albemarle and forced Wilkison out of political power.[57] Chowan men no longer directed affairs in the region.

Durant had died by early 1694, and Culpeper died at around the same time.[58] They must have been happy to see the Albemarle community at large back in control of its own destiny. The members of the next generation would have to carry the torch themselves. The memories of the Interregnum and its freedoms were more distant but had not lost their meaning. And as those freedoms came under attack, the settlers again prepared their defenses.

*Part Two* ◄◄

# The Second Generation

As the seventeenth century turned to the eighteenth, an era of hierarchical rule began all over the British empire. A group categorized as High Church Tories reclaimed power in Britain and sought to remove the last vestiges of egalitarian thinking and policy from government both in England and throughout the British domain. Their authoritarian politics shaped new policies—renewed attacks on piracy and smuggling and on religious tolerance, for example—and justified and supported the development of slave societies in the mainland American colonies, with power located in the hands of the great elite landowners.

This development spelled disaster for the Africans who were soon captured by the tens of thousands and forced to endure the horrors of the Middle Passage and a lifetime of captivity. Resistance also came from northern Carolina's small white farmers. Their peers in Virginia tolerated their changing society, for in return they received redress from the grievances with which they had been burdened under the Berkeley regime, but the farmers of Albemarle had not suffered so. They had nothing to gain and everything to lose from the imposition of a slave society and the accompanying concentration of power, reinforced by an Anglican Church to which they did not subscribe.

◄◄

As this new era opened in the late 1690s, Albemarle's society and economy had evolved considerably. One of the first steps toward building a new regime came with Governor Phillip Ludwell's belief that northern Carolina's governmental infrastructure lacked a proper sense of law and order. He contributed forty pounds of his own money toward the construction of public buildings—"Churches, Court Houses and Prison"—all institutions of authority.[1] He called for a public levy to cover additional costs. The people of Albemarle did not look favorably on taxation, especially for the purpose of erecting churches, courthouses, and prisons. Nonetheless, in the fall of 1694, Harvey ordered that a list of tithables be drawn up so that officials could assess the rate of taxation per person.[2]

The head of household had to pay a poll tax on each tithable in his household. The total revenue needed had been estimated at 195 pounds, and the breakdown came to five shillings per head. As surviving receipts from the mid-1690s show, five shillings would have bought one dose of an anodyne pill or a doctor's attendance for half a day. The same money could have been used to purchase two pounds of gunpowder with four pounds of shot or to buy food at a boardinghouse for a month. Those who attended a court hearing on someone else's behalf usually received two shillings per day expenses.[3]

Normally, people paid in what were known as the "commodities of the country": "In this as in all other parts of the province, there is no money," reported a missionary. Between 1677 and 1687, as the price of tobacco collapsed, Albemarle farmers diversified considerably. Dressed pork, wheat, "Indian" corn, whale oil, and deerskins served as currency. "Good Sound fat Clean drest neat poarke" was the most common of these media of exchange, with eight pounds of pork per shilling the standard rate in 1694.[4] Deerskin prices fluctuated during the 1690s, with buckskins' value varying from two to three shillings each and doeskins fetching between eight pence and two and a half shillings.[5]

The decision to diversify agriculture had been very wise, for Virginia continued to rely on tobacco and therefore, because of the low prices it fetched, slave labor. Albemarle's farmers sold their provisions to their northerly neighbors and via Boston to Europe and the Caribbean. While some surviving information comes from propagandists hoping to attract settlers, farming in northern Carolina at the turn of the eighteenth century apparently was not terribly strenuous. Even allowing for such exaggerations as those penned by John Lawson—"Every thing seem'd to come by Nature, the Husbandman living almost void of Care, and free from those Fatigues which are absolutely requisite in Winter-Countries, for providing Fodder and other Necessaries"—keeping hogs did not require much labor. They ranged freely in the woods, eating their fill of acorns and nuts and occasionally fruit. The number of cattle and sheep also increased, judging by the amount of court time taken up with recording farmers' brands. Horses became more commonly used, though still a valuable commodity. The production of naval stores, soon the colony's chief source of revenue, did not yet constitute a big percentage of exports.[6]

Lawson based his account on his observations during the first decade of the eighteenth century. He cannot be regarded as an impartial reporter, for he became a land speculator and participated in politics. He expressed some displeasure at the settlers' lack of diligence or entrepreneurship; in his opinion, "some of the Men are very laborious, and make great Improvements in their Way; but I dare hardly give 'em that Character in general. . . . Our Merchants are not many, nor have those few there be, apply'd themselves to the *European Trade*." Lawson's revelations confirm the nature of the Albemarle community, then in its second generation. Community members did not share the values of the ambitious planter or the capitalist merchant, so familiar to students of the colonial history of Massachusetts and Virginia. North Carolinians were not Calvinists. They viewed hard work neither as its own reward nor as a duty toward God.[7]

≺⋅≻

The proprietors appointed John Archdale as the next governor of both Carolinas in August 1694. Archdale, the Quaker proprietor who had served briefly as governor during one of Sothell's absences in the mid-1680s, now served full time. Archdale, in Charles Town by the fall of 1695, did not come to the northern region for more than a year, spending that time sorting out land laws and quitrent terms in southern Carolina.[8] Thomas Harvey continued in the post of deputy governor. A fair man, Harvey excused himself from court hearings when the cases involved his relatives and kept a balance between different interests in the colony. But his job was not easy. In the late spring of 1696, he begged Archdale to come to Albemarle. Custom apparently required that assembly meetings be adjourned until a new governor's arrival, and with his delay in South

Carolina, the Albemarle residents grew restless. The issuing of land patents under way during Ludwell's tenure had been postponed until the new governor could put his signature to the documents. Harvey worried that "if your honr be not present or at best special instructions from ye Honor to satisfy the Inhabitants, particularly in the assurance of their land I doubt very much wee shall not be able to keep this Governmt in peace any longer."[9] With good reason, Harvey did not have a great deal of confidence in his authority over the population. He had witnessed rebellions against governors in 1677 and 1689. In February 1695, a resident was found guilty of "Misbehaviour and abusive language Especially against the Honorable Thomas Harvey Esquire." The man was sentenced to "publickly upon his knees crave the Honorable Deputy Governors Pardon."[10] As Harvey explained to Archdale, "There doe appear great animosity in the Country already and If things will be worse, when, I crave leave once agine to your Honor to hasten your coming if possible the peace of the Country very much depends upon it."[11]

He also wanted Archdale to sort out certain economic issues. "If your Honr cant come[,] to send full Instructions of the qt rent in the Comoditye of the Country[,] for price last settled viz of porke at one penny & tobacco 3 farthings p pound is soe ill taken that the country will not continue it except yr Honr presence here may prevail upon them."[12] If pork was valued locally at eight shillings per pound, farmers clearly would not have accepted the proprietors' rate of a penny a pound. Of course, all such values were moot to some degree, for rarely did colonists in any proprietary colony regularly pay their quitrents. Governors and deputy governors were supposed to subtract their salary and expenses from the collected quitrents and then send the remainder to England for the proprietors. But as Harvey complained to Archdale two years later, "Concerning the qt rents . . . there is very little come to my hands & far as I am Informed the receivers have got in very little. Severall psons dispute the paying them. . . . [T]here hath not come into my hand's soe much as will defray the Charge and expenses wch I have inevitably been put to this year either by the qt rents or anything else." In fact, never in the proprietary period did the lords receive any quitrent payment from the settlers of northern Carolina.[13]

Archdale finally appeared in Albemarle late in 1696. He brought some of the peace Harvey craved by authenticating the Great Deed of Grant and honoring its terms. He held sessions from February through May 1697, continuing the process of the previous few years whereby many residents, old and new, had their landholdings confirmed and recorded.[14]

The only other business Archdale ever conducted in Albemarle was to create the new precinct or county of Bath. The Pamlico Indians had suffered a shattering epidemic in 1695, and in the year following, white settlers spread south across Albemarle Sound and toward the Pamlico River.[15] Albemarle had maintained very amicable relationships with neighboring native people since 1660, and open communication continued. In 1694, during Harvey's term as deputy governor, the court heard complaints from "the Chowan Indians that they are much injured by the English seating soe near them." With peaceful relations so crucial, the court addressed the Indians' complaints with an order that further encroachment on their lands cease immediately. Those already living on farms could stay, but "what entries are already made and not yett settled shall be void."[16] Those who had hoped to move west went south instead, taking up the land formerly inhabited by the disease-torn Pamlicos. The results would be momentous.

When Archdale departed northern Carolina, everything seemed to be at peace on political, religious, and ethnic grounds. But all these issues simmered. With broad-based land rights and political representation secured, battles in the 1690s and beyond included the old one for freedom from customs duties and a new struggle for freedom of religion. The nature of the colonists' relations with Native Americans also became an issue. The Chowan clique wanted more land, even if obtaining it led to violence with Indians. Levellers wished to avoid the inequities of power that would surely follow inequity of wealth. Quakers sought to maintain their right to practice their faith. Durant's generation had not had to fight for that right; the proprietors had promised toleration, and no attempt to construct a religious building, let alone establish a tithe-extracting church, had succeeded.

The following twenty years were dominated by the religious issue, for another element cemented the connections among the Chowan men: their Anglicanism. Albemarle as a whole seemed extraordinarily secular, with Quakerism the only religion practiced at all in 1696 and the established church not welcomed. Those who espoused its establishment, with the requisite tithes, already felt isolated from their neighbors. In the seventeenth century, when religion and politics were deeply enmeshed, the Anglican Church formed a bulwark of support for maintaining the traditional authority of the gentry, affirming patriarchy and reinforcing an orderly social hierarchy. The church could also be used to shut dissenters out of political office. These political rather than religious aspects of the church appealed to the men of Chowan, for no evidence suggests they were devout believers. Despite their wealth, not until the turn of the next century did Edward Smithwick donate one acre for the construction of St. Paul's Parish Church in Chowan. The first list of vestrymen reads like a reunion of Sothell's regime: Henderson Walker, Thomas Pollock, William Duckenfield, William Wilkison, and the sons of James Blount.[17]

# FIVE

## CHALLENGE OF
## THE ANGLICANS I
Church Establishment,

1695–1707

In the face of a new attempt to enforce the Navigation Acts at the turn of the eighteenth century, the people of Albemarle shared common ground. But fault lines soon appeared. John Archdale's encouragement of settlement in the area south of Albemarle Sound opened the eyes of the Chowan planters to the possibilities inherent in Indian lands. Both for growth in the size of their own holdings and for speculation, the clique sought to expand the settlement zone.

Holding them back was the decades-old agreement between the original settlers and the neighboring Indian groups. Peace had been maintained for forty years by an adherence to the boundaries delineated by this agreement, and the popularly elected assembly had shown its loyalty to those agreements as recently as 1694. The act forbidding expansion to the west of Chowan precinct particularly enraged the members of the clique. To pursue their goals they needed to take control of the assembly. But how?

To secure Indian land and enable the shift to a plantation economy, planters needed political change, to put "the state in the planters' service," in the mode of South Carolina.[1] But first they needed religious change to enable political change. The answer lay in the Anglican Church.

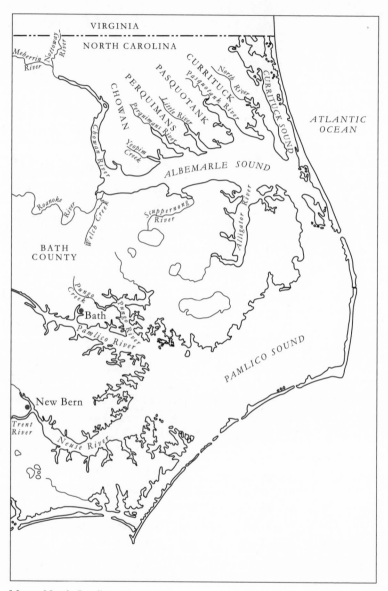

Map 2. North Carolina, 1695–1713

*Source*: Adapted from Maurice A. Mook, "Algonkian Ethnohistory of Carolina Sound," *Journal of the Washington Academy of Sciences* 34, no. 6 (June 1944): 183.

If the Chowan planters could establish the church, Quakers would be disqualified from holding office, costing the small farmers their most educated and articulate representatives. So began the campaign for establishment, not for reasons of faith but for political goals. This campaign was not an isolated Albemarle affair; throughout the British empire, a resurgence of elite rule took the shape of what one historian has classified as a "religious offensive": a fight to clamp down on religious dissenters, who were perceived as hostile to landed wealth and as a serious threat to obedience.[2] In the southern American colonies, the campaign to establish a church would allow the formation of a slave society. The leveling settlers in the Great Dismal Swamp, however, would put up as fierce a fight as anyone.

→←

While Thomas Harvey remained deputy governor, he held the small colony together. Binding the Albemarle farmers against customs collection had never proved difficult in the past and did not do so now, when English authorities launched a new campaign to enforce duties. In the 1690s, Edward Randolph traveled on a mission to bring the American colonies under tighter control of the Crown. Back in 1679, he had gone to New England as a royal appointee to ensure that governors there would take oaths to uphold the Navigation Acts. Unsuccessful, Randolph pushed for the revocation of the Massachusetts charter in 1684. Not surprisingly, he found himself imprisoned when that colony rose against Sir Edmund Andros during the Glorious Revolution. Randolph returned to England after being released in 1690 and secured a commission as surveyor-general for the American colonies to oversee all customs officials in British North America. He faced the challenge of bringing greater order and compliance to the system, a goal he believed would be best achieved by revoking all proprietary charters and bringing all colonies under direct royal control.[3]

In 1692, Randolph sailed to the Chesapeake. Affairs in royal Virginia at first met with his approval, but he got a rude awakening on his travels north. From Maryland to New England, he could barely find any customs officials, never mind juries willing to convict anyone charged with avoiding the Navigation Acts. Randolph was reviled everywhere, and Maryland officials issued a warrant for his arrest. He found refuge in

Virginia, where his old friend, Andros, now served as governor. Yet even in Virginia, the customs corruption appalled Randolph. He returned to England in the summer of 1695, and in October he submitted a report on "illegall trade" to the English customs commissioners.[4]

Randolph's return coincided with a new threat to the royal coffers: the establishment of a Scotland-based trading company that would not impose customs duties. The new company provided an easy means for goods to get into England from America. The House of Lords turned its attention to the whole matter of colonial customs administration, and in December 1695 Randolph submitted a set of proposals for its improvement. His paper included the suggestion that "North Carolina be annexed and put under the care and inspection of his Majesties Governor of Virginia." Randolph believed that the consolidation of colonies, on the Dominion of New England model, led to easier management from England.[5] Strong lobbying from William Penn and the Jersey proprietors as well as those of Carolina killed these proposals, but Randolph's memo brought about the passage of a new Navigation Act in April 1696. This measure called principally for stricter enforcement by creating vice admiralty courts in the colonies and requiring the king's approval for the appointment of all proprietary governors. In May 1696, the new Board of Trade assumed the role of the former Committee of Trade and Plantations.[6]

Randolph continued to send reports and suggestions for the admiralty court personnel to the Board of Trade over the next year. He even meddled in proposing royal-appointed attorneys general for proprietary colonies, an action that fell outside the scope of the 1696 act. He again recommended that Virginia officials receive jurisdiction over North Carolina, claiming in one memo that "North Carolina has no Attorney Generall."[7] In another, he accused Archdale of being "a favourer of the illegal Trade" in South Carolina and objected that Charles Town was "free to all, from all places."[8] Randolph stopped in Albemarle only briefly, if at all, and his sketchy information gave him the impression that "North Carolina has 60 or 70 scattered families, but under no regular government." He asserted that smugglers "frequented" Currituck and Roanoke inlets and claimed that "Pyrats & runaway Servants resort to this place from Virginia."[9] For these reasons, he believed, the region should be brought under Virginia's control. The Carolina proprietors balked both at this idea and at the proposal that the Crown appoint attorneys general for proprietary colonies. Again with Penn at the forefront, the proprietors used their considerable influence at court to prevent such an incursion into their authority, but they were forced to acquiesce to the formation of vice admiralty courts.[10]

Deputy Governor Harvey received papers indicating the new law and instructions and promised in early 1696 to "take all the Care I can in that matter," which, in the Albemarle tradition, would be none.[11] Displeased about the formation of a Virginia vice admiralty court with jurisdiction over North Carolina, the proprietors, although sympathetic, advised him that "it is better at this time to suffer it, then to give any occasion of a dispute."[12] Despite the efforts of the British treasury, the normal evasion of customs in North Carolina continued. Two cases of customs evasion reached the North Carolina courts in 1698, with juries finding for the accused in both cases.[13]

Virginia authorities remained as reluctant as they had been for the previous forty years to set foot in the Dismal Swamp, so Albemarle's residents easily evaded the vice admiralty courts. On the Outer Banks on February 2, 1698, the wreck of a royal ship, the HMS *Swift*, tested the new provisions. Now back in Virginia, Randolph was dismayed to hear of the disaster, for he awaited transport on the *Swift* to the Carolinas, where he planned to administer an oath whereby the governors would swear to uphold the new Navigation Act. The inhabitants of Currituck precinct, conversely, believed that the wreck was their great fortune and that the wild weather and dangerous coastline had brought them another windfall.

The unmanned frigate blew ashore the Outer Banks after a winter storm in Virginia had prompted the crew to abandon ship. As was the custom, local residents, aided by Indian and black slaves, set out to salvage all they could from the wreck. They stripped the *Swift* of everything, including weaponry ("two Musqetts," one pistol, and two swords) and the clothing abandoned by the crew (shoes, stockings, "Briches," and "one gown and petticoat").[14] Notably, the locals burned government papers from Whitehall.[15] The captain might have accepted having the goods stripped from the ship, but the Currituck men and women had removed everything of value, permanently demobilizing the vessel. They "spoil[ed] and deface[ed]" the vessel, hacked at its hull, and then blew a hole through it "with one great Gun."[16]

Realizing that a royal ship had to be treated with more care than the average privately owned vessel, Harvey arrested some of the culprits and charged them with theft of the goods. In late March, a jury declared six people including an Indian slave not guilty and convicted three men. Thomas Young was sentenced to the branding of a T on his "Left Thum."[17] Roger Snell earned the same punishment but pleaded for clemency on account of his ill health and received a suspended sentence.[18] The court also convicted Captain Anthony Dawson, whose home had previously served as the seat of the precinct court in Perquimans. Probably considered the ringleader, Dawson was condemned to death, but after begging for mercy, he was banished instead.[19] Further charges against some of the men for the destruction of the ship ended in acquittals, although "One Negro of the said Capt. Anthony Dawson" was found guilty of firing the gun. The slave, obviously a scapegoat, received "thirty one stripes on his bare Back."[20]

Governor Harvey claimed to Archdale that the parties involved had been tried "to the utmost of their demerit." The captain of the *Swift* wanted further inspection of the hulk in hope that it could be saved. Harvey again claimed to have done all he could to help, marshaling "Some of the ablest men we have." He also "joyned with them Some Masters of Vessels that did not belong to this Country to Survey the Ship." Harvey could not pretend that Albemarle residents would be impartial observers of the wreck of a royal ship. And indeed, he could not get the lower house of the assembly to help. He asked them to approve a levy for the aid of the ship but "had much adoe to make the house of burgesses to take the matter soe much as into their consideration." The burgesses adjourned rather than approve a tax to help His Majesty. After Harvey and the council brought pressure, the assembly finally approved only the appointment of the surveyors.[21]

Despite Harvey's best efforts to appease Randolph, the Englishman fumed. As Harvey reported, Randolph wrote to the Carolinian, delivering "such reproach abuse and threatening as I believe hath not been heard." Harvey worried about the affair's ramifications for North Carolina's independence. "We know not wt ugly representacons he may make or wt accusation he may frame out of a pce'll of direct lyes that he has put up he seems to be Maliciously sett against us."[22] Randolph later referred to the incident as one more reason North Carolina should become a royal colony, but the proprietors' power outweighed his.[23]

◄◄

So the community held fast against any encroachment by customs officers. But the old differences of the Sothell years soon reopened. During Archdale's short stay in North Carolina, as the Albemarle region now increasingly was called, a reinvigoration of the Quaker church had occurred. At the same time, ambitions grew for Albemarle's big planters, based chiefly in Chowan although others resided in every precinct. They wanted what they felt their peers in Virginia and South Carolina already had: ever more land, ever more slaves, and control of the reins of government. They wanted respect and deference from those lower in the social order. They wanted to be gentlemen. Thus, they identified themselves as Anglicans and sought an established church that upheld hierarchy and the primacy of landed wealth. One of the first Anglican ministers admiringly described them in 1704 as a distinct group, "really zealous for the interest of the Church, [they] are the fewest in number, but the better sort of people."[24] Nothing held them back more than the prevailing ascendancy of the Quakers, who believed in peace with their Indian neighbors and in nonostentatious living and who refused to doff their hats to anyone. This egalitarian philosophy had to be broken by the combined institutions of church and state.[25]

A window of opportunity opened with Harvey's death in July 1699. At the time, the council was composed of Francis Toms, Daniel Akehurst, and Richard Sanderson, who had represented Perquimans, Pasquotank, and Currituck precincts, respectively, during the 1690s. The three members met and elected Henderson Walker as their new president, or acting deputy governor. Walker was chief justice and a former member of the old Chowan clique who apparently had earned the trust of the councillors.[26] Both Toms and Akehurst were Quakers and must have believed that Walker respected Albemarle's traditional religious freedom. Just six months earlier, in January 1699, Toms had brought a Quaker missionary to meet Harvey "and others of the Council," and the missionary had been "respectfully received and entertained." The Quaker councillors therefore may have felt that religious toleration remained safe in Albemarle.[27]

Their trust was misplaced. Walker moved quickly to change the balance of power Harvey had so carefully maintained. George Durant's son, John, a justice during Harvey's term in office, continued in that capacity only for a few more months. Immediately after Harvey's death, Walker brought his Chowan neighbor, William Wilkison, in from the political cold to serve alongside him on the bench.[28] By March 1700, Akehurst and Sanderson were gone from the council, and two more of Walker's allies, Thomas Pollock and William Glover, had replaced them on that body. Walker's brother-in-law, Samuel Swann, became chief justice, with council meetings held at his house.[29] Walker and Swann had married two sisters, the daughters of Sothell's sheriff, Alexander Lillington. Power in Albemarle had again shifted to the west, back into the hands of the men who had gained from the corruption of the 1680s.

Why did the people of Albemarle allow the Chowan clique to regain power? Over the next four years, some citizens publicly protested Walker's government and received punishment in court for their actions.[30] But many residents may have thought it impossible for the new council to bring back the type or level of corruption of the Sothell years. During the 1690s, most had secured legal title to their land, and they had shown their ability through the assembly and juries to protect their rights and values. Indeed, the new councillors had to be careful not to overplay their hand. Even the proprietors had supported the ousting of Sothell. So at first, despite the shift of personnel at the top, nothing seemed to change in Albemarle's everyday affairs. The precinct court of Perquimans ran as it had in years past. The same justices presided over the usual cases of small debts, recorded livestock marks, and appointed overseers of highways and bridges. Even the new "Generall Court house," finally constructed in 1700, was located in Perquimans, and the one Quaker serving as justice on the higher court subscribed rather than swore an oath.[31]

Nevertheless, change was in the air. The new council prorogued the assembly in late 1700 and worked to obtain favorable election results in September 1701.[32] Council members pleaded with England to send a minister to preach the Anglican Church's line on societal order, someone around whom they could rally. They intended to use the church to break the dissenters. Earlier, in 1699, the proprietors sent notice that the Reverend Dr. Thomas Bray, commissary to the bishop of London, was coming to the region.[33] Bray, who spent time in Maryland, did not personally visit Albemarle, but he sent catechism books, and in 1700 he dispatched the first Anglican minister to the area, Daniel Brett.[34] The following year, Bray founded the Society for the Propagation of the Gospel to provide additional clergy for England's "foreign plantations."

In November 1701, the Albemarle Assembly passed the Vestry Act and the Act against Sabbath-Breaking. The Vestry Act ordered the building of Anglican churches and provided for a minister's salary to be raised through tithe collection.[35] How Walker could get such an act through the assembly is not completely clear, but corruption played a part. By Walker's admission, the election was rigged. He explained two years later in a letter to the bishop of London, "we did, about this time two years, with a great deal of care and management, get an Assembly, and we passed an act for building of churches and establishing a maintenance for a minister amongst us."[36] The details of that "great care and management" are not available, but the act passed by a narrow majority.[37]

However the election had been managed, the settlers of Albemarle refused to accept it passively. Brett, the new minister, was hardly the best man for the job. Arrogant and excessive, even according to Walker, Brett's manners allowed the Quakers to rally allies in opposition to him, exactly the reverse of what the council had hoped. Walker claimed "it hath been a great trouble and grief to us who have a great veneration for the Church, that the first minister who was sent to us should prove so ill as to give the dissenters so much occasion to charge us with him."[38] The claim of "great veneration" should be taken with some salt, for the wealthy Chowan men could have built a church in the previous decades if doing so had suited their priorities. They clearly designed this political move to enhance their power and crush the leveling philosophy of Quakerism. One month after the passage of the Vestry Act, the first meeting of St. Paul's Parish took place in Chowan precinct. The list of the Chowan vestrymen included the usual suspects: Walker, Pollock, Wilkison, William Duckenfield, and two members of the Blount family.[39]

Despite Rev. Brett's "most horrid manner," the Chowan vestrymen contracted a local carpenter to build a church, finally completed to their satisfaction in December 1702. They had hoped to fund the construction without applying too much pressure on the largely secular population, "first endeavouring to raise the said money by contribution." However, they also immediately put in place a system for the collection of twelve pence from "every Tythable in the precinct" to go toward the salaries of a minister and reader.[40] An unpopular cause, the parish bills totaled seventy pounds by late in 1702, while the kitty held fewer than seven pounds. A list of 283 tithables had been drawn up, and Wilkison volunteered to collect five shillings from each of those who owed, an amount that was reduced a few months later to four shillings, "the Reader being gone."[41] During 1703, as Wilkison attempted to collect the money, opposition built up around the entire colony.

The Vestry Act was the main issue of the assembly election in September 1703. Unable to control this election, Walker wrote to the bishop of London for help. The proprietors had never ratified the Albemarle Act, and Walker pleaded, "We have an Assembly to sit the 3d November next, and there is above one half of the burgesses that are chosen are Quakers, and have declared their designs of making void the act for establishing the Church."[42]

Church establishment was stymied for the present. Events in England, however, again played an important role in the Albemarle political scene. In January 1702, Lord John Granville succeeded as Palatine, the title given to the head of the proprietary board. A High Church Tory, Granville supported the Glorious Revolution (any Protestant being better than James) but thought William had not done enough to tie together church and state. Queen Anne's assumption of the throne in early 1702 encouraged Granville, for she was a staunch Anglican. He wanted to squelch not only Catholicism but all dissenters.[43]

In June 1702, Granville appointed Nathaniel Johnson as the new governor of both Carolinas.[44] Johnson, a military officer, lived in South Carolina and was a prominent "Goose Creek man," a term used to refer to slaveholders from Barbados who had acquired large landholdings in the area known as Goose Creek and who had been influential in the politics of the colony almost since its inception.[45] Like Granville in

England, Johnson and his faction practiced the Anglican faith, and one historian of South Carolina describes him as "usually act[ing] in internal affairs as if he thought dissenters were as great a menace as Spanish soldiers." Johnson appointed one of his best friends, Robert Daniel, to the post of deputy governor of North Carolina.[46]

Given Daniel's positions on church and authority and on land and slaveholdings, Henderson Walker had no problem handing him the reins of power in July 1703.[47] No difference in philosophy separated the Chowan clique from the Goose Creek men. Walker retained his position on the council until his death the following year. Yet his back was against the wall, for the newly elected assembly could overturn anything the council put into place.

Practicing Quakers did not make up a majority of the colony's electorate, but many citizens sympathized with the Quakers and trusted that their principles would lead them to be good representatives of small farmers. A few well-to-do men of Pasquotank precinct complained to Daniel and the council that the Quakers, "by their fair promises of Small Leaveys & other Specious prtences of standing up for the good and welfare of the Country have Seduced and drawn away Severall of the Meaner Sort and Meanest Capacities of the Inhabitants of this prcinct and by Such Sinister and pernicious meanes increased their numbers and consequently gotten Votes and procured themselves to be Elected Members of the House of Burgesses." The majority of the Pasquotank population evidently was of the "meaner sort," preferring lower taxes and representatives who looked out for the people's welfare: Quakers held more than half the seats in the House. The Pasquotank Anglicans wanted the council either to declare that election campaigning would invalidate a candidate or to use the oaths of office as a way to rid the assembly of the Quakers.[48] The Quakers always had been free to subscribe their allegiances by signing in a book—a right protected by the Fundamental Constitutions. For the moment, the council refrained from enforcing the oaths, for even by mid-1704, they had not received ratification of the Vestry Act from the proprietors.

A new Anglican minister, the Reverend John Blair, arrived in Albemarle in January 1704. The Society for the Propagation of the Gospel subsidized his travel and upkeep, but both he and the society expected that his new parish would furnish him a living. He went first to St. Paul's Parish in Chowan, where Walker, Wilkison, and the others welcomed the clergyman and promised him that the Vestry Act had provided that ministers would receive thirty pounds a year, paid for by a public tithe. But Blair received a rude awakening when the assembly held its next session, five weeks after his arrival.[49]

The assembly would not even address the issue of money for Blair's maintenance. According to Blair's account, the proprietors' failure to ratify the Vestry Act in essence allowed the Quakers to deestablish the church. And he sustained little hope that the act would ever again pass the assembly, for the Quakers would "endeavor to prevent any such law passing for the future, for they are the greatest number in the Assembly, and are unanimous." Blair divided the Albemarle population into four "sorts." First were the Quakers, "the most powerful enemies to Church government." Second came their allies, the "would be Quakers, if by that they were not obliged to lead a more moral life than they are willing to comply to." The third group comprised "something like Presbyterians," while the fourth group, Anglicans, were "fewest in number." The first three factions, Blair wrote, "although they be of different pretensions, yet they all concur together in one common cause to prevent anything that will be chargeable to them, as they allege Church government will be."[50]

The harried minister not only found it difficult to get paid but also had to endure a very demanding Anglican group. The Anglicans believed that since the Society for the Propagation of the Gospel had paid Blair's travel costs, he was obliged to serve them throughout the colony, whereas the minister himself hoped to settle in Chowan and attend only to St. Paul's Parish. His description of travel from one precinct to another (and indeed from Virginia just to get to Albemarle) showed that transportation had improved little since George Fox's 1672 trip. Blair explained that the Anglican residents of Perquimans, Pasquotank, Currituck, and the "new colony of Pamtico" demanded that his meetings to preach and baptize must be held only "on the Sabbath, for they won't spare time of another day, and must be in every ten miles distant, for five miles is the furthest they will bring their children, or willingly come themselves." Their "great veneration" of the church accommodated little inconvenience.[51]

Deputy Governor Daniel was an Anglican and very concerned with establishment, so he kept his attention on solving the problem of power in the assembly. He had appointed new justices a few months after his arrival, including two men new to the colony, John Porter and Christopher Gale. Porter came from a Virginia Quaker family but at first kept his religious views to himself.[52] Christopher Gale, another newcomer and a slave owner, quickly moved into North Carolina's government circles by an opportune marriage to Sarah Harvey, the second wife and widow of the late deputy governor, Thomas Harvey.[53] The wives of the leading men of the colony had traditionally been very involved in local politics. Gale did not share the mentalité of the men of Culpeper's Rebellion, however, and perhaps did not give his wife's opinions and property the respect those men had done. By 1706, while her husband served as a justice and attorney general, Sarah Gale gave another man her power of attorney.[54] She wanted him to represent her in protecting—presumably from Christopher Gale—both her dower rights and the five-hundred-acre "Estate for life" Harvey had left her.[55]

Governor Daniel was dismayed to see that the old Vestry Act had languished and that the Quakers and their sympathizers now held the majority of seats in the House of Burgesses. Late in 1704, a new weapon fell into his hands. An English "act to declare the oath coming in place of the abrogated oath etc." demanded that all assemblymen take the oath of loyalty to the new sovereign, Queen Anne, before taking their seats.[56] When at least four of the representatives "refused to take the Oaths appointed by Law" because doing so would betray their religious beliefs, he dismissed them and called for a new election in Pasquotank precinct.[57] All five Pasquotank burgessmen were Quaker. The only one not dismissed was Thomas Symons, who also served as a justice on the General Court and who had previously been allowed to subscribe or sign his name in a book rather than swear.[58] He may have decided to swear for the sake of maintaining some representation. As Quakers comprised at least four of the five burgessmen from Perquimans precinct, Daniel probably ousted them, too, and called for new elections there.[59]

The results of the early 1705 elections have been lost, but events later in the year indicate that Albemarle's voters reelected the Quakers. The representatives must have been prevented from taking their seats. To secure the doors against the Quakers, Daniel's new assembly passed "An

Act Qualifying Members of the House of Burgesses and All Persons of Office and Trust."[60]

But the measure did not immediately take effect. During the winter, Governor Johnson in Charles Town replaced Daniel as deputy governor with a more pragmatic man, Colonel Thomas Cary. The Quakers had complained to Johnson, but the reasons for Daniel's replacement remain unclear. Cary was related to prominent Quaker John Archdale and was a friend of Johnson's.[61] The governor may have regarded Cary as someone who could keep the peace between the feuding religious groups while allowing Daniel to return to his South Carolina estates. Cary published his official appointment on March 21, 1705.[62] Nonetheless, the change in deputy governor presented no cause for a Quaker celebration. Despite his Archdale family connection, Cary's initial actions did not appear to indicate that his administration would differ in tenor from that of his predecessor. The proclamation of his commission declared that "all persons of Office and Trust within this Government Shall Continue in their respective Stations."[63]

Cary made few personnel changes at the local levels of court and council during his first year. Walker had died in 1704, and his influential widow quickly remarried Edward Moseley, who had come from South Carolina, where he served as clerk to the council and therefore would have known Cary.[64] Moseley must have been a charmer, for he had no land. His new bride's family took legal action to protect her property so that he could not give her wealth away to anyone else.[65] However, marrying Walker's widow instantly made Moseley a major Chowan landowner, and Governor Cary granted him a seat on the council before the end of 1705. Moseley also became a vestryman at St. Paul's Parish in Chowan.[66] The only other new officeholder was another St. Paul's vestryman, John Arderne, a kinsman of William Duckenfield. Arderne had recently acquired twenty-three "Negro Indyan and Mallotta Slaves" from Duckenfield.[67] Cary filled the other administrative positions with Swann, Glover, and Pollock—clique members all. The campaign for church establishment obviously would go on as planned.[68]

Only one factor indicated that Cary might have a more relaxed attitude toward dissenters than Daniel and the St. Paul's Parish vestrymen. Thomas Story, the Quaker missionary who had visited the colony in

1699, returned in April 1705 and lodged at the homes of the leading Quakers. Emmanuel Low, John Archdale's son-in-law and attorney for his North Carolina property and business interests, introduced the missionary to Cary.[69] The missionary and the governor "had much discourse about matters of government" at Low's house, and Story explained how other governors had found ways to relax the enforcement of severe laws against dissenters. Cary gave the impression that he too was "very inclinable to favour us so far as in any Construction could be consistent with his Office."[70] Yet back in England, Archdale grew concerned enough about the establishment trends in London, Charles Town, and Albemarle to purchase another proprietary share. He had sold his first share when he left the colony in 1696, believing that he had left the Quakers in a secure position. In June 1705, however, he retook a seat on the proprietary board, ready to argue for the replacement of Governor Johnson in Charles Town and the continuation of the Carolinas as a haven for dissenters.[71]

In Perquimans and Pasquotank, the Quakers remained the political choice of the majority of residents. Councillors Swann and Glover lived in Perquimans and endeavored to have an Anglican church built, but they met with little success.[72] They had found twelve individuals to serve as vestrymen for that parish, but a visiting minister, William Gordon, expressed pessimism regarding any Anglican zeal among supposed adherents in the area. He found "most, if not all of them very ignorant, loose in their lives, and unconcerned as to religion." Gordon conceded that the practicing Quakers lived lives of better Christian example than any Anglicans in the precinct and had thus made more converts. Gordon felt that the church had more hope in Pasquotank, where the reader had built a reputation for "discreet behavior," in contrast to the series of unsuitable ministers at St. Paul's Parish.[73] Another reverend, Henry Gerrard, was appointed to St. Paul's in the fall of 1705 and within six months had been accused of "several Debauched practices."[74] Such questionable morals among the Anglican ministry made it difficult for proponents to pursue the case for establishment. And for those in Albemarle with little religious fervor and even less superfluous money, the Quaker men who offered to serve as their political representatives guaranteed the removal of any tithes.

Cary's all-Anglican council again moved against the Quakers. A meeting of the North Carolina Assembly had been held in November 1705, with Quaker representatives apparently refusing to take oaths or remove their hats. In the council's words, these burgesses committed "many repeated Affronts Manifest Contempts and Deceits." At the next council meeting, held at Moseley's house on December 3, the governor and council issued a proclamation for the "Speedy Calling" of another election.[75] They also divided Bath County into three precincts, Pamptecough, Wickham, and Archdale, each of which could elect only two assembly members; each of the old Albemarle precincts had had five representatives.[76]

The assembly that met on January 21, 1706, forbade those refusing to take the oaths from taking their seats. The Anglicans of North Carolina finally had an assembly without Quakers. The assembly put into effect the 1705 act controlling membership of the House of Burgesses and all officeholders. The legislature could now proceed with formal establishment of the Church of England and pursue the anti-Indian measures of which the Chowan Anglicans had dreamed. North Carolina also finally got the town the proprietors had long advocated. The village of Bath, laid out in lots by John Lawson on a creek of the Pamlico River, was incorporated in March. By the early summer of 1706, Cary felt he had put affairs in order and returned home to South Carolina, leaving Councillor Glover of Perquimans in charge with the title "president." The Anglican clique apparently had won.[77]

Yet the fight was not over. The religious struggle also had been playing out in South Carolina. Dissenters in that colony resisted Governor Johnson's heavy-handed attempts to establish the Anglican Church. Johnson had unscrupulously engineered passage of several acts in the South Carolina Assembly that removed all dissenters from office by requiring conformity to the Church of England. In a move that qualified his religiosity, Johnson then masterminded the passage of another bill that put church ministers under the civilian authority of a board of his choosing.[78]

Action then moved across the Atlantic. Despite Archdale's efforts, Granville and the proprietary board ratified the South Carolina acts. The South Carolina dissenters dispatched Joseph Boone to London to plead their case against the church's establishment.[79] In March 1706, he appealed to the House of Lords citing the toleration clauses of the original charter, and the acts were repealed.[80] (The Crown was tempted to seize the opportunity to regain control of the Carolinas, citing the passage and ratification of the acts as an example of misgovernment by the proprietors. Royal officials considered issuing the long-feared writ of quo warranto to revoke the proprietors' charter, but in another example of the proprietary board's power at Whitehall, those proceedings were dropped.)[81] When word of establishment's repeal reached Charles Town, Governor Johnson reluctantly accepted the decision.[82]

While Boone represented the southern colony's dissenters in England, the Albemarle Quakers sent an emissary to London to complain about their treatment. John Porter sailed in 1706, before the news of the repeal had reached America. With Archdale's help, Porter convinced the proprietors to remove Cary from office and to issue new blank deputations for the council positions. The proprietors had never heard "the Least Account of the State and Condition of our Province & of our Revenues there" from Cary, and they believed Porter a reliable man to entrust with the choice of councilmen.[83] The news of Cary's dismissal did not reach the Carolinas until the summer of 1707. Porter had not hurried back. In fact, he lingered in England until that fall.[84]

# SIX

# CHALLENGE OF
# THE ANGLICANS II
Native American Resistance,

1695–1707

The Chowan clique's campaign to establish the Anglican Church and disbar Quakers from public office had the ultimate goal of taking over Indian lands. While the Chowan faction waged that campaign against other settlers, conflicts with local Indian groups also arose. The members of Albemarle's first generation had always believed in honest and peaceful dealings with their Indian neighbors. The original settlers purchased their lands directly from the Yeopim Indians and only later got deeds issued by the first governor after the charter. Various Indian leaders in the region adopted the names of English leaders over the decades: Durant, Blount, Sothell, and King Charles were all chiefs of different tribes during the first fifty years after European settlement. The 1672 pact with the Tuscarora and other smaller groups required that white settlements stay north of Albemarle Sound. That agreement held for almost forty years. In 1686, during John Archdale's first term as deputy governor, he reported to George Fox, "We at present have peace with all the nations of the Indians; and the great fat King of the Tuscaroras was not long since with me."[1] But along the western edges of Albemarle, the Anglican planters' designs required much greater landholdings, and Native Americans stood in the way. Most aggravating were those Indian groups living in Chowan precinct: the Chowan and Meherrin.

Another development also threatened the Native Americans' amicable relationship with Albemarle. In the late 1690s, an epidemic to the south of Albemarle Sound resulted in a wave of English migration into that area. In recalling his second term as governor, in the mid-1690s, Archdale discussed a "consumption . . . in my time at the River Pemlicoe, and some nations adjoining," explaining that a "great mortality" had occurred, in accordance with God's plan. He said that Englishmen settled the area "in two or three years, although at that time not one family was there."[2] But Archdale did not fully understand the importance of the old treaty, and when he heard of the epidemic among the Pamlico Indians, he believed God had sent the disease to free up that region for English settlement. By creating Bath County in 1696, he set in motion a trend that would cost everyone in North Carolina dearly.

≺≺≺

That "new colony" of Pamlico or Bath County attracted a flood of settlers, very few of them old residents moving south across Albemarle Sound. The wealthy Chowan men eagerly claimed tracts, but Virginia accounted for most of the land-hungry arrivals. According to the president of the Virginia Council, as that colony had moved toward a slave labor economy, "the number of white servants is so inconsiderable" that those poorer whites who might otherwise have been servants or farm laborers "daily remove into our neighboring Colonies, especially to North Carolina."[3] Freed servants also left Maryland in great numbers during the 1690s.[4] Those who came to North Carolina moved not into the large swampy peninsula due south of Pasquotank but further west and south, between the Pamlico and Neuse Rivers, a considerable distance from the old Albemarle settlements. In exasperation, missionary John Blair complained that it would be easier to get from England to Holland than from Durant's Neck to Pamlico. "Beside a pond of five miles broad, and nothing to carry one over but a small perryauger, there are about fifty miles desert to pass through, without any human creature inhabiting in it."[5]

The expansion of settlement into Bath County led to huge new problems for the colony. Despite the epidemic, many Indians remained in the region. Moreover, other tribes to the west and south of Bath County, notably the Tuscarora, looked askance at the influx of Europeans so close to their land. Blair described them as "a great nation of Indians . . . no less than 100,000, many of which live amongst the English, and all, as I can understand, a very civilized people."[6] His population guess was vastly exaggerated (the tribe numbered fewer than 10,000) but indicates that the settlers knew that the formidable Tuscarora constituted more than a mere remnant of some disease-torn nation. Third, the area's new white population had issues with the older settlers in terms of land rights and representation.

Several different tribes, including the Bear River (or Bay or Matchapungo), still occupied parts of Bath County. Little trouble arose at first. An increase in the fur trade indicates that good relationships with Albemarle settlers persisted, building on a level of trust developed during a generation of peace. Tensions began to rise during the summer of 1699, when rumors flew as far as Virginia that Bear River Indians had murdered several people traveling by canoe and stolen their property.[7] The Albemarle Assembly discussed the matter, and in September, Henderson Walker, who had just taken over the reins of government, dispatched a delegation of representatives to investigate. The Indians cooperated: "All the Indians that could be suspected freely upon the first summons surrendered themselves," and the delegation "returned fully satisfied that that canoe was lost by extremity of wind and sea."[8] The delegation and the Indian leaders negotiated articles of agreement for dealing with any future problems. The terms of that agreement, however, indicate that the balance of power was firmly weighted toward the European settlers. The Bear River Indians agreed to send any of their own accused of crime "into the English Government or to some Officer," to ally themselves with the English in disputes with other Indians, and to appear at the July General Court and pay tribute of two deerskins. Members of the Bear River tribe could carry out "reasonable salvage" of any wrecks as long as they led the sailors to an English plantation.[9]

Another incident in the spring of 1701 showed the Indians loath to completely surrender their sovereignty on the grounds of any complaint. Walker heard a report that some lost Englishmen had been physically threatened by Bear River Indians who had at first offered to help them find their way. The settlers escaped but were shaken enough by the experience to report to the council, which issued a warrant for the culprits.[10] The settlers sent John Lawson to meet with King Sothell to resolve the matter. Lawson reported that the delegation members "were extraordinary sivil." The Indians produced the old articles and denied the account as it had been told. According to their version of events, the accused had been trying to help the English, but they had given the Indians "3 Clay potts full of Rum." One of the Indian delegation explained that he had warned the wayward men that "if they made the Indians drunk they would be rude." One of the Bear Rivers became intoxicated and after "hearing them talk of Ashley River, made him afraid of being taken thither," for he assumed the English intended to take him south to sell as a slave.[11] (Charles Town, at the mouth of the Ashley and Cooper Rivers, was engaged in a brisk and brutal trade, exporting hundreds of Native American captives to the West Indies and the northern mainland colonies, where they were sold as slaves to finance the purchase of enslaved African workers, who were then imported to South Carolina.)[12] The Indians consequently fled, and in the panic, guns fell into the water, but no threats had been intended.

Lawson was a new man to the colony but felt qualified to liaise with the Bear Rivers for he had recently spent time among various native groups. Lawson had come to the Carolinas in 1700 in search of fame and fortune. He got both, living fast and dying young, as was the case for so many colonial-era adventurers. Contracted by the lords proprietors to survey the backcountry of their still largely unexplored colony, Lawson set off from Charleston on December 28, 1700, seeking to record as much as possible about the flora, fauna, minerals, and people he encountered. He crossed into present-day North Carolina about three weeks later, went as far north as what is now Hillsborough, and then turned east. Lawson arrived at the Bath County settlements on February 23, 1701. The following month, he applied for a land grant in the region. By June, he represented the colony in its meeting with the Bear Rivers about the canoe incident. He constructed his first cabin on the banks of the Neuse River, and within a few years, he had acquired land on the banks of the Pamlico, too.[13]

Lawson later described King Sothell of the Bear Rivers as "a great Politician . . . the most Cunning of any Indian I ever met." The Bear Rivers refused, however, to send to the Albemarle Council the men accused of threatening the lost Englishmen, and the matter appears to have been dropped. But both the Indians and the "English," as the native nations always referred to any European settler, gradually came to the realization that the alliance was untenable.[14]

New deputy governor Robert Daniel's arrival from South Carolina in the summer of 1703 did not improve Indian-white relations. The Core Indians lived west of the Chowan, where the Roanoke River flowed into Albemarle Sound. They hunted in the area recently designated as Bath County and thus came into conflict with the new settlers, who complained to the Albemarle Council that "many robereys outrages and injurys are dayly committed." The settlers believed that the Cores were "slaves to the Tuscorouda," so the council first dispatched Walker to meet with the Tuscarora chiefs to seek "satisfaction for the Injurys done," authorizing Walker to threaten force.[15] Daniel called up a militia and declared war on the Core in the fall of 1703, probably a feint by the colonial authorities. The Tuscarora's fighting forces remained significant enough to render the administration unwilling to take them on.[16]

The threat of military action did little to calm matters in the Bath County region, for it drew counterthreats from Indian towns willing to call Daniel's bluff. By October 1703, the local Indians had come to believe that the English would attack, and worried settlers dispatched a letter to their Bath representative in the assembly. According to one settler, "The Indians are now fully Resolved for to make trial of it for to see which is the [h]ardiest, and Samuel Slockum saith that several other Indians has told him that there is 2 pertiqlar towns dos intend for to make war." This account triggered a great deal of fear among the settlers, "so much that they are for leaving the Country arount."[17]

The authorities offered little response, so by the end of the winter, the settlers drew up a more serious petition to Daniel and the council. "Wee have great reason to beleve," they declared, "that the neighbouring towns of the Tuscororah Indians are of late Dissatisfied with the Inhabitants of this place." Word spread that the Bear River Indians had been in talks with the Tuscarora and "beleve that they are Indevouring to perswade them that the English here designs a war against them."[18] These groups, traditional enemies, might unite in the face of a common foe.[19] The mention of the Tuscarora significantly raised the threat level. One contemporary estimate credited the Tuscarora with at least twelve hundred warriors.[20] No one wanted that fight. The Bath residents pleaded with Daniel to intervene: "Sum of the Chiefs of the Indians would Cum in to your Honors if you would Spedily please to Send a good Interpreter here with orders what to doe."[21]

By the end of the summer of 1704, a meeting between Daniel and the Tuscarora had been arranged. That meeting disclosed another moment of colonial possibility: the Tuscarora admitted that three fur traders from Virginia, at least one of them a free black man, were "encouraging" them to "cutt off the Inhabitants of Pamtico & News."[22] Daniel wrote to Virginia authorities to complain, but at a hearing before the Virginia Council the following month, the traders denied all charges. The council let them go, choosing to believe the word of "Hubert a Negro" over that of Daniel, the aristocratic planter and deputy governor. Skeptical council members requested that the "hon. Coll. Robert Daniel be desired to send hither what Proofs he has agt. them."[23] Relations between the Virginia and North Carolina governments could not have been frostier, and those pushed to the margins, both Indian and black, could benefit.

Daniel's 1704 meeting with the Tuscarora resulted in a new peace treaty that included the proviso that no alcohol would be sold to the Indian nation. The North Carolina Assembly passed a law to that effect, although according to Lawson, "it was never strictly observ'd."[24] The agreement certainly held off the Tuscarora, but it could not help the new settlers deal with the many smaller attacks by the Bear Rivers and other groups in the area. Through the fall and winter of 1704–5, Bath County residents begged Daniel for relief. The Indians needed ammunition for their hunting as well as for the war that might come. After learning that the English would not sell ammunition to the Indians, they broke into private homes to steal it, sometimes in parties as large as sixteen.[25] The Bath residents complained that the local Indians also stole hogs, and by early 1705 the settlers asked the council "to see us defended from these barbarous heathen, And that wee may not live in such dayly Jeapordy of our lives."[26] Yet local court hearings revealed another reason for the animosity. As the settlers moved onto Indian lands along the Pamlico River, they agreed to purchase the property from the natives. But the newcomers expected to make only token payments, and many apparently reneged on the contracts. "Henry Hoborn says he owes the Indians for his land. . . . The people are all willing to pay the Indians for the lands, but they demand such great prices, that they cannot buy of them."[27] Along the Neuse River, matters were the same. Settlers there protested that Indians "likewise are seated in severall Commodious places of this River to the great disadvantage thereof. Demanding unreasonable prices for their Land which we are neither willing or able to give them."[28]

Confirmation that the increasing hostility between natives and whites arose from dishonest trading came from Lawson, one of the main promoters of the Bath County region. Daniel appointed Lawson as surveyor in Bath County, a lucrative office given the influx of settlers. Lawson was impressed by the Native Americans, particularly their stature and bearing. He wrote at length about their height, straight posture, "their Gate sedate and majestick," and their superior eyesight. They did not win Lawson's full approval, however, for he decried that "they never work as the English do, taking care for no further than what is absolutely necessary to support Life. In Travelling and Hunting, they are very indefatigable; because that carries a Pleasure along with the Profit."[29]

Lawson ridiculed Indian religion, writing "what strange ridiculous Stories these Wretches are inclined to believe," but he was no hypocrite: "For all our religion and Education, we possess more Moral Deformities, and Evils than these savages do," he noted. He admitted the settlers' and traders' fraudulent transactions and blamed them for all troubles that had arisen between the natives and colonists: "All the wars, which we have had with the Savages, were occasion'd by the unjust Dealings of the Christians towards them." The movement of new settlers into the Bath County area apparently did not provoke friction as much as did the dishonesty of those settlers.[30]

⫸⫷

In 1707, the assembly passed a renewed debtor law, "An Act to Encourage the Settlement of This Country," that began, "The Inhabitants of this Government by reason of their fewness are subject to the dayly Insults of the Heathen owing their Lives and safety's to the courtesy of the Heathen rather then their own strength, therefore for the more speedy peo-pling the said Tract of Land."[31] By that year, Daniel's replacement, Dep-uty Governor Thomas Cary, had returned to South Carolina to attend to his estate, and William Glover served as president of Albemarle. Quaker dissidents had finally been removed from political office, so Glover and his friends decided to deal with several issues touching their interests. Like the act of the 1660s, the 1707 legislation granted debtors from other colonies who took up residence in North Carolina safety from prosecu-tion for their debts for five years. An exception was made for those either indebted to the queen or from Virginia. North Carolinians saw no need to further rankle their northern neighbors.

Word of the law quickly reached Maryland, for in June the governor of that colony, John Seymour, protested loudly to the Board of Trade in England. Seymour was very concerned that "great numbers" would "flye from this Province thither."[32] He subsequently admitted that the North Carolina act offered "an extraordinary inducement" to the citizens of Maryland, "the generality whereof are much indebted to the Merchants in England & others."[33] In June 1708, Seymour wrote again, still pleading for help with the matter.[34]

The council then moved against the Indians of the Bath County re-gion. Glover went with Christopher Gale to threaten the Indians in the Pamlico River area. John Norcom publicly joked that "they (meaneing the said president and Mr. Gale) went for nothing but to Knock the Indyan Women," a statement that reflected the North Carolina commu-nity's attitude toward the colony's current leadership. Gale heard of Nor-com's remark and had him arrested and subjected to "tenn Lashes on his bare Back publickly." The Anglicans brooked no disrespect.[35]

Bath County's new residents did not want war, for they were heavily engaged in the Indian trade and of course would be on the front lines of any armed conflict. The Quakers and the people who voted for them in Pasquotank and Perquimans precincts sought to maintain peaceful rela-tions and to honor the old agreements not to expand settlement. But the chief interest of the Anglicans, especially the slave-owning Chowan clique, lay in the business of land speculation and planting.[36] The Indians occupied land white settlers wanted; the continuing native presence represented unrealized profit. The members of the Chowan clique and their ilk increasingly looked for ways to exert their growing power. While the Bath County region filled up with settlers, the Chowan planters confronted the natives of the western portion of Albemarle.

The Chowan (or Chowanoke) Indians had been the most powerful Algonkian-language tribe in coastal North Carolina in 1585. By the turn of the eighteenth century, however, they had been reduced to a shadow of their former selves.[37] In 1694, the Albemarle courts had halted further encroachment on the western Chowan Indian lands in response to a complaint from the Indians. No Englishman could settle within four miles of the Chowan Indians' town.[38] Yet in 1696, tensions mounted between one of the Chowan clique, William Duckenfield, and the Indians who lived close to his expanding property. Duckenfield wrote to an official to explain his absence from the assembly: "The indyan's plays the Roge with Me[.] [T]he[y] have almost Kild all my hoggs. . . . I could well find in my heart to Sheare Sum of them out of there lives. . . . I rather find hogs bones or hog flesh or cows, if this be Suffered, there will be nea living." Duckenfield sent out a search party in hopes of finding dead livestock that would enable him to justify killing the culprits, but the searchers found only a cabin. The Chowan planter had a patent issued by Seth Sothell for land close to the native settlement and knew that the 1694 court order revoking any lands granted but not seated in the area threatened his claim. However, he intended to assert that because he had built a log house on the property, the court order did not apply to him.[39]

With Walker, Duckenfield's Chowan neighbor, in charge, such excuses became unnecessary, and the court order meant nothing. During Walker's term as president (1699–1703), the definition of landownership again was thrown open to question. The 1694 agreement specified a four-mile buffer zone, but no survey was conducted, and no boundaries were marked. The farmers who settled closest ran into trouble, for the Chowan still felt entitled to hunt in their traditional spaces. One group of farmers blamed the Indians for "destroying their Stocks burning their houses and other hostilities under pretence they are under yor Honrs protection."[40] The farmers petitioned the council to survey and mark off the Indian land to avoid further disputes. Walker happily complied. The Chowan Indians were granted a six-mile-square reservation.[41] Ten years after Duckenfield's letter made clear the Chowan planters' desire to be completely rid of their neighbors, the then-starving Indians pleaded for help to the council. John Hoyter, the chief or spokesperson for the Chowan nation, explained that the surveyor, Captain Thomas Leuten (another vestryman of St. Paul's Parish), had laid out some land.[42] The survey was, however, "wholy Contrary to the Intent & Meaneing of the s[ai]d Order." Leuten had located the worst tract in the region. "No part or parecell of the s[ai]d Land in the s[ai]d tract Layd out will produce Corn being all pines & Sands and Desserts." Hoyter, in a plaintive but futile plea, asked the council to remember "that he is not a stranger nor a foriner but [this] is his one Nativ ples [place]."[43] By 1709, the Chowan Indians were reduced to a fighting force of fifteen warriors.[44]

By 1704, the Yeopim Indians also lived on a reservation. They too had worked out an agreement with the council during Thomas Harvey's leadership that guaranteed them security from new settlers on their land, and the administration now felt it necessary to mark the boundaries.[45] Governor Daniel approved of the idea of creating reservations and carried the idea back to South Carolina, where planters decreed reservations for their "friendly" Indians beginning in 1706.[46]

To complicate matters further, the Virginians continued to claim jurisdiction over certain nations in the vicinity. In 1680, the Meherrin had signed a treaty of tributary status with the Virginia government.[47] But the old debate over the boundary between Virginia and North Carolina had never been settled, and the Meherrin took advantage of the confusion. Their settlements gradually moved south into the lands where the Carolinians had pushed out the Chowan Indians. In April 1703, Walker expressed to the Virginia Council Carolina colonists' growing complaints about the Meherrin "destroying their Stocks and burning their timber and houses, refusing to pay Tribute or render obedience to that Government." The Virginians responded that they would handle any complaints about Meherrin behavior.[48] By 1705, officials had drawn up a reservation for the Meherrin. Much to the dismay of the Chowan planters, the entirety of the reservation was located within the chartered area of Carolina, just west of the Chowan River.[49]

One of the first council orders of Glover's presidency, issued in August 1706, commanded some of the Meherrin to "remove all their Effects to the other side of Moherrin River." Most of the tribe already lived in a town on the north side of the river, and now all must do so. The change not only freed up much of their land but also put "all their young men . . . under the imediate inspection of their own Governors to prevent their private Mischeifs that may be more Easily done and Concealed in Single and Seperate Familys." The Meherrin town also had to pay a tribute for the privilege of living in North Carolina.[50] Thomas Garrett, another St. Paul's Parish vestryman, delivered the August 1706 order to the Indians, making clear "the danger they would bring upon them selves if they did not hasten." The Meherrin pleaded for more time, arguing that "it would Ruin them to Remove now." According to Garrett, they stated that since "now is the time a year to gett skins," they were about to embark on a hunting trip. Furthermore, they declared, they no longer had "Anny land to go tow." The beleaguered Meherrin promised to procure alternative land and move by the spring, but they "desired that we might make no lise [lies] of them." They protested that they had been deceived before, despite the fact that they "did not give a mis behaving word to Anny body."[51] At a November council meeting, the Chowan clique reluctantly allowed the Meherrin to stay put until the spring of 1707.[52]

If the settlers thought the Meherrin would give up their lands without a struggle, they were mistaken. When the spring of 1707 arrived, the Indians did not move quietly but first demanded payment for the land they had cleared and then reminded Virginia officials that the Meherrin had always recognized that colony's sovereignty. The old debate on the exact location of the border between the two colonies had been revived over the course of 1706, and the Meherrin exploited Virginia's rage that North Carolina's surveyors had laid out tracts on lands Virginia officials considered within their jurisdiction.[53]

The Virginia Council contacted the North Carolina Council in April, none too politely offering the reminder that the Meherrin were "entituled to her Majestys protection." If the North Carolinians could prove that individual citizens had threatened the Indians without the approval of the council, and if those individuals were punished, the Virginians would overlook the whole matter. However, if the government had waged this campaign against the Meherrin (as the Virginians knew to be true given the demand for tribute), Virginia "must be oblieged to take other measures to assert her Majestys Right, and do Justice to the Said Indians."[54]

The Carolina council foresaw some of this opposition and had Edward Moseley collect depositions from older residents. In June, officials assembled more testimony describing the Meherrin as recent settlers in the area under contention. The North Carolina Council defended its actions to the Virginia Council, including the depositions as supporting evidence. As newcomers themselves, the Meherrin should be made to return from whence they came rather than "be Suffered to possess the mouth of a Navigable River." The North Carolinians questioned on principle "whether near a hundred familys of her Majestys Subjects of Carolina should be disseased of their freehold to lett a few Vagrant and Insolent Indians rove where they please." Moreover, they argued, men of warrior age should be in towns, under closer supervision of the nation's elders, and no white Carolinian "should be left to the Merciless Insults of Savage people."[55]

Before the Virginians could send an official response, the frustration of Chowan's large slave owners reached a boiling point. Resenting Meherrin control of so much land, Thomas Pollock took matters into his own hands in August. Without authorization, Pollock commanded a troop of some sixty men in an attack on the Indian settlement. Instead of assaulting the people living in scattered settlements whom the council had ordered to move into town, the troops struck the town itself. They captured thirty-six men and brought them to a small fort, holding them there for two hot days during which time, according to the Meherrin, "for want of water they were almost destroyed." Pollock claimed to have acted on the orders of the queen of England and demanded that the Indians "remove from that place." To drive home the point to certain captives, he ordered the destruction of cabins, belongings, and crops before releasing the men.[56]

Word of the raid reached the Virginia government in early September. A colonel in the Virginia militia went immediately to meet the "Great men" of the Meherrin and to plead with them not to take retaliatory action. His orders said to "assure them" that the Virginians "will take care to protect them."[57] Colonel Edmund Jenings, president of the Council of Virginia, then composed a biting letter to his counterpart in North Carolina. Jenings highlighted the differences between the two colonies and the long-simmering acrimony. He first responded item by item to the June letter with its depositions and defense of the demands and threats made against the Meherrin. He enclosed opposing depositions from "Two of our ancient Inhabitants" who had known the area before "the proprietary Government of Carolina had a being." These testimonies were more reliable than the depositions, he argued, not merely because of the length of time the Virginia witnesses had lived in the region but also because the two men had "such honest reputations." The North Carolina witnesses, conversely, had originally come from Virginia, and "little Credit . . . ought to be given to such persons whose understandings and Characters were known here to be none of the best before they took Shelter in Carolina."[58]

Jenings scoffed at the Carolinians' claim that they could trace Indian history and titles to land, describing such items as "imaginary Indian writeings and Records," and became sarcastic when discussing the possibility that the Meherrin would pay tribute to North Carolina: "We admire to heare it offered that a Clandestine Treaty between the Government of Carolina and the Maherine Indians should Create a Title to their Lands or be a pretence for Exacting Tribute from them who were long before Tributary to her Majestys Dominion of Virginia by Virtue of a Treaty which has the Royall Approbation." Nothing outranked the Crown, and the Virginians repeatedly cited their status as a royal colony as proof of the merit of their claims. Having made his argument for jurisdiction, Jenings then charged that "the Government of Carolina have been the Agressors."[59]

The letter's tone grew more furious as Jenings turned to Pollock's actions and especially his claim to the Meherrin that he had been authorized by the queen. The Meherrin were "not to be Considered as a Nation of Savages" but as "her Majestys Subjects." They would be defended as such. Jenings had "little Doubt of our Ability to effect our Resentment had not our duty to her Majesty a greater influence on us than our Vanity to show our Power. . . . [I]t Seems our Lenity has been misinterpreted." He cautioned North Carolina that the Meherrin might bring in "Forreigne Indians to Revenge their wrongs" and that any war that might result had been instigated only "to Satisfye the Selfish interest of Collonel Pollock and some few insatiable people who aim at the

Indians land." Jenings demanded not merely reparations but also the punishment of Pollock, "as such an insolence deserves." Failure to do so would be interpreted as governmental approval of Pollock and lead to "what we shall hereafter be obliged to do." The warning was not spelled out, but the letter concluded, "We doubt not her Majestys gracious approbation of our proceedings."[60] Taking his threat seriously, the Chowan men subsequently left the Meherrin alone.[61]

Virginian administrations had a forty-year history of despising their southern neighbors, many of whom had lived in the Chesapeake "before they took Shelter in Carolina." Albemarle always had been a troublesome refuge for runaway African and Indian slaves, servants, debtors, and political malcontents who sought freedom and respite from the aristocratic, authoritarian philosophies and actions of a long succession of governors in Jamestown and Williamsburg. The Dismal Swamp had protected them from capture or prosecution. Increasingly bitter, until now Virginia had done nothing but make disparaging noises about "those very mutinous people." It was terribly ironic, therefore, that they finally threatened war on behalf of Native Americans and that the man who finally brought them to make the threat was Thomas Pollock, the North Carolinian with the greatest planter ambitions.

By the fall of 1707, the stage was set for a showdown. The Anglican Chowan clique had grabbed power and set out to run North Carolina along the lines they wanted: a society securely led by the largest slave owners, where the Indian problem would be dealt with decisively and where the lower ranks would be told at each Sunday service to defer to their social betters. Virginia's and South Carolina's prominent planters had solidified their power despite opposition from small farmers and dissenters.[62] Now it seemed that North Carolina would mirror its neighbors. But Albemarle had by this time an almost fifty-year tradition of resistance to such men and their values. Settlers in the region had waged many successful struggles to keep planters out of power and to maintain a more egalitarian community. Pacifist philosophy notwithstanding, the Quakers and their leveling allies would not surrender without a fight.

Albemarle's farmers had learned to use the English proprietors to their benefit. Over the decades, the Carolinians had played on the lords' ignorance of realities on the ground and had manipulated the tensions between proprietors and Crown. The region's residents had capitalized on the diversion of English attention to more profitable South Carolina. They had faked deference many times, sending emissaries or letters promising both devotion and money when doing so suited their needs but had never delivered either. Now for the last time, they had sent a delegate, John Porter, to plead their case against the vestrymen of St. Paul's Parish. As on so many previous occasions, he convinced the less-than-attentive proprietors that the appointed governor was unworthy of the post and should be replaced. Porter returned to North Carolina with the power—in the form of blank lords' deputies assignations— to throw out the Anglican Council and reestablish a Quaker-Leveller government.

A third group of Carolinians might play a crucial role in the impending battle. The Native Americans had lived peacefully alongside their European neighbors until the opening of the Bath County region south of Albemarle to settlement in 1695. But the years since had seen nothing but friction between the small Indian groups and the new settlers. Moreover, as the Chowan men's landowning ambitions had grown, serious conflict spread along the western edges of white settlement. The Meherrin had used the traditional hostility between Virginia and North Carolina to their advantage, and for the moment Pollock and his Anglican partners had been forced to back off. Now loomed the question of the powerful and numerous Tuscarora. Would they unite with the other Indian groups? Would they take sides in the white men's struggle for power? Or would they view the "English" as a single threatening entity and watch from the sidelines as the foreigners fought among themselves?

# SEVEN

# CARY'S REBELLION,
# 1708–1711

The eighteenth century opened with the Anglican slave owners in power in Albemarle and their hierarchical worldview holding sway not only in North Carolina but throughout the southern mainland colonies. But just as in John Culpeper's day, the region's small farmers refused to internalize those values. Understanding the advantages of living in a remote, inaccessible area, this dissenting majority fought to retake their assembly and their rights. The three-year episode known as Cary's Rebellion revealed that most European settlers in North Carolina opposed the conversion of their colony from a society with slaves to a slave society.

Thomas Pollock's Anglicans, obliged to retreat temporarily, slowly learned that only military force would allow them to realize their vision of a plantation economy in North Carolina. They would need help from elites of the other southern colonies who had already achieved that goal. Albemarle gives us a chance to observe closely the process—a nexus of colonial governments, state church, and military force imposing an inequitable social and political order supported by violence.

◄◄

In the summer of 1707, Thomas Cary happily served in the South Carolina legislature in Charles Town, presumably receiving some of the government fees collected by William Glover, North Carolina's deputy governor. When Cary learned that the proprietors had fired him, he quickly returned north to see how things stood. Meanwhile, John Porter claimed his seat on the council as the current Ashley family deputy. He used blank deputations to swear in two other Quakers, Gabriel Newby and John Hawkins, but did not reveal that he had more blank deputations. Porter moved cautiously, carefully assessing who could be brought over to his side. At an October 20, 1707, meeting, a compromise allowed Cary to serve, and the new council was composed of Glover, Cary, Porter, Hawkins, Newby, and Francis Foster, an Anglican. They chose Glover as president.[1]

While Cary had been an ally of the Chowan clique during his first term in office, he was not happy about the turn of events that had put Glover in charge. A pragmatic politician, Cary now befriended Porter, and together they reached out to the disaffected—the same people against whom Cary had worked during his first administration. Cary and Porter were helped by their enemies. Glover's work over the winter rallied much of the North Carolina population around Cary. To rid themselves of the Quaker threat, Glover and Pollock issued writs for a new election, and the Anglicans used the old technique of requiring government officers to swear oaths to achieve an assembly willing to pass the Vestry Act.[2] Newby and Hawkins refused to take the oaths and were removed from the council. Pollock took one of their seats. Porter, never the most devout Quaker, swore the oaths to ensure himself a place at the decision-making table. With the disgruntled Cary, he formulated a plan.[3]

Cary and Porter built an alliance among powerful men that gained the support of the settlers of the Bath region. Given Pollock's title of "colonel" and his demonstrated ability to raise a Chowan militia force against the Meherrin, moving slowly against him seemed prudent. The ever-charming (and land-hungry) Edward Moseley later came on board, as did Foster.[4] But North Carolina's yeoman farmers were unlikely to give political support to slave owners unless they espoused a popular cause. So although Porter was the only dissenter among the councillors, his group became the Quaker party. The support of most of the residents of Perquimans and Pasquotank hinged on the toleration question.

In the spring of 1708, matters came to a head, and the Quakers and their friends cemented their alliance with Cary. As Glover related the story, the arrival of two zealous new Anglican missionaries sparked a coup that brought about the overthrow of Glover and Pollock. The missionaries dispatched by the bishop of London and the Society for the Propagation of the Gospel, William Gordon and James Adams, arrived in North Carolina in April.[5] Glover and Pollock threw their full public support behind the two churchmen. With the Vestry Act again in play, the Quakers recognized the new drive to establish the Anglican Church. As Glover and Adams explained, "The unhappy troubles which the enemy, alarmed at the coming over of these worthy gentlemen, has raised" began "immediately."[6] Gordon described the Perquimans Quakers' reaction to his arrival: "They doubled their efforts and contrivances against my endeavours; their meetings amongst themselves were more frequent."[7]

The Albemarle Council met in May and received word that the dissenters would not stand by and let church establishment proceed. On May 13, the council issued a proclamation: "Information is Made unto us that as well in the County of Bath as In this County severall persons have Conspired to raise Insurection against the peace." The council ordered all government officers to "prevent hinder and suppress All Riotts Mutenys And Insurections."[8] A day later, the councillors appointed various friends, including Moseley, as justices. Porter and Cary signed off on these decisions but made other plans behind the scenes. Cary may have wanted the reins of government (and the requisite fees that would come his way). Porter, while undoubtedly politically ambitious, held a genuine belief in religious toleration and stood firmly loyal to the Quakers. Given the discontent apparent throughout the colony, the moment had come to move publicly against Pollock and Glover.[9]

Porter was accused of masterminding the coup by Rev. Gordon, whose reports are one of the best sources for the events in the spring and summer of 1708. The Anglican minister, however, can hardly be regarded as a neutral observer. The newcomer was not seasoned in Albemarle politics, so his critique of Porter—"his many tricks to advance the interest of the Quakers, and the confusion and disturbance of which he was the chief or only occasion"—must be viewed in that light.[10] North Carolinians had always been prepared to resist encroachments on their religious liberties and, more importantly, on their political freedoms. Porter ranked among the most visible rebels, certainly, but the depiction of him, or Cary, whose name traditionally has been attached to this retaking of power, as a demagogue leading an ignorant mob distorts the reality. The two men represented an informed population whose members had eschewed the controlling values of Virginian society and taken difficult steps to escape it. They would not let their precious freedoms, eked out in the Great Dismal Swamp, be surrendered easily.

Porter still possessed some unused blank deputations and at one of the extra meetings about which Gordon complained secretly put several to good use. With one, he made the deposed Newby, a longtime Perquimans resident and prominent Quaker, John Archdale's deputy. The other deposed Quaker, Hawkins, also signed a new deputation.[11] The council met in July, and with Cary in their camp, the dissenters comprised a majority. To the shock of Glover and Pollock, Porter's men declared Glover's election as president illegal and therefore void.[12]

Cary became the new president of North Carolina. The colony erupted in an uproar as Pollock sought to marshal his supporters. Moseley and Foster declared themselves in favor of the Cary government. The justices who remained loyal to the Anglican regime held court and published an official protest from Pollock that included a stern warning to the councillors who were "overthrowing the present Government . . . that whatever Evil Consequences Confusion And Disorder does thereupon follow may lye at their Doors." Pollock then called up a militia.[13]

Several witnesses mention the death of one man in the armed struggle that followed.[14] All surviving accounts of the events of July and August 1708 and of the next few years were written by Anglicans: the ministers, Pollock, and the Virginia governor. Of these reporters, only Pollock had lived long enough in North Carolina to understand the egalitarian politics of his opponents. To the outsiders, the new order seemed incomprehensible. "The proceedings of the several partys which look liker the freaks of Madmen than the actions of men of reason" was Edmund Jenings's verdict in a September letter to the Board of Trade.[15] Rev. Adams defended Pollock's decision to resort to violence: "Our old worthy patriots, who have for many years bore rule in the government with great applause, cannot without concern and indignation think of their being turned out of the council and places of trust, for no other reason but because they are members of the Church of England, and that shoemakers and other mechanics should be appointed in their room, merely because they are Quaker preachers."[16] However, neither Scripture nor devotion to the Lord dictated Anglican actions. The Chowan parish had difficulty achieving a quorum for vestry meetings, and the wealthiest men in the colony were embarrassed by the appearance of the chapel they had built, with its "smallness and rough and unfit workmanship."[17]

While both sides sent letters across the Atlantic to ask for the proprietors' support, the Carolinians tried to settle things themselves. The violence proved limited and short-lived; a compromise between Pollock and Cary decreed that assembly elections would be held in October. This new body would have the right to decide whether the presidency should go to Glover or Cary. There were now twenty-six assembly seats: five from each of the four old Albemarle precincts (Chowan, Perquimans, Pasquotank, and Currituck) and two each from the three Bath County precincts (Pamptecough, Wickham, and Archdale). In the October elections, Bath, Perquimans, and Pasquotank voted for Cary supporters. Currituck's five seats went to Pollock men, while the election in Chowan was contested. In each precinct, each party seems to have nominated a whole slate of candidates, and voters chose which group would represent them. Now that Moseley had declared for the Cary party, he led that slate in Chowan. When the assembly met on October 11, both groups of Chowan candidates claimed legitimacy. The Cary-majority House of Burgesses accepted Moseley's group, and he became speaker of the House. According to the "articles of agreement" drawn up by Cary and Pollock, the House should choose between two councils, one led by Glover, the other by Cary. Unsurprisingly, they chose Cary as the new president. Porter, Foster, Newby, and Hawkins formed his council. The assembly held a two-week session and then adjourned until the following July.[18]

Glover wrote an official letter of protest, decrying the legality of any government that would not take oaths of loyalty to the Crown. He issued a challenge to take the matter to England. "I . . . do offer myself as the Queen's prisoner . . . Provided, that the said Col. Cary and Mr. John Porter, who have been the chief instruments of these unhappy troubles, will be obliged with good security in the sum of two thousand pounds personally there to appear and prosecute me." They ignored his challenge. For now, the real leader of the Anglican planters, Pollock, went into self-imposed exile in Virginia. Pollock never claimed to be under physical threat but merely said that he refused to live under an illegal government. He left close allies in North Carolina to report on proceedings there while he plotted counterrevolution.[19]

While North Carolina's Quakers and Levellers celebrated their victory on both banks of Albemarle Sound, the news traveled to London with Rev. Gordon. Knowing that Gordon's version of events would not read in their favor, the Cary party also sent letters outlining their side of the story. The death of stalwart High Churchman Lord Granville in December 1707 worked in the Cary supporters' favor. Archdale had transferred his proprietary share to his daughter, Mary Danson, and her husband, John. The latter took an active role in representing the Quaker interests at the proprietary board meetings. Not that there were many meetings, or at least much discussion of North Carolina affairs, during 1708. Still awaiting profits from the area, the lords continued to pay little attention to North Carolina. Those Carolinians who had watched proprietary operations over the years knew that the lords "would not be willing by openly joining either party, to foment, the difference."[20] As usual, they thought the best response would be to send over a new man from England to serve as a neutral governor and settle the colony. Accordingly, they appointed Edward Tynte as governor of both North and South Carolina in December 1708. He did not move to Charles Town until almost a year later, and he died seven months thereafter without ever going to North Carolina.[21]

≼≁

John Lawson and Christopher Gale were in England in 1709, Lawson hoping to publish his book. It is unclear when they departed North Carolina or how much of the political turmoil there they had witnessed. While in London, the two men became involved in a major land transaction. More than ten thousand German refugees flooded London in 1709, the majority escaping from their homelands in the Lower Palatinate region, which had been devastated first by French forces and then by a harsh winter that had destroyed the area's orchards. Other Europeans also flocked to the British capital, including many Swiss. In April, the Carolina proprietors sold ten thousand acres to a group of Germans and Swiss under the leadership of Baron Christopher de Graffenried.[22] As the refugees wore out their welcome encamped at Blackheath, near

London, the queen offered to help pay their costs of transportation. De Graffenried purchased five thousand acres for himself from the proprietors for fifty pounds and received the title "landgrave." Lawson and Gale helped lead the expedition, Lawson as surveyor-general of the colony and Gale as receiver-general. They prepared to set sail in January 1710.[23]

Meanwhile, North Carolina enjoyed a peaceful spell under Cary's government. The establishment of the church was null and void, although the Anglicans remained legally free to have any services they desired.[24] However, the reader, Charles Griffin, who served the parish after Rev. Gordon's departure, allegedly fell "into the sin of fornication, and joined with the Quakers' interest" during 1709. With the Anglicans' political plans dashed, the parish apparently held no further meetings for several years. The last surviving Anglican minister in the colony, Rev. Adams, lived in Currituck, feeling very sorry for himself. "We are now ruled by such as are generally friends only to drunkenness, irreligious and profane," he complained to his senior at the Society for the Propagation of the Gospel. "Had the government continued as we found it, there had been churches built by now; but since the Quakers and their accomplices have got to the helm, all such thoughts are laid aside."[25] This statement was true, for no tithes would be collected from the general populace to pay for Anglican churches under this administration. Not only average parishioners but wealthy slave owners who served as vestrymen were unwilling to contribute out of their own pockets. By 1711, St. Paul's Parish Church in Chowan housed livestock, making it, according to the next missionary, "a loathsome place with their dung and nastiness which is the peoples regard to Churches."[26]

In fact, along with the abolition of tithes, few taxes at all were collected. Cary and the council had decided on a levy "amounting to so small a [sum] as 6/ two pence," a decision that according to Cary "has mightily Pleased the inhabitants of this county."[27] While the North Carolinians wisely diversified their economy and supported themselves through crops and livestock and increasingly with the naval stores of pitch and tar for which the colony would become famous, few lived with superfluity.[28] The Virginia government remained upset that so many of the colony's "poorer sort" emigrated to North Carolina, where they would find "persons of the like circumstances & principles."[29] The colonists still had no hard currency: "Every one buys and pays with their commodities," explained Rev. Gordon, "of which corn, pork, pitch and tar are the chief." Gordon based his unfavorable impressions of the colonists' lifestyles not just on their irreligiosity. They had plenty of pork and beef and corn bread to eat, but according to the minister, "they are so careless and uncleanly that there is but little difference between the corn in the horse's manger and the bread on their tables. . . . [N]ot but that the place is capable of better things, were it not overrun with sloth and poverty."[30]

Gordon had never been a servant, as so many North Carolinians had in their lifetime. They knew hard work very well, having labored for many years for no more than subsistence. Having obtained their freedom, their own land, and enough to eat without overly exerting themselves, the former servants chose leisure time over wealth. The Cary Rebellion, as the overthrow of Glover and the Chowan clique has been called, was not just about religious freedom. In 1708, too few of Cary's supporters were practicing churchgoers for that to have been the sole cause. The protection of their long-cherished political and economic freedoms motivated them. They wanted the liberty of choosing representatives who shared their egalitarian outlook and class interests.

The clearest statement of their views appeared in a February 1709 petition to the council from some Currituck squatters. They accused William Reed, a close associate of the Chowan clique, of less-than-gentle quitrent collection:

The umbell petion of we in habiters on the sand banks Cumplaineeth whereas we have liveed and setelled upon sufrens and Could have no patin nor no asurans of the land we live upon But william Reed Cam Last spring with theretenings and threts with tekeing a way our goods if we did not pay or give him our [b]ills for nine yeres quitrents in fresh porke or other wayes he would sell our houses that we live in and by that menes he has got most of our bills now your umbel petioners desiers and preis that your honers would be plesed to teke it in to your serus Consideretion that we are pore pepill and would willingly pay our Rents when we can have patins for our sand all that we desire of your honers is that we Shall be Relesed out of our bondeg.[31]

The petitioners received a hearing at a sympathetic council meeting. The old Albemarle tradition of not paying quitrents to absentee landlords remained in place, and those who did not even have title to their land naturally would be the least likely to pay. The threat of losing one's home for nonpayment seemed like a return to the days of the Sothell regime. Cary ordered Reed's arrest.[32]

The Great Deed of Grant promised low rents only in the area north of Albemarle Sound, and the proprietors had been firm in their instructions in the 1690s that such low rents should not be extended to any other area of settlement. A petition from the Pamptecough representatives to the assembly declared such inequities "highly unreasonable" and had the backing of the House of Burgesses. The Cary council had a firm base of support in Bath County, and it probably granted this request to lower their quitrents.[33]

In sharp contrast to the immediately preceding period, no documents record any disputes or trouble with any Native American group during Cary's administration. With the Quaker philosophy of peace and fair dealings back in place and the aggressive actions of Pollock and his allies curtailed, North Carolina returned to its tradition of respectful, peaceful coexistence.

However, the imminent arrival of hundreds of German and Swiss refugees to take up land along the Neuse River threatened this harmony. About one hundred families—some 650 people—set sail from Gravesend in two ships. De Graffenried remained behind to prepare another expedition. Lawson and Gale supervised the mission. Although the Atlantic crossing normally took about a month, their voyage, hard hit by storms, lasted three. Roughly half of the refugees died from "spotted fever" along the way. According to Lawson, "One reason & the chiefest was seeing they were twice as many as ought to have been on a healthful ship." Close to the Virginia shore, a French privateer seized much of the remaining provisions. The destitute Palatines received aid from Virginians and set out overland for North Carolina.[34]

De Graffenried later claimed that Pollock generously helped the new settlers at his plantation on the Chowan River. In fact, however, Pollock was still in exile in Virginia and heard through other sources that Lawson was back in Carolina in April. De Graffenried offered this false claim as cover for the fact that he later gave a mortgage to Pollock for all the refugees' land. Pollock probably sold supplies to the settlers over the next year or two, but he could not have helped them on their original trip. Lawson brought them to the juncture of the Neuse and Trent Rivers and busied himself laying out tracts of land for farms and a town. He immediately found himself embroiled in the political war.[35]

Lawson aided the settlement as surveyor, and Gale was supposed to use the quitrents to furnish them with supplies. But the two men could not officially take up these positions—and collect the attending fees— until the letters appointing them had been seen by "the Governor for the time being Or President and Council and Assembly in North Carolina." The proprietors' only response was to say that Tynte would settle matters.[36] Tynte reached Charles Town in late 1709, but by March 1710, Rev. Adams had begun "to despair of his coming" north.[37]

Pollock, always in contact with allies in Carolina, sent several letters in April and May to warn Lawson and Gale not to recognize Cary's authority but instead to take their appointment letters to Glover. While one friend had suggested that the arrival of the new officeholders might be an opportunity "to concert such proper methods as may put the government again on its proper foundation," the ever-wily Pollock remained cautious. He informed Glover that the Chowan planters did not have the power to construct a council without authorization in writing from the proprietors. Pollock felt that he and his allies should "consider and duly weigh all circumstances, in retaking the government" until a new governor or deputy governor had assumed authority. He hoped that Lawson and Gale would at least stay neutral until then.[38]

Lawson certainly wanted to avoid taking sides. He tried to evade the Cary government by staying busy settling the new arrivals. Moseley was the acting surveyor-general, and he and Lawson received appointment as North Carolina's representative in the long-delayed effort to draw the boundary between North Carolina and Virginia. In April, the Crown ordered the creation of the Boundary Commission. The Virginians were eager to get started, but the tension between Lawson and Moseley delayed the initial meeting from June 9 until August 30. (In fact, the two men rarely met the Virginians together; almost every time the commission convened between August and October, either Lawson or Moseley begged off.) In late August, Edward Hyde arrived in Williamsburg with letters from the proprietors declaring him deputy governor of North Carolina.[39]

Hyde used his name to great advantage as he led others to believe he was directly descended from Hyde, Earl of Clarendon, one of the original proprietors, whose daughters had married into the royal family. A distant relation to Clarendon and therefore to the current queen, Hyde greatly exaggerated the connection. However, his name gave him much clout in North Carolina, for the power of the British Crown inspired appropriate levels of fear. De Graffenried thought Hyde "a near relation to Queen Ann." Pollock expressed delight to hear that such a "great and good character" had come to Carolina. The new governor of Virginia, Alexander Spotswood, echoed the sentiment, applauding that there was now "in the Government of Carolina a Gentleman whose word can be depended on," worthy of "the respect due to his birth and Character."[40]

High birth or not, Hyde's papers indicated that he must be officially commissioned deputy governor by Tynte in Charles Town. But Tynte had died in June. This left Hyde in a precarious constitutional position, and he decided to wait in Virginia until he could get confirmation of his appointment from England. He consulted with several Carolinians who came to see him in Williamsburg, including Lawson and Rev. Adams, and he met with Lawson and Pollock at Pollock's Blackwater, Virginia, location in September. By December 1710, Hyde felt it safe to go to North Carolina.[41]

The best account of the early months of 1711 comes from the Reverend John Urmston, who had come to serve St. Paul's Parish in the summer of 1710. At about the same time, Rev. Adams gladly fled North Carolina, saying, "I have lived here in a dismal country about two years and a half, where I have suffered a world of misery and trouble, both in body and mind."[42] The colony never offered Anglican missionaries any pleasure, but while Adams had mostly borne his woes quietly and tried to fulfill his mission despite them, Urmston was quite another type of man. He scarcely had a thought or feeling he did not think worth expressing and often did so in extremely colorful language. Ill prepared for life in the American wilderness, he complained, "Had I servants and money I might live very comfortably," but "I am forced to work hard with Axe

Hoe & spade." His North Carolina neighbors could not "endure to see any body live as well as themselves without having undergone the slavish part and learnt to live independent of others. [They] think there is no difference between a Gentleman and a labourer."[43]

The greatest shock had come from discovering that the Carolinians expected Urmston to serve a colony where respect for Anglican ministers was greatly wanting. "This is a nest of the most notorious profligates upon earth. . . . [T]hey think I am beholden to them," he protested, obviously having expected the opposite situation. "Everybody would have a Church by his own door every Sunday or not at all," and when it came to contributing to Urmston's maintenance, his neighbors showed enormous reluctance: "Any thought of raising money either for building the Churches buying a Glebe or providing for Minister that is the Great Buggbere here they are not to be at any charge nor much trouble." Urmston's anger at his treatment by Chowan's Anglicans rose in an unpunctuated torrent of prose. There would be no payment in currency, of course:

> They usually pay Ministers with the refuse the worst pay in the country is good enough for us. . . . Well, if I would continue to come among them as I had hither to done two Sundays in four and give them two Sermons in the Week day in order to which I must ride 100 miles and forced to quarter in some sorry house or other not fit to lodge a Man in for 11 or 12 days they would be kind for the future but having been ill used by them already I pressed them to give me some assurance not being willing to trust to their generosity they very liberally offered me £25 for the year or proportionable till such time as they had a Minister which I refused and am resolved if I must starve I'll not thereunto add Slavery.[44]

Until Hyde's arrival in December 1710, North Carolina's residents had apparently lived as they liked, with far too little authority and control for Urmston's taste. They simply "did and said what they list," and he characterized the era as a latter-day commonwealth: "Olivers days come again." Fifty years after Cromwell, everyone, including High Church opponents, still viewed the Interregnum as a time of great freedom, when radical Protestants had held the upper hand and the authority of the traditional established church and government had been fiercely challenged and successfully undermined. Similarly in North Carolina, the courts had ceased to meet during Cary's administration. The settlers of Pasquotank comprised, in Urmston's eyes, "a very factious mutinous and rebellious people most of them allied to the Quakers and at all times at their Beck ready to oppose either Church or state."[45]

When de Graffenried finally landed in the fall of 1710 with the second set of Swiss refugees, he verified that the proprietors had indeed appointed Hyde. And when Hyde crossed the disputed boundary and was offered a place of residence by Chowan planter William Duckenfield, "the aweful respect to [Hyde's] family and interest overawed others."[46] Even Cary recognized that the proprietors had chosen Hyde as deputy governor despite the ambiguous legal position Tynte's death had caused. Hyde called an election for a new assembly, resisting the harsh realities that Urmston had learned in his short stay in the colony. Despite what most long-term residents might have told him, the new governor accepted advice only from the Chowan clique. He would not allow the seating in the assembly of any Quaker who remained unwilling to swear the oaths of allegiance, and he saw to it that a new act to establish the Church of England passed. Opposition again mounted quickly. While Urmston vented his frustration with the lack of decorum at vestry meetings—"The Vestry met at an Ordinary where rum was the chief of their business"—a more serious threat arose to his church and to the new government that had established it.[47]

By March 1711, Cary and Porter again headed a popular movement to protest Hyde's actions and dissolve the assembly. They opposed not merely the establishment of the church but the refusal to allow Quakers to have a voice at any level of government. They based their argument on Hyde's lack of official commission.[48] On March 6, Virginia's Governor Spotswood described Hyde as being "upon so precarious a footing and his authority so little" that his survival in office seemed in serious doubt.[49] In an attempt to stop the popular movement, the assembly quickly passed two laws. The Anti-Sedition Act made it illegal to "speak any seditious words or speeches or spread abroad false news, write or disperse scurrilous Libels against the present Government," or "instigate others to Sedition Caball or meet together to contrive invent suggest or incite rebellions, Conspiracys Riotts or any manner of unlawfull Feuds." The second act, aimed personally at Cary and Moseley, ordered them to turn over any money they had collected while in office.[50] Very little quitrent money had ever been paid in North Carolina, and Cary's administration had ordered the arrest of one quitrent collector, so it seems highly unlikely that much public money ever came into his hands. Even Spotswood believed the act "perhaps too severe to be justify'd," commenting that its motivation arose from "their resentment of their ill usage during Mr. Cary's usurpacon." Articles of impeachment for "high crimes and misdemeanours" were brought against Cary and Porter, and Hyde's supporters arrested the two men. But, as Spotswood related, the members of the Hyde faction soon "found their power was too weak to enforce the execution of the laws they had passed."[51]

Cary and Porter escaped in May, before their trial. Cary went to his Pamlico home in Bath County and gathered his supporters. His backing reached well beyond his neighbors to include some of the Quaker leaders of Perquimans and Pasquotank precincts, including Emmanuel Low and Gabriel Newby. Hyde and Pollock quickly assembled their own force in Chowan, claiming that Cary had kept all the quitrent money for himself and threatening to march on Pamlico to arrest him and Porter. On May 27, Hyde brought some eighty men across Albemarle Sound into Bath County. They camped overnight and marched on Cary's farm the next day, only to find that he had fled downriver. By the time they reached his new locale, Cary had gathered forty armed men and fortified the place with cannon. Hyde retreated on June 1.[52]

Richard Roach, an English merchant, had sailed into Albemarle Sound and come to the aid of the rebels with a cargo that included guns and ammunition. The traders who for decades had guided their small sloops through North Carolina's treacherous shoals and inlets staunchly opposed hierarchal governments. Too often, men who publicly avowed loyalty to church and Crown and to law and order also avowed loyalty to Navigation Act enforcement, a position that motivated some settlers who had little interest in the politics of religion. Imported goods already fetched outrageous prices in Carolina because of the transportation difficulties and the fluctuating values given to the commodities that circulated as currency. Adding on tariff duties might put rum beyond the colonists' reach. The alliance of the traders and the settlers, so strong in the days of Culpeper's Rebellion, was renewed. Roach put his cargo at the disposal of Cary and his supporters. Cary used the weapons, including six large guns, to arm a brigantine and a smaller barco longo.[53]

Pollock and Hyde knew that the weight of popular opinion was against them. With even some practicing Quakers willing to take up arms, the Hyde faction lacked the manpower to confront Cary and defeat him militarily. They named de Graffenried, whose new Bath County settlement was now called New Bern, to the post of "colonel and commander of the County of Bath." The Cary adherents had warned New Bern's desperate settlers, hit so hard by sickness and hunger, to stay neutral, and they had no desire to take up arms against any one. De Graffenried went to Pollock's plantation to meet with Hyde's council and swore his loyalty, but de Graffenried had little to offer in terms of material assistance.[54]

Hyde and the council were well aware of Cary's new munitions. Cary had not armed the brigantine secretly; perhaps he hoped to intimidate the council into surrendering. Instead, they asked Spotswood in Williamsburg for help.[55] The Virginians traditionally had hesitated to have anything to do with North Carolina's affairs, but things had changed since the last popular uprising there. Virginia had a great many more slaves in 1711 than had been the case in 1689, increasing anxiety among white residents of that colony. Just a year earlier, in the spring of 1710, planters had thwarted a widespread slave insurrection in which the rebels planned to escape to the North Carolina section of the Great Dismal Swamp.[56] In the months thereafter, Spotswood warned the Virginia House of Burgesses that slaves "by Their Dayly Encrease" were becoming "Most Dangerous." Inadequately prepared for this threat, Spotswood noted, "the Strength of Your Country and the State of your Militia . . . is so Imaginary a Defense, That we Cannot too Cautiously Conceal it from our Neighbours and our Slaves." Spotswood accommodated no delusions: "Freedom Wears a Cap which Can Without a Tongue, Call Togather all Those who Long to Shake of The fetters of Slavery."[57] The Virginia council decided to get involved because members feared that some of these "Neighbours" might have a "bad influence . . . on this

Colony by encouraging the servants and negroes and other persons of desperate fortunes to run from hence in hopes of protection from the party in arms there."[58]

On June 13, the Virginia governor offered the services of a mediator, John Clayton. Spotswood dispatched Clayton to Carolina on June 20 with two letters. The first letter had two copies, one each for Cary and Hyde, and offered Clayton as a moderate and impartial negotiator.[59] The second letter was to be given to Cary only if he rejected the offer of mediation. The tone differed markedly and made clear Spotswood's intentions in support of Hyde. "So long as I have any power at hand," wrote the governor, "I shall not suffer him to ly imprisoned by a Plebeian Route."[60]

Hastening south, Clayton delivered the first letter to Hyde and the rest of the council on June 25 at Pollock's plantation, which had been fortified with a militia guard. The next day, Clayton went to see Cary. A truce was called and a meeting arranged for the following day. Only the Hyde party's version of events has survived: Hyde and de Graffenried claimed that when Clayton returned from Cary with the details of the conference, the planned location was determined to be unsuitable. Another letter proposing an alternative site supposedly was sent but did not reach Cary because of bad weather. Whatever the reasons, when Cary sailed in the next day, his opponents did not meet him. According to Hyde, Cary then took up a position with his boats that would have isolated the Hyde council, proving to its members that their adversary could not be trusted. "Our passage back [would have] been Cutt off," Hyde lamented. When Clayton delivered the second, threatening letter from Spotswood on June 28, Cary sent the mediator packing.[61]

The men holed up at Pollock's plantation became frightened.[62] Hyde, the council, Lawson, and de Graffenried were outnumbered and outgunned. They could drum up no more local support. They knew that Cary was aboard the large-gunned brig, sailing straight for them, and wrote to Spotswood begging for military help: "We earnestly request you will be pleased to assist us with what armed force can be spared from your Government." They would pay and supply any troops Virginia could send. But the grave situation might need more: "If you could spare us some Marines it would strike greater Terrour in the people."[63]

Marines—regulars from the royal armed forces, posted off the coast of Virginia—would indeed raise the fight to a new level. For colonial militia-men to fire on Crown forces not only would challenge a professional navy but would constitute treason, a capital offense: "greater Terrour," indeed. Within a week, the Virginians agreed to send both a detachment of their own "Militia of our Frontier Countys" and some of the Royal Marines.[64]

Cary's small army attacked before the marines arrived. At dawn on June 30, they fired some of the guns at Pollock's house. The men were inexperienced with such weaponry, and the semidarkness did not work in their favor. The initial shots did little damage. A landing party tried to get ashore on two smaller accompanying boats, but the council in the house had full view of these actions and fired on the landing boats. At the same time, the rebels spotted one of de Graffenried's servants. The sighting shocked Cary's men, for they had believed that the Palatines would be neutral in the battle. Only de Graffenried and the servant were actually lodged at Pollock's, but in the firing and the confusion, the rebels may have believed that the entire colony of Germans and Swiss had taken up arms. The rebels abandoned the attempt to land, climbed back on board the brig, and sailed off. For some unknown reason, they put in further along the sound, and most of the men went into the woods, leaving three men with the brig. The council guards found and captured the men, the boat, and all the guns and ammunition.[65]

Rev. Urmston, holed up on his farm in Chowan, still did not know of the capture of the brig a week later and described the situation on July 7: "War being revived among us we are all in confusion there is no stirring abroad Colonel Hyde has done all that in him lay to bring the Country into good order and promote religion but is therefore hated and threat-ened with fire and sword and all of his party." Ten days later, Urmston was somewhat heartened, having learned that Cary had been repulsed at Pollock's.[66]

The rebels faced a desperate situation but did not give up. They re-treated to the safety of Bath County and drew up a new plan. Their cause did not lack for public support, but the news of the defeat and loss of the brig left many backers reluctant to fight. As word leaked out that the Royal Marines and Virginia militia were on their way, Cary and Porter lost even more manpower. But one potential ally remained untapped. In mid-July, Porter went to meet the Tuscarora.

The Indians had plenty of reasons for joining a coalition with the rebels. The Quaker-backed force represented a community of people who for fifty years had maintained peace with their native neighbors. The men of Chowan had consistently broken with this tradition. Pollock had shown his true colors with his attack on the Meherrin in the summer of 1707. Other supporters of Hyde, such as Lawson and de Graffenried, had recently expanded settlement into the Neuse River area, edging ever closer to Tuscarora territory. Porter explained that the new governor, Hyde, had firmly thrown in his lot with these land-hungry men, and Tuscarora land would surely be next on their list for annexation. If the warriors of that nation would organize quickly to help Cary's forces, victory would be assured and the old Indian-Quaker relationship could continue. Porter personally appealed to the Tuscarora to attack Chowan precinct, since that area housed the greatest concentration of Anglican planters. According to his enemies, Porter specifically requested that the Indians "cut of Man, Woman and Child on the Western Shore of Chowan, that has been the only subjects to her Majesty that on all occasions has expressed their Loyalty."[67]

The problem was time. Porter had to go to several towns, making his pitch for a coalition force. Two identifiable groupings of Tuscarora, Upper (located primarily in the Tar-Pamlico and Roanoke River Valleys) and Lower (the larger group, living along the Neuse), had formed by this time. The Tuscarora wanted to hear all input and work out a consensus before making such a drastic move as to take on the Europeans. According to Spotswood, "The Indians own that the proposal was accepted by their young men," but the elders of the nation were "Suspitious of some trick." English traders and land speculators did not have a good record of honest dealing with the natives of North Carolina. Porter might be leading them into an ambush. Even if the Tuscarora agreed, such a major expedition would require time, both to build a consensus and then to devise a strategy.[68]

While the Indians deliberated, the Royal Marines did not delay. Word reached Virginia in mid-July of the capture of the brigantine and the dispersal of the rebels into Bath County. Spotswood decided not to send his militia on foot, knowing "the almost insuperable difficultys of marching Forces into a Country so cutt with great Rivers and without any conveniency of carriage." Instead, he sent only the marines from the guard ships off Williamsburg.[69] The Redcoats sailed into Albemarle Sound during the third week of July. Their captain went to Pollock's plantation, where the council asked him publicly to threaten "the greatest severity" toward any rebels who did not return to their homes.[70]

The rebels knew that they could not take on the British Navy. It appeared that Britain's royal government, so long unaware or unconcerned with a small colony in a swamp, was no longer prepared to condone a political entity under its jurisdiction that so contravened all its values. Clinging to a last desperate hope that the proprietors would help, Cary, Porter, and the rest of the rebel leaders took flight, trying to get to England by way of Virginia. The council had issued an amnesty to "all who had been maliciously enticed by the leaders," knowing that the rebels had too many supporters for all of them to be arrested.[71] On July 24, Spotswood issued a proclamation "for seizing and apprehending Col. Thomas Cary and other Seditious and Fractious persons" in Virginia. He charged them with taking up arms against the established government and with holding "a Traitorous Correspondence with the Tuscarora Indians." The proclamation further decreed that any North Carolinian caught "Issueing Seditious principles into her Majesties Subjects of this Colony" would also be imprisoned.[72] Though Porter escaped, Cary and some of his associates were captured and sent to England aboard a man-of-war to face trial.[73]

Was North Carolina's Quaker-Leveller republic no more? If so, it had not been defeated easily. Despite constant attacks from within and without, the ex-servants and debtors had defended their rights in a society of their own creation. The English Revolution's Levellers had sought political representation, religious toleration, landownership, and equality of birthright, ideas picked up and championed by many of the Quakers who had replaced the Levellers on the English political scene. When Rev. Urmston described North Carolina in 1711 as "Olivers days come again," he told us more than he knew. One hundred years before the

American Revolution, North Carolinians had resisted British taxation in any form and prevented the establishment of a culture of deference within their own boundaries.

Such a society was more than the powerful men of the British empire could tolerate, for it stood as a lingering threat to their right to govern and as a temptation to the discontented on whose labor they had become so dependent. Spotswood took a step without precedent: launching a military campaign, however limited, against the British subjects of another colony. He subsequently wrote many letters justifying his action: "It is no small concern to me to find in two or three of our frontier countys where the Quakers have got the greatest footing such a reluctancy to undertake anything against Cary and his Party, which I understand is owing to the crafty insinuations of that sort of People, who not only have been the principal Fomenters of the distractions in Carolina but make it their business to instill the like pernicious notions into the minds of her Majesty's subjects here and to justify all the mad actions of that Rabble by such arguments as are destructive to all Government."[74]

In another letter, he listed the reasons for taking the further step of bringing the neighboring colony under permanent royal jurisdiction. "Since the Country of North Carolina has long been the common Sanctuary of all our Runaway Servants . . . since they labor under such a total Absence of Religion . . . since the Quakers are a numerous people there . . . since it has been the common practice there to resist and imprison their Governor," the proprietors' lackadaisical governance had to be replaced with the Crown's firm hand.[75] His assessment of North Carolina cannot be faulted; it certainly had never been a friendly place to church or state or even to planter.

Spotswood also bore more personal motivations. The Virginia governor repeated on several occasions the charge that Cary "had the madness to insinuate to the Gentleman I sent to him that Mr. Hyde might expect the same fate Collonel Park had in Antegoa." Just six months earlier, Virginia-born Daniel Parke, the royal governor of Antigua, had dissolved the island's popular assembly. In response, the island's burgesses led a force to his house and killed him. All subsequently won reelection. Several years earlier, the lieutenant governor of Nevis had been killed, and the man who shot him had been acquitted. Governors in the Atlantic colonies had reason to be nervous. If Spotswood stood by and allowed Hyde to suffer a similar fate, the Virginia governor's own life could be in danger.[76]

At least temporarily, however, the worst danger seemed to have passed. Pollock had emerged victorious, if only with the aid of an imperial force. He and Hyde and their supporters settled in to reestablish Anglican authority as best they could. Doing so proved difficult. North Carolina's dissident population was not inclined to obedience. Hyde finally received the official paperwork required to establish himself as the rightful governor and called a new assembly. However, he still could raise no revenue. De Graffenried appealed to Hyde for funds to help the Palatines; after all, one of the charges against Cary was that he had not used the quitrent money to help the refugees, as the proprietors had instructed. Hyde quickly learned the reality about collecting quitrents in the colony. Without these payments, the costs of government could scarcely be met, let alone yield him a profit. According to de Graffenried, the governor explained that "he was so pinched and straitened, that he hardly had enough to supply his own wants."[77] His control over his colony was about to be further tested.

# EIGHT

# ONE FINAL FIGHT
# FOR FREEDOM,
# 1711—1713

In early August 1711, the violent times seemed to have ended, and the people of the North Carolina countryside returned to tending their farms and livestock. No records survive to tell us what they said to each other about the defeat of Cary's Rebellion, about the invasion of their colony by the Royal Marines, or about the establishment of the Anglican Church and the tithes that would surely follow. Only their behavior in the ensuing two years indicates the feelings of the majority of North Carolina farmers toward the Anglican-planter regime.

At the end of the summer, surveyor John Lawson approached Baron Christopher de Graffenried and Chief Justice Christopher Gale about a scouting trip up the Neuse River to look for new lands, make a reconnaissance among the Indian towns, and perhaps find an easier route to Virginia than the current passage through the swamp. Gale backed out at the last minute as a consequence of an illness in the family, but Lawson and de Graffenried set off in mid-September with two black slaves and two Indian guides. The summer had been dry, and the river flowed slowly, so they did not travel far on the first day. On the morning of the second, Lawson sent one of the Indians ahead on horseback to scout a place to start a road to the north. The Indian went to nearby Catechna, one of the biggest Lower Tuscarora towns. The Tuscarora then sent out a party to capture Lawson and de Graffenried and escort them to the town.[1]

Catechna was the seat of King Hancock of the Tuscarora, who mistook de Graffenried for Governor Edward Hyde. After capturing the two Europeans, Hancock dispatched messengers to invite many local Indian chiefs for an "Assembly of the Great," a major pan-Indian conference that included the leaders of many of the region's groups, not merely other Tuscarora. The Indians of Bath County, such as the Core and Bay Rivers, sent their chief men.

The Indian leaders now believed that John Porter's warnings should have been heeded. The governor who Porter had predicted would come after their lands accompanied the hated surveyor of the Neuse River, patrolling close to their territory. The long-suffering smaller Indian groups confirmed Lawson as the man responsible for laying out the farms in their territory. The attendees swore an intertribal alliance and agreed to take the offensive. Indian elders sentenced Lawson, de Graffenried, and their two slaves to death; the Swiss man escaped execution only by finally persuading them he was not the governor. Kept prisoner for the next six weeks, de Graffenried watched as Lawson and the others met tortuous deaths.[2]

At dawn on September 22, 1711, what is known as the Tuscarora War began with an attack on isolated plantations along the Pamlico and Neuse Rivers in Bath County. Some five hundred warriors engaged in the coordinated attacks, but only one part of the force was Tuscarora. All the Indian groups that had been in conflict with the settlers for the past sixteen years played an active role. In a two-hour period, they decimated Bath County. More than a hundred Europeans—mostly men—met their deaths on the first day. The Indians took women and children prisoner, destroying homes and crops along the way and leaving devastation in their wake.[3] The Swiss and Germans of New Bern, living much closer to each other, were left alone. They had worked hard to build a town and community of outlying farms and had reportedly made a good start. Now vulnerable, too, they joined the ravaged people of Bath County who gathered in eleven scattered garrisons and kept watch day and night. Small and inconclusive battles were fought outside the forts over the next few months.[4]

Little documentation records the first few weeks after the initial attack, but we know a series of smaller raids on farms and plantations around the region followed the September 22 fighting. No military response emerged from the majority of North Carolinians. The big question—whether Porter's proposed alliance between the Indians and the Cary rebels was in force—cannot be answered conclusively. All the contemporary accounts and documents from the period of the war come from the Anglicans—Virginia governor Alexander Spotswood, Thomas Pollock, and Hyde. We cannot know, therefore, whether Tuscarora and Quaker delegates met for further negotiations. The actions of North Carolina's population over the next eighteen months, however, overwhelmingly suggest that Cary's forces at least agreed to stay neutral while the Indians retook Bath County and southwestern Chowan. The agreement held until armed men from outside colonies again brought about the defeat of all those who resisted a stratified plantation society.

Spotswood first addressed the potential alliance. "I will not affirm that the invitation given those Savages some time ago by Col. Cary and his Party, to cutt off their fellow subjects (tho that heavy charge is proved by divers testimonys and firmly believed in Carolina) has been the only occasion of this Tragedy." He told the Board of Trade that Hyde had difficulty in raising a militia, even after such a dire attack. The Quakers of Carolina willingly bore arms against Hyde but "now fly again to the pretence of Conscience to be excused from assisting against the Indians."[5] Most citizens of Albemarle never attended Quaker meetings yet still refused to sign up to fight against the Tuscarora. They believed—correctly—that they had nothing to fear. There would be no assault on Perquimans, Pasquotank, and Currituck Counties.

While the Virginians busied themselves ensuring their safety by scheduling peace talks with nearby Tuscarora towns, Gale went to South Carolina to beg for help. After a stirring recounting of the events and a blurring of the reasons the North Carolinians could not defend themselves (he made no mention of Quaker pacifism), Gale asked the South Carolinians "to permit and encourage so many of your tributary Indians as you think proper, to fall upon those Indians our enemies." While the leading colonists to the north and south distinguished between friendly and enemy Indians, Gale claimed that all Core and Tuscarora Indians likely were "knowing and consenting to what was done." In early November, the governor, council, and House of Burgesses in Charles Town agreed to send a force of Indians under Colonel John Barnwell (later nicknamed Tuscarora Jack) as soon as possible.[6]

Barnwell, accompanied by a small band of colonial soldiers and about five hundred Indians with an array of tribal affiliations, arrived in the Bath County region at the end of January 1712.[7] They first attacked what turned out to be a village uninvolved in the war and won a victory over fifty women, children, and old men, for the village's younger men were gone. Most of the South Carolina Indians seized enough booty and prisoners to sell as slaves to be satisfied with their foray north and promptly deserted. Barnwell was more jealous of their spoils than distressed about their departure: "While we were putting the men to the sword, our Indians got all the slaves & plunder, only one girl we gott . . . nothing left for the white men but their horses tired & their wounds to comfort them."[8]

Barnwell led the remaining two hundred men to the besieged town of Bath, where he arrived on February 9. He planned to launch an attack on Chief Hancock's central town of Catechna. About seventy local men joined his force, but to Barnwell's disgust, the North Carolina government did not furnish them with any food or ammunition. They were forced to live off the land until they made it to the new stockade Hancock had built near Catechna. Fort Neoheroka, designed by "a runaway negro . . . named Harry . . . sold into Virginia for roguery & since fled into the Tuscaruros," proved impenetrable. On March 6, Barnwell and Hancock declared a cease-fire, with Hancock agreeing to release some prisoners in exchange for Barnwell's retreat. They arranged a rendezvous twelve days later to deliver more prisoners and to sign a peace treaty. Barnwell's force headed toward New Bern, passing through Core Town, "the most lovely pleasantest, Richest piece of land in either Carolina upon a navigable River," according to Barnwell. During the respite there, Barnwell sent his account to his superiors in South Carolina. He had little complimentary to say about anyone from North Carolina but did not blame Governor Hyde, "for the people regard him no more than a broom staff, they pay much more deference to my cutlass." Barnwell had grasped the nature of North Carolina society in a nutshell.[9]

When the Tuscarora did not turn up for the scheduled meeting on March 19, Barnwell considered the truce broken. He set up a new encampment around Core Town, called Fort Barnwell, to prepare for the next round of fighting. Hyde sent word on April 1 that more militiamen and two sloops of supplies were on their way, which brightened Barnwell's spirits, but he was sorely disappointed with the insolent northerners, who had come only to avoid a five-pound fine Hyde threatened to levy on those who refused to serve. The reluctance of the Albemarle men to obey orders, let alone fight, had Barnwell describing them as "impertinent, imperious," and "cowardly." "They began to grumble for better victuals which putt me in such a passion at all kind of ill usages since I came here that I ordered one of their majors to be tyed neck & heels & kept him so, and whenever I heard a saucy word from any of them I imeadiately cutt him."[10]

With such discipline, Barnwell laid siege to Fort Neoheroka. Both sides grew increasingly desperate for food over the ten days of the siege, and on April 17, they agreed to another cease-fire. Barnwell made great demands on the Tuscarora: they would have to turn over their leaders, including Hancock, as hostages to demonstrate good faith; release all prisoners; destroy Neoheroka; provide future tribute payments to North Carolina; and restrict Tuscarora living and hunting territory. He won the release of thirty-two prisoners, including two negroes, "one of which being a notorious Rogue was cutt to pieces immediately." The victim may well have been Harry, the brilliant architect of Neoheroka, whose "subtill contrivances for Defence" thoroughly impressed Barnwell when he later inspected the fort from inside. With the further handover of some militant Indian leaders, it looked like Barnwell had exacted tough terms.[11] Yet he knew that any settlement short of complete military victory would not please his superiors. An aroused North Carolina Council had passed a resolution in February vowing not to grant peace to any Indian who had participated in the September 22 massacre "but rather to extirpate them according to the laudable custom of South Carolina."[12] The South Carolina colonel defended the peace terms, arguing, "If North Carolina had but furnished me with but 4 days' provision more I had in spite of all enemys, without firing many gunns more, entirely made a glorious end of the war."[13]

Satisfied with his accomplishments, Barnwell set off for New Bern, planning to depart from there to South Carolina. At New Bern he expected to receive payment for his expenses. Indeed, since he was now among those who coveted the rich farmland as a valuable asset, he even hoped for a generous prize from the people of North Carolina in the form of Core Town. Unfortunately for both Barnwell and the Cores, Governor Hyde had decided that he wanted the beautiful bottomland. When the land grant reward did not materialize, the violent and vindictive Barnwell sought another kind of spoils. He invited many of the Indians with whom he had concluded the treaty to a "friendly meeting" at Fort Barnwell but then massacred the men, taking nearly two hundred women and children back to Charles Town to be sold as slaves. His treachery rendered the Indians of North Carolina more vengeful than ever.[14]

Governor Hyde had done his best to force the people of North Carolina to fight the Indian coalition. Although he had council support, he was powerless in the face of the assembly. Meeting in late 1711, after the massacre, with all Quakers prevented from serving as burgesses, the assembly still refused to approve any measure that would support a war. As Spotswood explained to the Board of Trade, "Because they cannot introduce into the Government the persons most obnoxious for the late Rebellion and Civil war, they will make no provision for defending any part of the Country."[15] Trying to get around the assembly, Hyde had decreed in March that "every member of the councill have full power and authority to impress men, horses, or canoos," but he still had little success.[16] In April, the commissioners appointed to requisition men and materiel were ordered to "make diligent search" and take all surplus corn from every family.[17] The commissioners found little. After Barnwell's departure, Hyde sent an emissary to South Carolina to explain why he had been unable to provide the relief force with needed supplies. The assembly bore responsibility, he explained, "a short time before Col. Barnwell's arrival, refusing to agree to the raising of men & provisions for the defence of the Country." He begged Charles Town to send an even bigger army, "if possible 1000 Indians," but not with Barnwell as commander. The emissary was told to tempt the South Carolinians with the potential for valuable plunder. "You must lay before them the great advantage may be made of slaves, there being many hundreds of (them,) women & children may we believe 3 or 4 thousand."[18]

At a July meeting, the council issued an official pardon for all but five leaders of Cary's Rebellion, perhaps hoping that doing so might persuade men to fight under their government.[19] This strategy also failed. In August, Hyde asked Captain Palin, a Pasquotank militia officer, to send him the names of the "Severall of the Militia of this Government" who "have deserted." Within a few weeks, Hyde claimed, he personally would "at the head of the main body of the forces of this County march myself into Bath County . . . & shall at Bath Town and Neuse fix my quarters during this war," promising to "end the war with honour or make such a peace as shall not reflect upon the British Glory." He offered to "dispense with the oath," believing that measure would "secure volunteers enough to enlist themselves." The particular "oath" to which Hyde was referring is not clear, but he undoubtedly felt that releasing Quakers from swearing any oath could only help increase militia recruits.[20] But this strategy was no more successful than his earlier efforts. Hyde died on September 8 without achieving any "British Glory." His death removed whatever mystique Hyde's name still carried in North Carolina and cast greater doubt on the council's legitimacy.

Thomas Pollock emerged reluctantly from the shadows and finally took on the mantle of power. Aware of the hazards faced by North Carolina's governors, he had always preferred to direct affairs discreetly from his Chowan plantation, and he pointed out that "in more peacible times I have refused" to serve as the colony's leader.[21] Once committed, however, he acted quickly. At the first council meeting of his presidency, held on September 12, 1712, he ordered the cruel Currituck quitrent collector, William Reed, to arrest "Thomas Cox Senr. & William Stafford Senr. Of Corretuck for that they did in a Mutinous maner Seduce & draw a side divers men who had Enlisted in the Service of this Government to the great Detirment of the present Expedition against the Indyan Enomy."[22]

Now fortified in his plantation, Pollock wrote to the proprietors on September 20 "to lay before you the true state of the country." He reported that the general pardon had done nothing to help instill loyalty to Hyde's administration, "the people still continuing stubborn and disobedient." The colony floundered, with the people of Bath County and Chowan precinct garrisoned for protection, all trade disrupted, and the government unable to pay its soldiers or afford support from any other colony. Hyde had tried his best, even issuing fines and securing an act from the assembly providing "that every person that would not go out in the country's service against the Indians should forfeit and pay five pounds towards defraying the charges of the war," yet "few or none would go out."[23] Pollock was also concerned about the next election and what it might mean for his power. He begged the proprietors to void the constitutional requirement that all laws must be renewed every two years, worrying that "we could never be able to revive [the Vestry Act] again." Church establishment had been obtained only with "great struggling," and although the Quakers currently were forbidden from the assembly, "yet, being the most numerous, they choose such members as are guided and directed by them."[24]

Pollock wrote more frankly to Lord Carteret, whom he served as deputy. Impugning the Quakers as the root cause of the reluctance to fight the Tuscarora, Pollock explained, "They neither will assist themselves or suffer others, but hinder and dissuade them, all they can, they having great influence on the common people." The five-pound fee had not worked, he reiterated, "most of all the people refusing still to go: the distemper hath been so epidemical that Governor Hyde could scarcely find any person that would undertake to levy the fines aforesaid." He asked the proprietor to pressure the colonists to the south to help.[25]

Despite his supposed high anxieties regarding his safety and the colony's continued existence, Pollock found time to slip a specific request into the letter. He asked that "if the Indians are conquered," he be granted "a seat of extraordinary land upon Neus River"—the area around Core Town. "Col. Barnwell, commander of the Indians from South Carolina, expected to have had it: Gov. Hyde had entered it, but by his death it is clear." Pollock claimed that Hyde and the council really wanted Pollock to have the land as payment for his expenses in pursuing the war, but someone else had laid claim to the tract. Pollock asked that the proprietors confirm in writing that he be allowed to grant the promising tract to his son. If he could not have the Meherrin lands, perhaps he could have those of the Cores.[26]

Throughout the fall of 1712, the Albemarle residents tenaciously stood by, refusing to muster militia and resources for the fight while Pollock's fears were being realized. As he waited and hoped for a second expedition from South Carolina to ensure his authority and his latest land grant, the Quakers planned to retake the government. Hyde had dissolved the assembly in May, but the October elections for the November assembly had not gone the way of the Chowan clique. "I hear few but quakers and their party are chosen Burgesses," the Reverend John Urmston reported, revealing his disdain for everything North Carolinian: "They give out already they'l have new Lords and new Laws. Or rather no Laws[. T]hat will best please the generality of our Gentry."[27]

From Pollock's vantage point, not only North Carolina's security but also its future character hinged on the military defeat of the Tuscarora nation. All now depended on whether South Carolina's gentlemen would step in to save the Anglican ascendancy.[28] Pollock had also again asked Virginia for aid, but after learning that Colonel James Moore, a leader of South Carolina's Goose Creek faction, was on his way north with around nine hundred Yamassee and other Indians, Pollock put all his energy and resources into ensuring that the new expedition would succeed. He ignored Spotswood's proffers of support. At a conference suggested by the Virginian and snubbed by Pollock, Spotswood intended to ask that the proprietors mortgage all lands north of Albemarle Sound in return for some clothing and one thousand pounds, with Spotswood retaining approval of the spending of that money. There was no charity from the northern neighbors.[29]

Some delegates from the Tuscarora came for peace talks in November 1712, and Pollock insisted that they return in January with those guilty of the massacre or at least hostages as a symbol of good faith. Moore's forces crossed the Cape Fear River in early December. But no matter what pressure Pollock could bring, "our Assembly would not consent to send round to Neuse a Sloop" with provisions to maintain the invading army while it waited to see if the peace negotiations would succeed.[30] The council requisitioned a total of only 135 bushels of Indian corn from the colony in December.[31] Pollock could not "find one hundred in the whole province" to join up with Moore, "some deserting the Country others absconding and the rest sheltering themselves under the Masque of Quakerism."[32] Pollock angrily informed Moore that he should bring his entire Indian army to Albemarle County to live off the land and crops of the people who refused to take up arms. Within a few weeks, Moore's forces had wreaked such destruction there that Pollock feared that some were "more ready to ryse upe against them, than march out against the enemy."[33]

Moore's army set off for Bath County in mid-January 1713. Winter weather, including "extraordinary deep snow," prevented the troops from engaging with the Tuscarora for almost two months, during which time Pollock struggled to find provisions for them. South Carolina finally sent beef and salt in February. But finding food was not the only problem facing Pollock. By late February, rumors abounded that the Five Nations would come from New York to aid the Tuscarora. If these rumors were true, Moore's forces would be impossibly outnumbered.[34]

One report from New York explained that the northern Indians believed that some of their own men had been captured and hung while hunting in North Carolina. Northern delegates certainly visited the region, for a Seneca, Anethae, was captured by Moore's Yamassee forces while in the company of a party of Tuscarora. Anethae would have been sold as a slave, but understanding the revenge the Five Nations might wreak, Pollock quickly purchased the Indian and arranged for his freedom and safe transport north. Pollock appealed to the governor of New York to ensure Anethae's return to "his own Country, that they may see and know the falsity of these reports."[35]

The campaign to take Fort Neoheroka began in early spring, and on the last day of March, Pollock received the news that the fort had fallen. Somewhere between six and eight hundred Indians had met their fate "in the laudable custom of South Carolina." Almost four hundred more had been taken prisoner, booty of the Yamassee. Pollock no longer had formidable enemies in arms. Since some Indian stragglers remained (Cores, who killed isolated settlers on the south side of the sound), he requested that Moore linger to clean up. Pollock could still procure no help from his own settlers; "as for white men," he told Moore, "you know how difficult it will be to raise any number out of this country."[36]

Spotswood encouraged Pollock to appoint Tom Blount, a friendly leader of the smaller Upper Tuscarora, as king of the entire Tuscarora nation if Blount agreed to turn in any members with seditious tendencies. "Make him King of all those Indians under the protection of North Carolina. This proposal will stir up his ambition," wrote Spotswood. "You may assure Blunt that . . . he shall be owned by [Virginia's] Govt. as the Chief of the Tuscarora Nations."[37] Most survivors among the Tuscarora, unwilling to accept the puppet Blount as their leader, "fled northerly" to join the Five Nations in June 1713.[38] However, warriors of the region's smaller bands—the Cores and Matamuskeets—continued to use violence to prevent white settlers from encroaching on tribal lands until a February 1715 treaty secured the Indians' property.[39]

Thus finally ended North Carolina's Quaker-Leveller republic. No leader emerged from the Quakers to plan another insurrection. Cary returned in May 1713, briefly worrying Pollock. The governor reported in September that "the opposite party . . . seems now to be more strong since Col. Cary came in."[40] But a year in an English jail seemed to have sapped Cary's will, and by 1714, he had departed for the West Indies. Pollock's administration continued to prosecute those who "in a mutinous maner did Contemn and resist the Lawfull authority of this Government being Imprest on an Expedition agt. Indyan Enemy."[41] By October 1714, Pollock claimed that the Quakers had abandoned their rebellious attitude.[42] With the 1715 passage of a new Vestry Act that established the Church of England and an act that required all members of the assembly to take oaths, the Quakers lost control of North Carolina's political machinery.[43]

The establishment of the church did not indicate any more religious devotion among the Anglicans than had previously been the case. In 1714, the leading men of St. Paul's Parish in Chowan admitted they had "but one sorry Church . . . never finished."[44] Even after establishment, Urmston continued to complain bitterly. "The Vestry's very averse to meet," he wrote to the Society for the Propagation of the Gospel, and "no care is taken for collecting" his stipend.[45]

The regular colonists, whom he called "a pack of profligate & loose people & zealous sectarists," were no more receptive to Urmston's requests for money, which apparently caused them only to ask "why did I not labour & make corn[. T]they saw no reason why I should not work as well as they."[46] Resistance to paying tithes would remain powerful, and the all-Anglican council never made collecting such funds a priority, given the risk of provoking popular struggle. Urmston lamented that "the Country will never be brought to make any provision for a Minister . . . as averse to be at any charge in the saving of their souls as their Country."[47]

The refusal to pay tithes marked the limits of the settlers' defiance of Anglican-planter control. The people of North Carolina seemed unlikely to win a fight for anything more. In fifty years of resistance, the ex-servants, debtors, and dissenters never had been defeated by enemies from within. But now powerful interests without had determined that the existence of their sanctuary posed too much of a threat. The powerful Anglican colonies to the north and south clearly were prepared to intervene—with Crown forces if necessary—against North Carolina.

Any lingering doubts about other colonies' willingness to become involved were answered in late 1718. South Carolina forces captured Stede Bonnet, a pirate, at the mouth of the Cape Fear River and brought him to Charles Town to be tried and hung. In November, Spotswood again sent the Royal Navy into North Carolina territory, this time to catch the last ally of the Atlantic Levellers, Edward "Blackbeard" Teach. The navy killed him and half of the crew of his ship, the *Adventure*, in the waters of Ocracoke Inlet. They brought the remaining crew members to Virginia, where a trial led to their execution.[48]

The lords proprietors appointed Charles Eden the new governor of North Carolina in June 1713, the first time the job had not been described as a "deputy governor," secondary to the governor seated in Charles Town. Pollock handed the reins of government to Eden in early 1715 but continued to serve as a council member. North Carolina adopted its first slave code in 1715. The government now firmly served the planters' purposes. The battle to control North Carolina had been successful—and lucrative. By the time of his death in 1722, Pollock was the largest landowner in North Carolina.[49] In 1710, even after fifty years of settlement in North Carolina, the colony had fewer than one thousand slaves.[50] South Carolina's Moore family (which included James Moore) soon moved hundreds of slaves into the Cape Fear region, creating a society in South Carolina's image.[51]

"That thereby the Countrey may have a free parlement."[52] John Culpeper's 1677 words mark the democratic aspirations of peoples everywhere. Albemarle's Levellers ultimately failed to prevent the rise of an
intolerant, hierarchical, slave society in their midst, but they nevertheless
should not be dismissed or forgotten. On the contrary: that two generations successfully built a society of free and equal people—government
of, by, and for the people—peacefully coexisting with Native Americans,
should proudly enter the annals of North Carolina history, a sign of the
possibilities of the colonial period and of the big principles ordinary
seventeenth-century people held dear. A full century before Virginia's
planters gazed out their windows at people they had purchased and
praised liberty, North Carolina's hardy, rough-hewn farmers had not
merely articulated but gallantly fought for their right to democratic, representative self-government.

# AFTERWORD

At first glance, the ideas of the English Revolution appear to have evaporated from the North Carolina terrain in the eighteenth century. The colony joined America's "Gulag Archipelago" as South Carolinians spread the slave society north, just as they would later expand it south into Georgia.[1] "The family," as the Moores became known, intermarried with Chowan clique families and converted wealth into political power. These South Carolinians, already groomed for economic and political dominance over others, claimed vast land holdings in the Cape Fear area and parlayed those estates into seats in the assembly.

The southern slave society's elites tried to disguise the grotesque brutality of the regime over which they presided. The gorgeous architecture of Charleston, homes filled with the best luxuries Europe had to offer, and sons educated at Eton together constituted a facade covering a system that allowed them to sell other people's—and occasionally their own—children for money. No system of social control could operate more effectively than the ever-present threat of destroying family bonds. The planters lived in a world of self-delusion, comforting themselves with the patriarchal idea that the slaves happily served them: "My Negroes are in more comfortable circumstances than any equal number of Peasantry in Europe, there is not a Beggar among them nor one unprovided with food, raiment & good Lodging, they also enjoy property; the Lash is forbidden; they all understand this declaration as a Substitute —'If you deserve whipping I shall conclude you don't love me & will sell you.' . . . Yet I believe no man gets more work from his Negroes than I do, at the same time they are my Watchmen and my friends; never was an absolute Monarch more happy in his Subjects than at the present time I am."[2]

There was no way to marry absolute monarchy and the republican ideas of Levellers and Quakers. Since the 1640s, these groups had rejected all titles and privileges of birth and refused to defer to any who claimed high social rank. Demanding a wide franchise, they sought to give political access to the common man. But North Carolina's elite planters combined legal expertise, control of local market networks, and the election machinery to manage the colonial assembly in tandem with the governors. That political domination included running the court system. The slave society completely contradicted every Albemarle principle.

However, North Carolina's planters could rarely compete with the finery of their southern counterparts, earning the colony the sobriquet "Poor Carolina" from contemporaries and future historians. Private tutors, never mind an English education, were much rarer than in South Carolina, while no one displayed Charleston's powdered wigs or porcelain.[3] Neither geography nor climate had limited the growth of planter wealth. Rather, the majority of the people who settled the region continued to resist the plantation complex. Eastern planters could not command the outward signs of deference from less wealthy white farmers, and the colony as a whole remained much less stratified than its neighbors.

North Carolinians never totally lost their leveling spirit, as the Piedmont's Regulation movement a few generations later testifies. Huge numbers of small farmers moved into the Piedmont in the 1740s and 1750s. Perhaps attracted by the Albemarle tradition, they brought with them a theology of equality in the sight of God. Politically, the backcountry farmers remained underrepresented in the colony as late as the 1770s, but they struggled against the emergent slave society. These farmers objected not because they carried modern liberal ideas about race relations but because a slave society devalued their labor and skills and especially because it meant the concentration of power in the hands of a few. Like the men of Cary's Rebellion, these small farmers viewed the planter elite as the source of their troubles, blocking their right to participate fully in their own government. The North Carolina Regulators organized a movement against political corruption in the late 1760s: "To sum up the whole matter of our petition in a few words it is namely these that we may obtain unprejudiced Jurys, That all extortionate Officers Lawyers and Clerks may be brought to fair Tryals—That the Collectors of publick money may be called to proper settlements of their accounts. . . . If we cannot obtain this that we may have some securities for our properties more than the bare humour of officers, we can see plainly that we shall not be able to live under such oppressions."[4]

The history of the Regulation's fight for fair and just representative government is told elsewhere, but slaveholders violently repressed any attempt to introduce equality and justice to the political system. The rich planters' raw military power again crushed a popular egalitarian movement.[5]

The ideas of the English Revolution survived even the public hanging of the Regulators, emerging again in Mecklenburg County, where citizens told their delegates to the state's Constitutional Convention in the late 1770s to "oppose everything that leans to aristocracy or power in the hands of the rich and chief men exercised to the oppression of the poor."[6] North Carolinians later refused to ratify the new federal constitution with its strengthening of centralized power.

The defeat of the Albemarle settlers in 1713 (and later of the Piedmont Regulators) does not constitute the usual uplifting American story of equality triumphing over hierarchy. A very few ruthless and aggressive men defeated these movements and imposed the plantation complex on the whole state. Yet many North Carolinians—red, white, and black—contested the slave society during the colonial period, recognizing that not only slaves lost. Almost everyone did. Given the barbaric practices of slavery, contemporary Tar Heelers should bear with pride the "Poor Carolina" legacy. However humble its origins, the Albemarle community believed in equality, representative government, and freedom of religion. These ideas, cherished by George Durant, John Culpeper, and all those very mutinous people, eventually became accepted as the quintessential American values.

# NOTES

## Abbreviations

CRNC     *Colonial Records of North Carolina*

NCHGR   Hathaway, *North Carolina Historical and Genealogical Register*

NCSA    North Carolina State Archives, Raleigh

## Introduction

1. Affidavit of Henry Hudson, Jan. 31, 1679, in Saunders, *CRNC*, 1:272. "Landgrave" referred to medieval German nobility; "Cassique" was a Spanish version of the Arawak word for chieftain. John Locke, prohibited from transferring English titles to the colonies, had suggested these designations for a potential colonial nobility and gentry.
2. Gura, *Glimpse*, 64. Gura acknowledges that the New England radicals never developed a political program akin to that of England's Civil War sects (79–82).
3. Edwin Churchill, "Mid-Seventeenth-Century Maine: A World on the Edge," in *American Beginnings*, edited by Churchill, Baker, and D'Abate, 245.
4. McConville, *These Daring Disturbers*, 13–27.
5. Urmston to Society for the Propagation of the Gospel, July 7, 1711, in Saunders, *CRNC*, 1:764, 770.
6. Nicholson to Lords of the Committee, Aug. 20, 1690, in ibid., 366.

## Prologue

1. Urmston to Society for the Propagation of the Gospel, July 7, 1711, in Saunders, *CRNC*, 1:768.
2. The historical debate over the causes of the English Civil War has spawned an enormous literature. Some of the most influential works include Hill, *Century of Revolution*; Stone, *Causes of the English Revolution*; Russell, *Origins of the English*

*Civil War*; Aylmer, *Rebellion or Revolution*; J. C. D. Clark, *Revolution and Rebellion*; Cressy, *England on Edge*; Manning, *English People and the English Revolution*. For a useful historiographical guide, see Richardson, *Debate on the English Revolution Revisited*.

3. Hill, "A Bourgeois Revolution?," in *Three British Revolutions*, edited by Pocock, 122; see also Hill, *World Turned Upside Down*; Underdown, *Revel, Riot and Rebellion*.

4. Richard Overton, "Some Articles," in *Levellers*, edited by Aylmer, 83.

5. Richard Overton, "Appeale from the Degenerate Representative Body . . . to . . . the Free People . . . of England," July 1647, in ibid., 87.

6. Hill, *World Turned Upside Down*, 72.

7. Ibid., 210, 212–13.

8. Ibid., 214.

9. Hill, *Experience of Defeat*, 126n. Although the Quakers are now most famous for their pacifist principles, pacifism entered Quaker doctrine only after the failed Venner Rising in 1664. Many Quakers resisted this new line preached by George Fox, their leader. Some had already departed to cross the Atlantic, "traveling," as Hill puts it, "to establish the Leveller/Quaker republic in America" (*Experience of Defeat*, 160).

10. George, *Women in the First Capitalist Society*, 53.

11. Mack, *Visionary Women*, 1; Moore, *Light in Their Consciences*, 125. See also Fischer, *Suspect Relations*, 49–52.

12. Hutton, *Restoration*, 71, 121–22.

13. Lawrence Stone, "The Results of the English Revolutions of the Seventeenth Century," in *Three British Revolutions*, edited by Pocock, 36.

14. Throughout this volume, I refer to this person as Shaftesbury, although he was known as Anthony Ashley Cooper until 1661, when he became Lord Ashley. In 1672, he acquired the title of Earl of Shaftesbury.

15. Hill, *Some Intellectual Consequences*, 13.

16. Thomas, *Slave Trade*, 201; Paschal, "Proprietary North Carolina," 74–75; Haley, *First Earl*, 230.

17. Thomas, *Slave Trade*, 14.

## Part 1

1. Hawks, *Embracing*; Ashe, *History*.

2. Lefler and Powell, *Colonial North Carolina*. Powell's 1977 text, *North Carolina*, skims over the first fifty years. Neither book provides footnotes. Osgood,

*Chartered Colonies*, remains by far the best treatment of proprietary North Carolina in a general colonial history, but North Carolina is still accorded less coverage than any other colony. Of the unpublished dissertations written on the period since 1963, none attempts a basic chronological narrative. Without a detailed study of all the surviving records, the analysis was flawed. Only an out-of-print monograph, Leaming, *Hidden Americans*, shows an understanding of the nature of the community, but Leaming paints a picture of the entire period, without a detailed breakdown of change over time. I hope that this book will be seen as a precursor to the recent historical literature on North Carolina: Fischer, *Suspect Relations*, Sensbach, *Separate Canaan*, and especially Kars, *Breaking Loose Together*. The North Carolina Regulation of the 1770s—a movement weaving strands of both theology and social class into its ideology of protest against the corruption of a plantation economy—can easily be seen as a later chapter in the story told here. Historians of Virginia will find common ground between my work and that of Brown (*Good Wives*), Holton (*Forced Founders*), and Parent (*Foul Means*). Their studies strip the last vestiges of romance from the Virginia gentlemen of the colonial period.

3. Greene, Brana-Shute, and Sparks, *Money, Trade and Power*, vii–xii.

4. Most if not all previous published research on the seventeenth century has leaned almost exclusively on the collected records of the period in Saunders, *CRNC*, vol. 1. This volume is also the chief source for this book, but I have supplemented it with court records, land records, and personal papers from the North Carolina State Archives in Raleigh, some papers from the Southern Historical Collection at the University of North Carolina in Chapel Hill, and the Quaker records housed at Guilford College in Greensboro. I have also used some published collections of the government records of both Virginia and South Carolina. Random records collected in the three volumes of Hathaway's *North Carolina Historical and Genealogical Register*, many of which have since been lost, were very useful, although dates were often missing and had to be calculated from internal information.

## Chapter 1

1. Gallivan, *James River Chiefdoms*, 20.

2. Leaming, *Hidden Americans*, 8–10; Lefler and Powell, *Colonial North Carolina*, 14.

3. Gallivan, *James River Chiefdoms*, 21; Garrow, "Mattamuskeet Documents," 5; Silver, *New Face*, 74–77.

4. Gallivan, *James River Chiefdoms*, 84, 91; Silver, *New Face*, 39–50.

5. Parramore, "Tuscarora Ascendancy," 312; Silver, *New Face*, 71–73; Gallay, *Indian Slave Trade*, 4.

6. Byrd, *Tuscarora Subsistence Practices*, 3–5.

7. Robbie Ethridge, "Creating the Shatter Zone," in *Light on the Path*, edited by Pluckhahn and Ethridge, 213.

8. Thomas Woodward to John Colleton, June 2, 1665, in Saunders, *CRNC*, 1:99. In 1711, it was reported that what had once been the main Currituck inlet had within thirty years become "quite stopped up with dry sand and people ride over it" (Ludwell and Harrison, "Boundary Line Proceedings," 11).

9. Ludwell and Harrison, "Boundary Line Proceedings," 6–10.

10. Meanley, *Great Dismal Swamp*; Matta, "Aquatic Insects of the Dismal Swamp," in *Great Dismal Swamp*, edited by Kirk.

11. Meanley, *Great Dismal Swamp*.

12. Quoted in Parent, *Foul Means*, 142; Billings, *Sir William Berkeley*, 202–3; Kulikoff, *Tobacco and Slaves*, 32–33; Edmund S. Morgan, *American Slavery*, 235–39, 246.

13. Brown, *Good Wives*, 149–52.

14. Parent, *Foul Means*, 36; Edward Price, *Dividing the Land*, 109.

15. Hening, *Statutes at Large*, 2:26.

16. Ibid., 1:532–33; William Berkeley to Richard Conquest, Aug. 8, 1660, in *Lower Norfolk County*, edited by James, 3:103.

17. James, *Lower Norfolk County*, 3:105, 141–46, 4:78–79.

18. Ibid., 4:78–79, 109–13; Weeks, *Southern Quakers*, 27n. The mother of John Porter, who would play a major role in Cary's Rebellion (see chapter 7) was among those fined in 1662 (Powell, *Dictionary*, 5:126).

19. Lawson, *New Voyage*, 190–92; Cumming, "Earliest Permanent Settlement."

20. Deed from King Kiscutanew to Nathaniel Batts, Sept. 24, 1660, Nathaniel Batts Papers, NCSA; George Durant Deed from Kilcacenen, Mar. 1662, in Saunders, *CRNC*, 1:19; Fenn and Wood, *Natives and Newcomers*, 25; Powell, *Dictionary*, 2:123.

21. Hawks, *Embracing*, 339.

22. Fox, *Journal*, edited by Nickalls, 642–43. For more on colonial-era frontier traders and interpreters, see Merrell, *Into the American Woods*.

23. Powell, *Dictionary*, 2:123–24; Leaming, *Hidden Americans*, 53.

24. Silver, *New Face*, 16–31; Merrens, *Colonial North Carolina*, 37–44; Lawson, *New Voyage*, 92–94.

25. Lawson, *New Voyage*, 156–57.

26. Ludwell and Harrison, "Boundary Line Proceedings," 10–11.

27. Urmston to Society for the Propagation of the Gospel, July 7, 1711, in Saunders, *CRNC*, 1:764.

28. Lawson, *New Voyage*, 90.

29. Mulcahy, *Hurricanes and Society*, 19.

30. Deetz, *Flowerdew Hundred*, 15, 53–55.

31. Urmston to Society for the Propagation of the Gospel, July 7, 1711, in Saunders, *CRNC*, 1:764.

32. Fox, *Journal*, edited by Nickalls, 645.

33. Urmston to Society for the Propagation of the Gospel, July 7, 1711, in Saunders, *CRNC*, 1:766.

34. Billings, *Sir William Berkeley*, 56–60, 272.

35. Billings, "Sir William Berkeley."

36. Powell, *Carolina Charter*, 35–36.

37. "The Second Charter Granted by King Charles the Second, to the Proprietors of Carolina," June 13, 1665, in Saunders, *CRNC*, 1:103.

38. "A Declaration and Proposals to All That Will Plant in Carolina," Aug. 25, 1663, in ibid., 45–46. Quitrents were a vestige of feudal obligation; instead of owing a portion of their crops or a certain number of workdays per year, tenants were "quit" of their duties if they paid a cash fee.

39. George Catchmany's Testimony, in Saunders, *CRNC*, 1:20.

40. "Instructions for Sir William Berkeley," in ibid., 1:51.

41. E. Lawrence Lee, *Lower Cape Fear*, 29–34. Lefler and Powell estimate the population at more than five hundred by 1663 (*Colonial North Carolina*, 32).

## Chapter 2

1. Roper, *Conceiving Carolina*, 19.

2. E. Lawrence Lee, *Lower Cape Fear*, 35–52.

3. A headright awarded a specific amount of land per person entering the colony, given to whoever paid for the passage of that person (Edward Price, *Dividing the Land*, 14).

4. "The Concessions and Agreement of the Lords Propryators of the Province of Carolina to and with the Adventurers of the Island of Barbados and Their Associates of England New England the Carribbia Islands and Barmothos to the Province of Carolina and All That Shall Plant There," in Saunders, *CRNC*, 1:87–89.

5. Thomas Woodward to John Colleton, June 2, 1665, in ibid., 100–101.

6. Sir John Colleton to Carteret, Sept. 9, 1665, in *Ye Countie*, edited by Powell, 6–8.

7. Weeks, "William Drummond"; Billings, *Sir William Berkeley*, 165–68; quotation from "Drummond to Deare Friend," Sept. 3, 1666, in Billings, *Papers*, 293–94.

8. Albertson, *In Ancient Albemarle*, 14–18.

9. Kulikoff, *Tobacco and Slaves*, 31–39.

10. "Articles of Agreement Concerning the Cessation in Virginia and Maryland and Albemarle at James City," July 12, 1666, in Saunders, *CRNC*, 1:141.

11. Edmund S. Morgan, *American Slavery*, 193–95.

12. "Coppy of a Commission to Sir William Berkeley to Constitute and Commissionate a Governor for Albemarle River," 1663, in Saunders, *CRNC*, 1:50.

13. Kulikoff, *From British Peasants*, 116.

14. Edward Price, *Dividing the Land*, 3n.

15. McConville, *These Daring Disturbers*, 14–18.

16. Lords Proprietors to Samuel Stephens, May 1, 1668, in Saunders, *CRNC*, 1:175; Edward Price, *Dividing the Land*, 23–24.

17. "Instructions to the Governor and Councell of Albemarle," 1670, in Saunders, *CRNC*, 1:182.

18. "William Berkeley to Assembly or Council of Albemarle," Mar. 7, 1670, in Powell, *Ye Countie*, 38.

19. "Acts of the Assembly of Albemarle Rattified and Confirmed by the Proprietors," Jan. 20, 1670, in Saunders, *CRNC*, 1:183–84.

20. Ibid., 184.

21. Veale, "Manner of Living," 244.

22. "Acts of the Assembly of Albemarle Rattified and Confirmed by the Proprietors," Jan. 20, 1670, in Saunders, *CRNC*, 1:185.

23. Ibid., 186.

24. Cheves, *Shaftesbury Papers*; Sirmans, *Colonial South Carolina*, 3–9.

25. "The Fundamental Constitutions of Carolina, Drawn up by John Locke," Mar. 1, 1669, in Saunders, *CRNC*, 1:187–88. Weir, *Colonial South Carolina*, argues that the Fundamental Constitutions make sense from the perspective of those for whom they were written—Barbadian planters with total control over hundreds of slaves.

26. "The Fundamental Constitutions of Carolina, Drawn up by John Locke," Mar. 1, 1669, in Saunders, *CRNC*, 1:202–3, 204.

27. Lords Proprietors to Samuel Stephens and Council, "Sending a Copy of the Fundamental Constitutions," Jan. 1670, in *Ye Countie*, edited by Powell, 34.

28. "Instructions to the Governor and Councell of Albemarle," 1670, in Saunders, *CRNC*, 1:181.

29. MacPherson, *Political Theory*, 247–52.

30. Cheves, *Shaftesbury Papers*. In Shaftesbury's papers, the voluminous correspon-

dence by all participants in the new Port Royal colony stands in sharp contrast to the absence of any mention of Albemarle in 1669–72.

31. "Peter Carteret's Appointment as Councillor and Assistant Governor for Albemarle; Peter Carteret's Appointment as Secretary and Chief Registrar for Albemarle," Dec. 3, 1664, in *Ye Countie*, edited by Powell, 3–5.

32. "Form for Deputation from Proprietor," July 1669, in Cain, *CRNC*, 334.

33. Governor and Council to Lords Proprietors, May 16, 1671, in ibid., 339–41.

34. Instructions to Governor, Apr. 27, 1672, Statement by John Harvey, July 11, 1672, both in Cain, *CRNC*, 342–43. Carteret never returned to Albemarle.

35. "Albemarle Acts of Parliament Sent Inclosed in a Letter of November 10, 1673," in Saunders, *CRNC*, 1:218–19.

36. Cheves, *Shaftesbury Papers*, 152, 160, 271; Sirmans, *Colonial South Carolina*, 16.

37. Pestana, *English Atlantic*, 81.

38. "Commission for Surveyor General," Dec. 30, 1671, in Saunders, *CRNC*, 1:211–12.

39. Cheves, *Shaftesbury Papers*, 160–61, 207; Craton and Saunders, *Islanders in the Stream*, 96; Rediker, *Villains*.

40. Pomfret, *Province*.

41. Peter Carteret's Account to Lords Proprietors, Dec. 3, 1674, in *Ye Countie*, edited by Powell, 62.

42. Woodward to Colleton, June 1665, in Saunders, *CRNC*, 1:100–101; Merrens, *Colonial North Carolina*, 26.

43. Wolf, "Proud and the Poor," 27–29.

44. "Extracts from the Journal of William Edmondson from the Years 1671–1672," in Saunders, *CRNC*, 1:215–16.

45. Fox, *Journal*, edited by Nickalls, 641.

46. Ibid., 641–42.

47. Ibid., 642.

48. Ibid., 643.

49. Ibid., 644.

50. Ludwell and Harrison, "Boundary Line Proceedings," 10.

51. Fox, *Journal*, edited by Nickalls, 641.

52. Fox, *Collection*, 55.

53. Parramore argues that the 1672 agreement "made of Albemarle a reservation for white people and such, in effect, it remained for the next thirty years" ("Tuscarora Ascendancy," 313).

54. Robert E. Gallman, "Changes."

55. Merrens, *Colonial North Carolina*, 20; Parker, *CRNC*, 2:xxx–xxxii; Lefler and Powell, *Colonial North Carolina*, 31–32, 174; Raper, *North Carolina*, 7.

# Chapter 3

1. Rankin's short account, *Upheaval*, narrates some of these events in a very different tone. Rankin acknowledges that his version "may appear weighted heavily on the side of the proprietary faction" (viii), meaning Miller and Thomas Eastchurch. Later historians of North Carolina (such as Lefler and Powell, *Colonial North Carolina*, 47) regarded the colony as divided into two factions, either for or against the proprietors. I feel that this approach sets up a false dichotomy. Most settlers wanted little interference from England. As long as the proprietors overlooked the colony, which was most of the time, the people of Albemarle had no problem with the lords. The settlers rebelled on two fronts, against the royal customs and against the governor who revoked their right to self-government.

2. The Atlantic world literature is extensive. See especially Pestana, *English Atlantic*; Hatfield, *Atlantic Virginia*; Games, *Migration*; Hornsby, *British Atlantic*; Steele, *English Atlantic*. None of these works deal at all with North Carolina.

3. Holmes, *Making of a Great Power*, 58–60, 440.

4. Ibid., 440.

5. "The Case of T. Miller, Z. Gilham &c Concerning the Rebellion of Carolina, by Sir Peter Colleton," Feb. 9, 1680, in Saunders, *CRNC*, 1:287.

6. Instructions to Governor, Apr. 27, 1672, in Cain, *CRNC*, 343.

7. Hatfield, *Atlantic Virginia*, 39–42.

8. Robert Holden to Commissioners of Customs, June 10, 1679, in Saunders, *CRNC*, 1:244.

9. Joshua Lamb Papers, NCSA; Affidavit of Henry Hudson, Jan. 31, 1679, in Saunders, *CRNC*, 1:272; Bailyn, *New England Merchants*, 148–51.

10. McCusker and Menard, *Economy*, 77. Although McCusker and Menard play down the extent of Atlantic smuggling over the entire colonial period, they acknowledge that in the tobacco trade, particularly in the first decades after 1660, avoidance of the Navigation Acts was significant.

11. Cheves, *Shaftesbury Papers*, 421, 424–25; Sirmans, *Colonial South Carolina*, 20.

12. Miller v. Riscoe Papers, NCSA.

13. Eastchurch to Carteret, Dec. 11, 1671, in *Ye Countie*, edited by Powell, 43.

14. Peter Carteret to Berkeley, Jan. 25, 1675, in ibid., 64–65. The published volume incorrectly identifies the recipient of this letter as George Carteret (Sirmans, *Colonial South Carolina*, 25).

15. Edmund S. Morgan, *American Slavery*, 203–10.

16. "Representation to the Lords Proprietors of Carolina Concerning the Rebellion in That Country," n.d., in Saunders, *CRNC*, 1:258.

17. Affidavit of Henry Hudson, Jan. 31, 1679, in ibid., 289–90.

18. "Carolina: Indictment of Th. Miller Recd. from the Commissioners of the Customs," July 15, 1680, in ibid., 314–15.

19. Affidavit of Henry Hudson, Jan. 31, 1679, in ibid., 289–90.

20. "Lords Proprietors to Present Government and Assembly of the County of Albemarle," Oct. 21, 1676, in ibid., 1:229.

21. Webb, *1676*, 26–29, 69–70; Edmund S. Morgan, *American Slavery*, 250–70.

22. "Lords Proprietors to Present Government and Assembly of the County of Albemarle," Oct. 21, 1676, in Saunders, *CRNC*, 1:228.

23. Ibid., 228–32; Affidavit of Timothy Biggs, May 1679, in Saunders, *CRNC*, 1:292.

24. Edmondson, *Journal*, 80.

25. "The Case of T. Miller, Z. Gilham &c Concerning the Rebellion of Carolina, by Sir Peter Colleton," Feb. 9, 1680, in Saunders, *CRNC*, 1:287.

26. "Affidavitt of Solomon Summers of Redriffe Shippwrite in the County of Surrey," Jan. 31, 1679, in Saunders, *CRNC*, 1:296–97. The sources for this chapter are mostly from affidavits of opponents of the rebellion, such as Miller, Timothy Biggs, and Henry Hudson, and their friends such as Summers. Summers did not witness most of the events about which he testified and seems to have related the story in accordance with Miller's instructions. Summers's deposition contains the phrases "as the deponent was there credibly informed" and "as your deponent supposeth." All the affidavits were submitted several years later in London, in connection with the trial of Culpeper. Significantly, Culpeper denied none of the facts of the case and argued only that his and his fellow rebels' actions were justified.

27. "The Remonstrance of the Inhabitants off Paspatancke to All the Rest of the County of Albemarle," Dec. 3, 1677, in Saunders, *CRNC*, 1:249; "The Case of T. Miller, Z. Gilham &c Concerning the Rebellion of Carolina, by Sir Peter Colleton," Feb. 9, 1680, in Saunders, *CRNC*, 1:287.

28. "T. Miller's Account to the Commissioners of His Majesty's Customes," Jan. 21, 1680, in Saunders, *CRNC*, 1:265–66.

29. "The Case of T. Miller, Z. Gilham &c Concerning the Rebellion of Carolina, by Sir Peter Colleton," Feb. 9, 1680, in ibid., 1:287.

30. Edmund S. Morgan, *American Slavery*, 273–75.

31. Haley, *First Earl*, 348–421.

32. "Representation to the Lords Proprietors of Carolina Concerning the Rebellion in That Country," n.d., in Saunders, *CRNC*, 1:256–60. It was not uncommon for colonial protesters to try to discredit their opposition by accusing them of collaborating with nonwhites or women. The numbers here

may be exaggerated, but given the nature of Albemarle society, the charge has some merit.

33. Affidavit of T. Miller, Jan. 31, 1679, Affidavit of Timothy Biggs, May 1679, both in Saunders, *CRNC*, 1:280, 292.

34. "The Remonstrance of the Inhabitants off Paspatancke to All the Rest of the County of Albemarle," Dec. 3, 1677, Deposition of Edward Wade, Aug. 22, 1679, Affidavit of T. Miller, Jan. 31, 1679, Affidavit of Timothy Biggs, May 1679, all in Saunders, *CRNC*, 1:249, 280, 292–93.

35. Two groups of independents in New Jersey also claimed the right to assemblies of their own choosing in the 1670s, defying the will of their governors and proprietors (McConville, *These Daring Disturbers*, 18).

36. "The Remonstrance of the Inhabitants off Paspatancke to All the Rest of the County of Albemarle," Dec. 3, 1677, in Saunders, *CRNC*, 1:248–49.

37. Affidavit of Henry Hudson, Jan. 31, 1679, in ibid., 272.

38. "Representation to the Lords Proprietors of Carolina Concerning the Rebellion in That Country," n.d., Affidavit of Henry Hudson, Jan. 31, 1679, Affidavit of T. Miller, Jan. 31, 1679, Affidavit of Peter Brockwell, Feb. 16, 1680, all in ibid., 259–60, 273, 280, 299.

39. "Representation to the Lords Proprietors of Carolina Concerning the Rebellion in That Country," n.d., Affidavit of T. Miller, Jan. 31, 1679, both in ibid., 1:259–60, 281–82.

40. Affidavit of Henry Hudson, Jan. 31, 1679, Affidavit of T. Miller, Jan. 31, 1679, Affidavit of Peter Brockwell, Feb. 16, 1680, all in ibid., 273–74, 281–82, 299–300.

41. Affidavit of Henry Hudson, Jan. 31, 1679, "Affidavitt of Solomon Summers of Redriffe Shippwrite in the County of Surrey," Jan. 31, 1679, both in ibid., 274, 298.

42. Rebel Council to Lieutenant Governor of Virginia, Dec. 27, 1677, in Cain, *CRNC*, 349.

43. Ibid., Jeffreys quoted on 349–50n.

44. Affidavit of Henry Hudson, Jan. 31, 1679, Affidavit of T. Miller, Jan. 31, 1679, Affidavit of Peter Brockwell, Feb. 16, 1680, all in Saunders, *CRNC*, 1:274, 282, 300.

45. Affidavit of T. Miller, Jan. 31, 1679, in ibid., 283.

46. Proposal by Timothy Biggs, Apr. 1678, Affidavit of Timothy Biggs, May 1679, Depositions of Timothy Biggs, 1678, Petition of Timothy Biggs to Earl of Danby, Lord Treasurer, Nov. 20, 1680, all in ibid., 247–48, 291–93, 309–11, 325–26. (Biggs, like Culpeper, had come to Albemarle by way of the Charleston area, where he had owned the town lot adjoining Culpeper's. Perhaps they

had formed some personal relationship, for Biggs never mentioned Culpeper by name in any of the affidavits he wrote during the next couple of years about the rebellion [Haley, *First Earl*, 418–19; Cheves, *Shaftesbury Papers*, 408]).

47. Proposal by Timothy Biggs, Apr. 1678, in Saunders, *CRNC*, 1:247–48, 291–93.

48. Ibid., 247–48.

49. "Representation to the Lords Proprietors of Carolina Concerning the Rebellion in That Country," n.d., in ibid., 1:261.

50. Haley, *First Earl*, 440.

51. Addition to Affidavit of Timothy Biggs, Aug. 15, 1679, in Saunders, *CRNC*, 1:293.

52. "The Case of T. Miller, Z. Gilham &c Concerning the Rebellion of Carolina, by Sir Peter Colleton," Feb. 9, 1680, in ibid., 288.

53. Affidavit of John Taylor, Jan. 31, 1679, "The Case of T. Miller, Z. Gilham &c Concerning the Rebellion of Carolina, by Sir Peter Colleton," Feb. 9, 1680, both in ibid., 1:276, 288.

54. "To All the Inhabitants or Any That May Arrive in the County of Albemarle, John Culpeper," Feb. 25, 1679, Affidavit of John Taylor, Jan. 31, 1679, both in ibid., 242, 276–77.

55. Affidavit of John Taylor, Jan. 31, 1679, in ibid., 277.

56. "Lords Proprietors to the Governor and Councell of the County of Albemarle in the Province of Carolina," Feb. 8, 1680, in ibid., 283–84.

57. "Carolina: Indictment of Th. Miller Recd. from the Commissioners of the Customs," July 15, 1680," in ibid., 316.

58. "The People of God Who Are in Scorne Called Quakers to the Lords Proprietors," Sept. 13, 1679, in ibid., 250–53.

59. "Carolina: Indictment of Th. Miller Recd. from the Commissioners of the Customs," July 15, 1680, in ibid., 316.

60. "Copie of an Order for Seizing Mr. Culpeper," Dec. 19, 1679, in ibid., 255.

61. "T. Miller's Account to the Commissioners of His Majesty's Customes," Jan. 21, 1680, in ibid., 266.

62. Commissioners of the Customs to Lords of Treasury, Jan. 22, 1680, King's Council Order, Feb. 4, 1680, both in ibid., 267, 270.

63. Report of the Lords of the Council, Feb. 7, 1680, in ibid., 275.

64. Minutes of the Committee of Trade and Plantations, Feb. 8, 1680, in ibid., 284–85.

65. "The Case of T. Miller, Z. Gilham &c Concerning the Rebellion of Carolina, by Sir Peter Colleton," Feb. 9, 1680, in ibid., 287–89.

66. "Answer of Capt. Gillam," Feb. 19, 1680, in ibid., 295.

67. Minutes of Committee of Trade and Plantations, Feb. 19, 1680, in ibid., 301.
68. "Commissioners of the Customs Proposall for Recovery of the Arrears in Carolina," Apr. 15, 1680, in ibid., 329–30.
69. "Record of Culpeper's Trial for Treason," in ibid., 331–33 (Latin trial transcript translated by Professor Ronald Witt, Duke University).
70. Petition of Thomas Miller to the King, June 29, 1680, in ibid., 303–4.
71. Haley, *First Earl*, 252, 433.
72. Petition of Timothy Biggs to the King, Feb. 19, 1680, in Saunders, *CRNC*, 1:295–96.
73. Quoted in Edmund S. Morgan, *American Slavery*, 239.
74. General Court, Mar. 27, 1680, in Parker, *CRNC*, 2:9.
75. Petitions of Thomas Miller to the King, June 29, 1680, July 7, 1680, both in Saunders, *CRNC*, 1:303–4, 308.
76. Petition of Timothy Biggs to Earl of Danby, Lord Treasurer, Nov. 20, 1680, in ibid., 325–26.
77. Petition of the Inhabitants of Albemarle County to the King, June 30, 1680, in ibid., 305.
78. "Carolina: Indictment of Th. Miller Recd. from the Commissioners of the Customs," July 15, 1680, in ibid., 313–21.
79. Minutes of Committee of Trade and Plantation, July 19, 1680, Peter Colleton to William Blathwayt, Aug. 9, 1680, both in ibid., 322, 323; Haley, *First Earl*, 581–87.
80. "Answer of the Lords Proprietors of Carolina," Nov. 20, 1680, in Saunders, *CRNC*, 1:326–28 (italics in original).
81. Minutes of Committee of Trade and Plantations, Nov. 20, 1680, in ibid., 328–29.
82. "Representation to the Lords Proprietors of Carolina Concerning the Rebellion in That Country," n.d., in ibid., 258.

Chapter 4

1. "Representation to the Lords Proprietors of Carolina Concerning the Rebellion in That Country," n.d., Patent from Gov. Jenkins, both in Saunders, *CRNC*, 1:259, 270–71; Parker, *CRNC*, 2:lviii. Shaftesbury's death also meant an end to one of the best documentary sources on the Carolinas. Much of what we know of the early years of settlement comes from the Shaftesbury Papers.
2. Haley, *First Earl*, 674; Lords Proprietors' Instructions to Henry Wilkinson, in Saunders, *CRNC*, 1:336.
3. Gordon to Secretary, May 13, 1709, in ibid., 712.
4. Blount Family Papers, Southern Historical Collection, University of North

Carolina, Chapel Hill; County Court of Albemarle, Mar. 10, 1683, in Parker, *CRNC*, 2:333.

5. County Court of Albemarle, Mar. 10, 1683, in Parker, *CRNC*, 2:333; Lords Proprietors to Seth Sothell, May 12, 1691, in Saunders, *CRNC*, 1:369.

6. County Court of Albemarle, Feb. 6, 1684, in Parker, *CRNC*, 2:342.

7. Haun, *Old Albemarle County North Carolina Book of Land Warrants and Surveys*, 71, 91–101, 113, 116. Working under the supervision of George Stevenson, Haun transcribed every land record in the NCSA.

8. Deposition to the County Court of Albemarle, July 11, 1684, in Parker, *CRNC*, 2:355–56.

9. County Court of Albemarle, Apr. 3, 1684, County Court, Dec. 3, 1684, Oct. 7, 1685, all in ibid., 346, 352, 362.

10. Lords Proprietors to Seth Sothell, Feb. 1685, in Saunders, *CRNC*, 1:350–52.

11. Powell, *Dictionary*, 1:38.

12. County Court, Oct. 7, 1685, in Parker, *CRNC*, 2:360–61.

13. Ibid., July 15, 1686, 369. This record is interesting in that the heading of the court hearing names Sothell as present, but a note at the end claims that it was "an Error of the Clerks" and that Sothell was not present. It seems strange that the clerk would mistakenly record the presence of someone so important. I assume that Sothell ordered his name struck from the record to make his action against Durant seem an objective decision by the court. The proprietors had warned him to separate himself from court proceedings. See Saunders, *CRNC*, 1:351.

14. Lords Proprietors to Seth Sothell, May 12, 1691, in Saunders, *CRNC*, 1:369; County Court, Dec. 1, 1686, in Parker, *CRNC*, 2:374–76.

15. County Court, Apr. 3, 1684, Dec. 1, 1686, both in Parker, *CRNC*, 2:345, 375–76.

16. Ibid., Dec. 3, 1684, 352–53.

17. Ibid., 355.

18. Ibid., Dec. 3, 1684, Oct. 5, 1687, 353, 378.

19. Ibid., Oct. 5, 1687, Dec. 14, 1687, 377, 379.

20. Ibid., Dec. 1, 1687, 374.

21. General Court, n.d., County Court, Dec. 14, 1687, both in ibid., 12, 380.

22. County Court, 1685, Oct. 5, 1687, both in ibid., 366–68, 377–78.

23. Hall, Leder, and Kammen, *Glorious Revolution*, 3; Reports on Quo Warranto in the Plantations, Apr. 1686, Shaftesbury to Craven, July 7, 1686, both in Saunders, *CRNC*, 1:352–53.

24. Hall, Leder, and Kammen, "Grievances against the Governor, 1687–89," in *Glorious Revolution*, 31.

25. As Steele writes, "Both Charles II and his brother, James, usually encouraged those who sought tighter control of the English Atlantic political economy in the name of the King" (*English Atlantic*, 17).

26. "Order for Passing a Law in the Plantations against Pirates and Privateers," in Saunders, *CRNC*, 1:347–48; Sirmans, *Colonial South Carolina*, 39–43.

27. Quotation from Linebaugh and Rediker, *Many-Headed Hydra*, 162; Rediker, *Villains*, 60–82. See also Rediker, *Between the Devil and the Deep Blue Sea*.

28. Sirmans, *Colonial South Carolina*, 45, 50; Saunders, *CRNC*, 1:354; Lords Proprietors to Seth Sothell, May 12, 1691, "Proprietors' Private Instructions to Collonell Philipp Ludwell Governor of Carolina," both in Saunders, *CRNC*, 1:368–69, 383.

29. Hall, Leder, and Kammen, *Glorious Revolution*, 12.

30. Ibid., 40–41.

31. Ibid., 105–6, 167–69.

32. Lords Proprietors to Seth Sothell, May 12, 1691, in Saunders, *CRNC*, 1:369. There are no records of exactly how or when Sothell was overthrown, but it must have been that fall. Sothell was still in power in July 1689, but news of his overthrow and imprisonment had reached England by early December (Cain, *CRNC*, 7:365).

33. Weir, *Colonial South Carolina*, 67–68; Gallay, *Indian Slave Trade*, 92–93.

34. Landsman, *Scotland*, 18–23; McConville, *These Daring Disturbers*, 20–22; Powell, *Dictionary*, 5:116–17.

35. Thomas Pollock Papers, NCSA; County Court, July 1686, Dec. 1687, both in Parker, *CRNC*, 2:369, 380; Lords Proprietors to Seth Sothell, May 12, 1691, in Saunders, *CRNC*, 1:369.

36. General Court File Papers, Feb. 1695, County Court, Apr. 1684, Miscellaneous Court Documents, all in Parker, *CRNC*, 2:155, 345, 413; Powell, *Ye Countie*, 10n.

37. "An Act of Assembly Made in the Year 1689 . . . against Probious Language Being Given against the Late Governor Lord Sothel," in *NCHGR*, 2:197.

38. Lords Proprietors to Seth Sothell, Feb. 14, 1685, Dec. 2, 1689, "Proprietors' Private Instructions to Collonell Philipp Ludwell Governor of Carolina," Nicholson to Lords of the Committee, Aug. 20, 1690, all in Saunders, *CRNC*, 1:352, 359–60, 360–61, 366.

39. Edmund S. Morgan, *American Slavery*, 206, 265, 275, 284, 288–89.

40. "Orders of Nobility in Carolina," n.d., in *NCHGR*, 1:586; introduction to Parker, *CRNC*, 2:lix; Miscellaneous Court Documents, n.d., in Parker, *CRNC*, 2:452.

41. "Captain Gibb's His Declaration," n.d., in Saunders, *CRNC*, 1:363–64.

42. Council to Governor, July 13, 1690, in Cain, *CRNC*, 366.

43. "Coll. Ludwell's Letter to the Lt. Gov. about North Carolina," July 19, 1690, in Saunders, *CRNC*, 1:364–65.

44. Nicholson to Lords of the Committee, Aug. 20, 1690, in ibid., 366.

45. "Proprietors' Instructions for Coll. Ludwell Governor of Carolina," in ibid., 376; Walter Clark, *Laws*, 12–13. Free blacks, the runaways with whom Virginia was always so concerned, may also have voted. Both the freeman franchise and the biennial assembly remained in effect until 1715.

46. "Proprietors' Instructions for Coll. Ludwell Governor of Carolina," in Saunders, *CRNC*, 1:378.

47. Introduction to Parker, *CRNC*, 2:lxxxiv; "John Huntt v. Thomas Taper, Miscellaneous Court Papers (1690–91)," in Parker, *CRNC*, 2:12n, 426; Instructions to Governor, Apr. 27, 1672, Council Order and Writ of Election, July 1689, both in Cain, *CRNC*, 342, 365; "Mrs. Wollard v. Edw. Smithwick," n.d., in Saunders, *CRNC*, 1:387.

48. General Court Records, Sept. 1694, in Saunders, *CRNC*, 1:414–15.

49. "Gov. Phillip Ludwell's Order Relating to Land Grants," Nov. 20, 1693, in *NCHGR*, 2:196; Patrick Henley's Petition to Phillip Ludwell, n.d., in *NCHGR*, 3:91.

50. Miscellaneous Items, n.d., in *NCHGR*, 3:141; Hofmann, *Province*, 3–14.

51. Edward Price, *Dividing the Land*, 109.

52. General Court Records, Nov. 1694, in Saunders, *CRNC*, 1:429; Council to Governor, Sept. 6, 1694, in Cain, *CRNC*, 369.

53. Haun, *Old Albemarle County North Carolina Book of Land Warrants and Surveys*, 52, 98.

54. Council to Governor, Sept. 6, 1694, in Cain, *CRNC*, 369.

55. General Court Records, Nov. 27, 1694, in Saunders, *CRNC*, 1:426.

56. Warrant of Arrest, Mar. 7, 1695, in Cain, *CRNC*, 370–71.

57. General Court, Nov. 1695, in Parker, *CRNC*, 2:205–7.

58. Court Records, Feb. 1694, Saunders, in *CRNC*, 1:393; Council Court, Feb. 1695, in Parker, *CRNC*, 2:126.


## Part 2

1. "Act of Assembly Relative to Court House," n.d., in *NCHGR*, 2:130.

2. General Court Records, Saunders, in *CRNC*, 1:428–29. Francis Toms, a Quaker on the Council, noted his dissent in the official record. In one of the biggest grievances of all the Interregnum sects, Quakers did not want to contribute to the building of Episcopal churches. The assembly had not specifically called

for a church tithe, but rather had agreed to a public levy, with a portion of the funds to go to church building. There is, however, no record of any construction of church or prison with Ludwell's money or any levy at that time. A courthouse was erected in 1700 but must have burned soon thereafter: by early 1702, courts again met at private homes (General Court, July 1700, in Parker, *CRNC*, 3:368; William S. Price, *CRNC*, 5).

3. "A Physician's Account," July 24, 1694, "An Account in 1699 Showing Prices of Goods," both in *NCHGR*, 2:113, 203.

4. "Bills Showing the Currency Used about 1696–97 for Quitt Rents &c," in ibid., 3:90–91; Records of Court of Chancery, Feb. 1695, in Saunders, *CRNC*, 1:455.

5. "Bond Payable in Deer Skins," Feb. 10, 1690, Records of Albemarle County, n.d., both in *NCHGR*, 3:81, 249; Miscellaneous Court Documents, n.d., in Parker, *CRNC*, 2:440–48. The missionary also said that the people reckoned "The difference of their money is to sterling as one to three" (Gordon to Secretary, May 13, 1709, in Saunders, *CRNC*, 1:715).

6. Lawson, *New Voyage*, 69–70, 88–90, 167.

7. Ibid., 90, 93.

8. Weir, *Colonial South Carolina*, 69–70.

9. [Harvey] to Archdale, [spring] 1696, in *NCHGR*, 2:222–23.

10. General Court Records, Feb. 1695, in Saunders, *CRNC*, 1:453.

11. [Harvey] to Archdale, [spring] 1696, in *NCHGR*, 2:222–23.

12. Ibid.

13. Harvey to Archdale, July 10, 1698, in *NCHGR*, 3:38; Paschal, "Proprietary North Carolina," 177; Bond, *Quitrent System*; Watson, "Quitrent System," 184.

14. Palatine's Court Records, Dec. 9, 1696, in Saunders, *CRNC*, 1:472; Hofmann, *Province*, 14–26.

15. John Archdale, "A New Description of That Fertile and Pleasant Province of Carolina, with a Brief Account of Its Discovery, Settling, and the Government Thereof to This Time, with Several Remarkable Passages of Divine Providence during my Time" (1707), in Salley, *Narratives*, 286; Palatine's Court Records, Dec. 9, 1696, in Saunders, *CRNC*, 1:472.

16. General Court Records, Nov. 1694, in Saunders, *CRNC*, 1:432.

17. Vestry Book of St. Paul's Parish, Chowan Precinct, Dec. 1701, in ibid., 543.

## Chapter 5

1. Gary L. Hewitt, "The State in the Planters' Service," in *Money, Trade and Power*, edited by Greene, Brana-Shute, and Sparks, 51.

2. Steele, "Board of Trade," 597.

3. Hall, *Edward Randolph*; Steele, "Board of Trade," 599. Some Rhode Island Quakers at the time linked the Anglican offensive with the campaign for charter resumption, but Steele's research effectively disproves that connection.

4. Hall, *Edward Randolph*, 129–54.

5. Randolph to Commissioners of the Customs, n.d., in Saunders, *CRNC*, 1:441.

6. Hall, *Edward Randolph*, 154–66; Hall, "House of Lords"; Steele, "Board of Trade," 608–10.

7. Randolph to Lords of Trade, Aug. 25, 1696, in Saunders, *CRNC*, 1:462.

8. Randolph's to Customs Commissioners, Nov. 10, 1696, in ibid., 467.

9. Ibid.

10. Petitions of Proprietors to King, n.d., in Saunders, *CRNC*, 1:470–71; Steele, "Board of Trade," 608–12.

11. [Harvey] to Archdale, [spring] 1696, in *NCHGR*, 2:222.

12. Thomas Amy to Harvey, Nov. 3, 1698, in Saunders, *CRNC*, 1:491.

13. Miscellaneous Court Documents, 1698, in Parker, *CRNC*, 3:517–20.

14. General Court, Mar. 1698, in ibid., 192–94.

15. Thomas Harvey to Archdale, July 10, 1698, in *NCHGR*, 3:36.

16. General Court Records, May 1698, in Parker, *CRNC*, 3:217.

17. Ibid., Mar. 1698, 193.

18. Ibid., 195.

19. Ibid., 197–98; Haun, *Old Albemarle County, North Carolina*, 10–18.

20. General Court Records, May 1698, in Parker, *CRNC*, 3:216–17. Harvey claimed that Dawson had come to Currituck several days after the looting had begun to secure the goods for the proprietors, which may be why he and his slave received the harshest treatment from an Albemarle jury (Harvey to Archdale, July 10, 1698). Further context on wrecking along the coast may be found in Margolin, "'Contrary to All Law and Justice.'"

21. Harvey to Archdale, July 10, 1698.

22. Ibid.

23. Randolph's Memo, Mar. 1700, Randolph to Lords of Trade, 1701, both in Saunders, CRNC, 1:527, 546–47.

24. "Mr. Blair's Mission to North Carolina," in ibid., 1:602.

25. Parent's chapter, "Baptism and Bondage," reveals how Virginia's large planters tried to use the "Anglican cosmology" to control their slaves (*Foul Means*, 236–64). See also Burnard, *Creole Gentlemen*, for similar developments in Maryland.

26. Walker to Governor of Virginia, July 28, 1699, in Saunders, *CRNC*, 1:511–12.

27. Thomas Story Papers, NCSA.

28. Commission of Justices, July 7, 1699, Mar. 20, 1700, both in Parker, *CRNC*, 3:327, 379–80.

29. Minutes of Council Meeting, 1700, in Cain, *CRNC*, 3.

30. General Court Records, July 30, 1701, in Parker, *CRNC*, 3:446; General Court Records, Apr. 1702, in William S. Price, *CRNC*, 11–13.

31. General Court, July 1700, in Parker, *CRNC*, 3:368.

32. Minutes of Council Meeting, 1700, in Cain, *CRNC*, 3.

33. Proprietors to Harvey and Council, Dec. 20, 1699, in Saunders, *CRNC*, 1:520.

34. Walker to Bishop of London, Oct. 21, 1703, in ibid., 571–73.

35. Vestry Book of St. Paul's Parish, Chowan Precinct, Dec. 15, 1701, in ibid., 543–45; General Court Records, n.d., in William S. Price, *CRNC*, 415.

36. Walker to Bishop of London, Oct. 21, 1703, in Saunders, *CRNC*, 1:572.

37. Gordon to Secretary, May 13, 1709, in ibid., 709.

38. Walker to Bishop of London, Oct. 21, 1703, in ibid., 572.

39. Vestry Book of St. Paul's Parish, Chowan Precinct, Nov. 12, 1701, in ibid., 543.

40. Ibid., 543–45. Readers were akin to deacons.

41. Ibid., Oct. 13, Dec. 15, 1702, 558–60, 561.

42. Walker to Bishop of London, Oct. 21, 1703, in ibid., 572.

43. Suttlemyre, "Proprietary Policy," 250–51.

44. Proprietors to Nathaniel Johnson, June 18, 1702, in Saunders, *CRNC*, 1:554.

45. Sirmans, *Colonial South Carolina*, 17–18; Peter Wood, *Black Majority*, 47.

46. Sirmans, *Colonial South Carolina*, 76–87.

47. Council Order, Nov. 2, 1703, Council to Governor of Carolina, both in Cain, *CRNC*, 393–94, 394–95.

48. Address to Deputy Governor and Council, in ibid., 396.

49. Vestry Book of St. Paul's Parish, Chowan Precinct, Mar. 9, 1704, in Saunders, *CRNC*, 1:596–98. Blair's troubles led him to write an account of his life in Albemarle; see "Mr. Blair's Mission," in Saunders, *CRNC*, 1:600–603.

50. "Mr. Blair's Mission," 601–2.

51. Ibid., 600–603. Bath County refers to the region south of Albemarle Sound. It is also called the Pamlico-Neuse region. The variant spellings "Pamtico," "Pamlico," "Pemlicoe," and "Pampticough" appear in the original documents.

52. There has been some debate over Porter's religion, with some historians arguing that he was an Anglican. The confusion stems from another John Porter in the colony, a wealthy slave owner from Pennsylvania, probably the Porter contracted to build the first Anglican church in Chowan ("John Porter's Rights," in *NCHGR*, 3:250). The parents of the John Porter discussed here were definitely Quakers and had suffered persecution in Virginia. Porter subscribed rather

than swore to oaths in court in 1705 (William S. Price, *CRNC*, 149, 180). He was not a particularly devout man, willing to swear oaths when politically expedient and concerning himself mostly with the political results of church establishment, such as the removal of Quaker representatives. A later missionary described him as "the son of a Quaker and he one in disguise" (Saunders, *CRNC*, 1:768; Powell, *Dictionary*, 5:126).

53. "List of Tithables, Perquimans Precinct," Jan. 30, 1703, in *NCHGR*, 3:84.

54. Daniel to Gale, Apr. 4, 1704, in William S. Price, *CRNC*, 122.

55. General Court Records, Nov. 28, 1706, in Cain, *CRNC*, 350.

56. Gordon to the Secretary of the Society for the Propagation of the Gospel, May 13, 1709, in Saunders, *CRNC*, 1:709.

57. "Proclamation Ordering New Election of Burgesses of Pasquotank," in *NCHGR*, 2:136.

58. General Court Records, Mar. 31, 1702, in William S. Price, *CRNC*, 6.

59. House of Burgesses to Deputy Governor and Council, in *NCHGR*, 3:60–61; Minutes of Perquimans Monthly Meeting of the Religious Society of Friends in North Carolina, Reel 1, Friends Historical Collection, Guilford College, Greensboro, North Carolina.

60. General Court Records, Mar. 27, 1705, in William S. Price, *CRNC*, 144.

61. Suttlemyre, "Proprietary Policy," 259.

62. "Proclamation by Deputy Governor and Council," Mar. 21, 1705, in Cain, *CRNC*, 405.

63. Ibid.

64. Salley, *Commissions and Instructions*, 151–54.

65. General Court Records, Aug. 4, 1705, in William S. Price, *CRNC*, 202–3.

66. Vestry Book of St. Paul's Parish, Chowan Precinct, Sept. 9, 1705, in Saunders, *CRNC*, 1:616.

67. General Court Records, Aug. 2, 1705, in William S. Price, *CRNC*, 204–5.

68. Council Meeting Minutes, Dec. 3, 1705, in Saunders, *CRNC*, 1:629.

69. "Gov. Archdale's Attorney," in *NCHGR*, 3:72.

70. Extracts from the Journal of the Life of Thomas Story, Story Papers.

71. Suttlemyre, "Proprietary Policy," 257.

72. William Glover to Lord Bishop of London, Sept. 25, 1708, in Saunders, *CRNC*, 1:689.

73. Gordon to Secretary, May 13, 1709, in ibid., 713–14.

74. Vestry Book of St. Paul's Parish, Chowan Precinct, Jan. 3, 1706, in ibid., 630.

75. "Proclamation by Deputy Governor and Council," Dec. 3, 1705, in Cain, *CRNC*, 407.

76. Council Order, Dec. 3, 1705, in ibid., 406.

77. Proclamation of President and Council, July 13, 1706, in William S. Price, *CRNC*, 472.

78. "The Humble Address of the Right Honourable the Lords Spiritual and Temporal in Parliament," Mar. 12, 1706, in Saunders, *CRNC*, 1:635–36.

79. "Humble Petition of Joseph Boone Merchant on Behalf of Himself and Many Other Inhabitants of the Province of Carolina," in ibid., 637–40.

80. "The Humble Address of the Right Honourable the Lords Spiritual and Temporal in Parliament," Mar. 12, 1706, in ibid., 636–37.

81. "At the Court at Windsor," June 10, 1706, "At the Court at St. James," June 26, 1706, both in ibid., 643, 644.

82. Salley, *Commissions and Instructions*, 192.

83. Ibid., 189.

84. Gordon to Secretary, May 13, 1709, in Saunders, *CRNC*, 1:709–10.

## Chapter 6

1. Archdale to Fox, Mar. 25, 1686, in Bowden, *History*, 415–16.

2. John Archdale, "A New Description of That Fertile and Pleasant Province of Carolina, with a Brief Account of Its Discovery, Settling, and the Government Thereof to This Time, with Several Remarkable Passages of Divine Providence during my Time" (1707), in Salley, *Narratives*, 285–86.

3. Jenings to Lords of Trade, Nov. 27, 1708, in Saunders, *CRNC*, 1:692.

4. Kulikoff, *Tobacco and Slaves*, 40.

5. "Mr. Blair's Mission to North Carolina," in Saunders, *CRNC*, 1:603.

6. Ibid.

7. Francis Nicholson to Henderson Walker, Nov. 8, 1699, in ibid., 515.

8. Henderson Walker to Francis Nicholson, Nov. 18, 1699, in ibid., 517.

9. "Articles of Agreement with the Bay River Indians," Sept. 23, 1699, in *NCHGR*, 1:598–99.

10. "Order from Walker Relating to Bay River Indians," May 14, 1701, in ibid., 597.

11. John Lawson to Walker, June 23, 1701, in ibid., 598.

12. Gallay, *Indian Slave Trade*, 313–14. Although there were Indian slaves in North Carolina throughout the proprietary era, neither slave labor nor the slave trade played a major role in the economy, as was the case in South Carolina. North Carolina's economy was more closely linked to that of Virginia, where African slavery predominated. In 1670, Indians had received free status in Virginia, where their land, not their labor, governed relations between natives and new-

comers. See Parent, *Foul Means*, 114. The long peace in Albemarle resulted from the limits of settlement until 1695.

13. Lawson, *New Voyage*, xi–xxii.

14. Ibid., 209–11.

15. Miscellaneous Court of Chancery Records, n.d., in Parker, *CRNC*, 3:511–12.

16. "A Majors Commission," n.d., "War Declared against the Core & Nynee Indians," 1703, both in *NCHGR*, 2:202, 204; Parramore, "Tuscarora Ascendancy," 307–26.

17. Lionel Reading to Barrow, Oct. 20, 1703, in *NCHGR*, 2:193–94.

18. Pamlico Residents to Governor and Council, Feb. 29, 1704, in Cain, *CRNC*, 401–2.

19. Archdale to Fox, Mar. 1686, in Bowden, *History*, 416.

20. Lawson, *New Voyage*, 242.

21. Pamlico residents to Governor and Council, Feb. 29, 1704, in Cain, *CRNC*, 402.

22. McIlwaine, *Executive Journals*, 2:390.

23. Ibid., 402.

24. Lawson, *New Voyage*, 211–12.

25. William Powell to Daniel, Oct. 20, 1704, in *NCHGR*, 1:437.

26. "Humble Petition of the Inhabitants of Matchapungo to Deputy Gov. and Council," n.d., in Cain, *CRNC*, 397–98.

27. Bath County Court, Nov. 22, 1704, in *NCHGR*, 1:441.

28. "Humble Petition of the Inhabitants of Neus Rivir to Deputy Gov. Daniel and Council," n.d., in Cain, *CRNC*, 396–97.

29. William S. Price, *CRNC*, 444; Lawson, *New Voyage*, 174–76. Lawson's interests dictated that he promote settlement in the region, and he certainly set out to do that. His journal and travelogue, *A New Voyage to Carolina*, is proprietary North Carolina's only book and an invaluable source, but it must be understood in the context of the writer as a booster for the colony. Thus, his praises may be exaggerated and his criticisms underplayed. He is, however, the best source for information about the native North Carolinians.

30. Lawson, *New Voyage*, 222, 243–44.

31. "An Act to Encourage the Settlement of This Country, [Carolina, North]," [1707], in Saunders, *CRNC*, 1:674–75.

32. Seymour to Lords of Trade, June 10, 1707, in ibid., 664–65.

33. Ibid., Aug. 16, 1707, 666.

34. Board of Trade to Her Majesty, Nov. 12, 1707, Seymour to Lords of Trade, June 23, 1708, both in ibid., 1:672–73, 682–83.

35. Minutes of Council Meeting, Nov. 1, 1706, in Cain, *CRNC*, 5–6.

36. Lowry, "Class," 151–53, 161, 165–66.

37. Garrow, "Mattamuskeet Documents"; Parramore, "Tuscarora Ascendancy," 309–11.

38. General Court Records, Nov. 1694, in Saunders, *CRNC*, 1:432.

39. Duckenfield to Glover, n.d., in *NCHGR*, 3:64.

40. Petition of Benjamin Blanchard, Mar. 1702, in ibid., 242.

41. Petition of Chowan Indians to President and Council, in ibid., 75–76.

42. Vestry Book of St. Paul's Parish, Chowan Precinct, Nov. 12, 1701, in Saunders, *CRNC*, 1:543.

43. Petition of John Hoyter, n.d., in *NCHGR*, 3:77.

44. Lawson, *New Voyage*, 242.

45. Council Order, Apr. 12, 1704, in Cain, *CRNC*, 403.

46. Gary L. Hewitt, "The State in the Planters' Service," in *Money, Trade and Power*, edited by Greene, Brana-Shute, and Sparks, 56–57.

47. Hatfield, *Atlantic Virginia*, 35.

48. McIlwaine, *Executive Journals*, 2:315.

49. Dawdy, "Meherrin's Secret History."

50. North Carolina Council to Virginia Council, June 17, 1707, in Cain, *CRNC*, 414.

51. Vestry Book of St. Paul's Parish, Chowan Precinct, Apr. 18, 1708, in Saunders, *CRNC*, 1:678; Thomas Garrett to Council, Oct. 17, 1706, in *NCHGR*, 2:110–11.

52. Minutes of Council Meeting, Nov. 2, 1706, in Cain, *CRNC*, 7.

53. Virginia Council Order, Apr. 19, 1706, Oct. 17, 1706, both in Saunders, *CRNC*, 1:641, 645, 646–47.

54. Virginia Council to Governor and Council, Apr. 30, 1707, in Cain, *CRNC*, 412–13.

55. Council to Council of Virginia, June 17, 1707, in ibid., 413–15.

56. Journal of the Virginia Council, Sept. 2, 1707, in Saunders, *CRNC*, 1:667–68; President and Council of Virginia to Governor and Council, Sept. 15, 1707, in Cain, *CRNC*, 418–20.

57. Journal of the Virginia Council, Sept. 2, 1707, in Saunders, *CRNC*, 1:668.

58. President and Council of Virginia to Governor and Council, Sept. 15, 1707, in Cain, *CRNC*, 418–20.

59. Ibid.

60. Ibid.

61. Dawdy, "Meherrin's Secret History," 404–6.

62. Hornsby, *British Atlantic*, 6; Peter Wood, *Black Majority*, 131.

# Chapter 7

1. Proclamation by President and Council, Oct. 20, 1707, Writ, Nov. 6, 1707, both in Cain, *CRNC*, 420–21.

2. Vestry Book of St. Paul's Parish, Chowan Precinct, May 5, 1708, in Saunders, *CRNC*, 1:679–80.

3. Thomas Pollock's Protest, General Court Records, July 1708, in William S. Price, *CRNC*, 403–4.

4. General Court Records, July 1708, in ibid., 405–6.

5. Gordon was to minister to Chowan and Perquimans precincts, while Adams served in Pasquotank and Currituck (St. Paul's Vestry Meeting, May 5, 1708, Adams to Secretary, June 10, 1708, both in Saunders, *CRNC*, 1:678–80, 681–82).

6. Adams to Secretary, Sept. 18, 1708, Glover to Lord Bishop of London, Sept. 25, 1708, both in ibid., 1:686–87, 689–90.

7. Gordon to Secretary, May 13, 1709, in ibid., 713.

8. Proclamation by President and Council, May 13, 1708, General Court Records, in William S. Price, *CRNC*, 402–3.

9. General Court Records, May 14, 1708, in ibid., 400–401.

10. Gordon to Secretary, May 13, 1709, in Saunders, *CRNC*, 1:710.

11. Memorandum, Apr. 2, 1708, "Appointment of Proprietary Deputy," 1708, both in Cain, *CRNC*, 428, 429.

12. Gordon to Secretary, May 13, 1709, in Saunders, *CRNC*, 1:710.

13. Thomas Pollock's Protest, July 24, 1708, in William S. Price, *CRNC*, 403–4.

14. The victim was probably a John Allcock, reportedly shot by John Feyerebendt (*NCHGR*, 1:454).

15. Jenings to the Lords of Trade, Sept. 20, 1708, in Saunders, *CRNC*, 1:688.

16. Adams to Secretary, Sept. 18, 1708, in ibid., 686.

17. St. Paul's Parish Vestry Meetings, July 1708, in ibid., 683–84.

18. Excerpt from Pollock's Letter Book, in ibid., 696–99; "Miscellaneous Items of Chowan Precinct," n.d., in *NCHGR*, 1:454–55.

19. Excerpt from Pollock's Letter Book, in Saunders, *CRNC*, 1:698–700.

20. Thomas Pollock to Chenin and Boyds, Apr. 16, 1710, in ibid., 724.

21. Proprietors Commission to Tynte, Dec. 9, 1708, in ibid., 694–96; Sirmans, *Colonial South Carolina*, 95.

22. Proprietors Contract with the Swiss, Apr. 28, 1709, in Saunders, *CRNC*, 1:707.

23. Minutes of Proprietary Board Meetings, Aug.–Sept. 1709, De Graffenried's Manuscript, n.d., both in ibid., 717–19, 907–9.

24. Assembly of North Carolina to Proprietors, July 1711, in ibid., 786.

25. Adams to Secretary, Oct. 1709, in ibid., 719–21.

26. Urmston to Society for the Propagation of the Gospel, July 7, 1711, in ibid., 769–70.

27. President to Council, Feb. 9, 1709, in Cain, *CRNC*, 430–31.

28. Williams, "English Mercantilism," 169.

29. Minutes, Virginia Council, Oct. 19, 1708, Jenings to Lords of Trade, Nov. 27, 1708, both in Saunders, *CRNC*, 1:691, 692.

30. Gordon to Secretary, May 13, 1709, in ibid., 713–15.

31. Petition to Governor and Council, Feb. 23, 1709, in Cain, *CRNC*, 431.

32. Minutes of Council Meeting, July 1712, in Cain, *CRNC*, 22; Court of Chancery, n.d., in William S. Price, *CRNC*, 463.

33. "Petition of Some Members of the House of Burgesses to the Governor and Council," n.d., in *NCHGR*, 3:74–75.

34. De Graffenreid's Manuscript, n.d., in Saunders, *CRNC*, 1:908–10; Lawson, *New Voyage*, xxx, n. 52; Lillian F. Wood, "Palatine Settlers on the Neuse and Trent Rivers, 1710," Apr. 1956, 2–5, Palatine Papers, NCSA.

35. De Graffenried's Manuscript, n.d., Thomas Pollock to Chevin and Boyd, Apr. 16, 1710, both in Saunders, *CRNC*, 1:910, 723–24.

36. Lords Proprietors to Governor, Council, and Assembly, Sept. 22, 1709, in Cain, *CRNC*, 435.

37. Adams to Secretary, Mar. 27, 1710, in Saunders, *CRNC*, 1:722.

38. Pollock to Glover, by Maule, Apr. 16, 1710, in ibid., 725–26.

39. "A Journal of the Proceedings of Philip Ludwell and Nathaniel Harrison Commissioners Appointed for Settling the Boundarys between Her Majestys Colony and Dominion of Virginia and the Province of Carolina," in ibid., 735–46. This commission never settled the matter; in 1729 another commission determined that the Carolinians had the rightful claim to the disputed areas.

40. "Pollock to Ed. Hyde Esq. Deputy Governor, Newly Come Out of England," Aug. 29, 1710, Spotswood to Hyde, Feb. 1711, Spotswood to Earl of Rochester, July 30, 1711, De Graffenried's Manuscript, n.d., all in ibid., 731, 753, 798, 912.

41. Adams to Secretary, Sept. 4, 1710, Journal of Boundary Commissioners, Spotswood to Hyde, Dec. 15, 1710, all in ibid., 733, 737, 740, 750.

42. Adams to Secretary, in ibid., 734.

43. Urmston to Society for the Propagation of the Gospel, July 7, 1711, in ibid., 764, 770.

44. Ibid., 763, 765, 770.

45. Ibid., 765, 768.

46. N.C. Assembly to Proprietors, July 1711, in ibid., 785.

47. Urmston to Society for the Propagation of the Gospel, July 7, 1711, in ibid.,

768–69; Spotswood to Board of Trade, July 25, 1711, De Graffenried's Manuscript, n.d., both in ibid., 780, 914–15.

48. Dennis to Secretary, Sept. 3, 1711, in ibid., 804.

49. Spotswood to Board of Trade, Mar. 6, 1711, in ibid., 755.

50. "Acts Pass'd in North Carolina 1711," in ibid., 787–94.

51. Spotswood to Board of Trade, July 25, 1711, Council to Board of Trade, both in ibid., 780, 806.

52. Dennis to Secretary, Sept. 3, 1711, in ibid., 803–4.

53. Spotswood to Lords Proprietors, July 28, 1711, in ibid., 795. See chapter 3 for the history of the political alliance of traders and settlers.

54. De Graffenried's Manuscript, n.d., in ibid., 916.

55. Spotswood to Board of Trade, July 25, 1711, in ibid., 780. As fellow Scots, Pollock and Spotswood had a much more civil relationship than Pollock had endured with the previous governor.

56. Parent, *Foul Means*, 151.

57. McIlwaine, *Journals*, 240.

58. Journal of the Virginia Council, June 13, 1711, in Saunders, *CRNC*, 1:757.

59. Spotswood to Cary and Hyde, June 20, 1711, Spotswood to Cary, June 21, 1711, both in ibid., 758, 759.

60. Spotswood to Cary, June 21, 1711, in ibid., 759.

61. Spotswood to Board of Trade, July 25, 1711, in ibid., 781; President and Council to Governor of Virginia, June 29, 1711, in Cain, *CRNC*, 438–39.

62. Ludwell and Harrison, "Boundary Line Proceedings," 17.

63. President and Council to Governor of Virginia, June 29, 1711, in Cain, *CRNC*, 438–39.

64. Spotswood to Board of Trade, July 25, 1711, in Saunders, *CRNC*, 1:781.

65. Journal of Virginia Council, July 5, 1711, Urmston to Secretary, July 17, 1711, De Graffenried's Manuscript, n.d., all in ibid., 762–63, 773–74, 917–18.

66. Urmston to Secretary, July 7, 1711, July 17, 1711, both in ibid., 766, 773–75.

67. Most historians have refused to believe that Porter's negotiations with the Tuscarora were possible. One of the most recent dissertations of this period, Lowry's, written in 1975, calls the idea "a ridiculous post-rebellion rationalization" and claims that "it defies plausibility to assume that Cary's party would have encouraged an Indian war" ("Class," 202). Lefler and Powell, *Colonial North Carolina*, omit the entire story of Cary's Rebellion and place the blame for the Tuscarora War on the coming of de Graffenried's settlers and on traders' deceitful dealings with the Indians. Parramore, "Tuscarora Ascendancy," shows an imperfect understanding of North Carolina politics, mentioning the Cary group's outreach to the Tuscarora but giving it little importance in the outbreak

of war. But the frequent mention of Porter's trip to the villages of the Tuscarora and the specifics of those visits in documents dated before the Tuscarora's surprise attack just weeks later make clear that no "post-rebellion rationalization" could explain events. Letters by Urmston, Spotswood, and Hyde written in July and Aug. 1711 contain repeated references to Porter's negotiations. See Saunders, *CRNC*, 1:774–76, 782–83, 796–98, 802, 806. De Graffenried's account (Saunders, *CRNC*, 1:920–22) written after the events, also supports the argument that the Tuscarora War was closely linked to Cary's Rebellion.

68. John E. Byrd and Charles L. Heath, "'The Country Here Is Very Thick of Indian Towns and Plantations . . . ': Tuscarora Settlement Patterns as Revealed by the Contentnea Creek Survey," in *Indian and European Contact*, edited by Blanton and King, 99–102; Hyde to unknown, Aug. 22, 1711, Spotswood to Lord Dartmouth, July 28, 1711, both in Saunders, *CRNC*, 1:802, 796–97.

69. Spotswood to Board of Trade, July 28, 1711, in Saunders, *CRNC*, 1:782–83.

70. De Graffenried's Manuscript, n.d., in ibid., 920.

71. Ibid., 918.

72. Virginia Proclamation, July 24, 1711, in ibid., 776–77.

73. Spotswood to Lords Proprietors, July 31, 1711, in ibid., 800; President and Council to Secretary of State, Aug. 22, 1711, in Cain, *CRNC*, 440–41.

74. Spotswood to Board of Trade, July 25, 1711, in Saunders, *CRNC*, 1:782.

75. Spotswood to Earl of Rochester, July 30, 1711, in ibid., 798.

76. Spotswood to Lords Proprietors, July 28, 1711, in ibid., 795; Natalie Zacek, "A Death in the Morning: The Murder of Daniel Parke," in *Cultures and Identities in Colonial British America*, edited by Olwell and Tully, 223–43; Burns, *History*, 419–23.

77. De Graffenried's Manuscript, n.d., in Saunders, *CRNC*, 1:921.

Chapter 8

1. De Graffenried's Manuscript, n.d., "A Letter from Major Christopher Gale," Nov. 2, 1711, both in Saunders, *CRNC*, 1:925–27, 825.

2. De Graffenried's Manuscript, n.d., "A Letter from Major Christopher Gale," Nov. 2, 1711, both in ibid., 929–33, 826.

3. Spotswood to Board of Trade, Oct. 15, 1711, in ibid., 810–11; Wayne Lee, "Fortify, Fight, or Flee," 732–33. Spotswood's reports were confused about the subjects of the Tuscarora attacks.

4. Ffarnifull Green to unknown, Oct. 26, 1711, Christopher Gale to unknown, Nov. 2, 1711, both in Saunders, *CRNC*, 1:815, 826.

5. Spotswood to Board of Trade, Oct. 15, 1711, in ibid., 811–12.

6. "The Memorial of Christopher Gale from the Government of North Carolina to the Honorable Robert Gibs, Governor and Commander-in-Chief, and to the Honorable Council and General Assembly," in ibid., 827–29.

7. Gallay, *Indian Slave Trade*, 267–68, describes the mix of Indians under Barnwell's command.

8. Barnwell, "Journal," 5:392–96; Parramore, "With Tuscarora Jack" (which provides an excellent analysis of Barnwell's journal).

9. Barnwell, "Journal," 6:43–48.

10. Ibid., 48–51.

11. Ibid., 51–54.

12. Minutes of Council Meeting, Feb. 1712, in Cain, *CRNC*, 9.

13. Barnwell, "Journal," 6:52.

14. Parramore, "With Tuscarora Jack," 134; De Graffenried's Manuscript, n.d., in Saunders, *CRNC*, 1:956. Gallay, *Indian Slave Trade*, 275–76, accepts Lefler and Powell's conclusion that North Carolinians attacked the Cores, but local forces had neither willing manpower nor resources.

15. Spotswood to Board of Trade, Feb. 8, 1712, in Saunders, *CRNC*, 1:834.

16. Minutes of Council Meeting, Mar. 12, 1712, in Cain, *CRNC*, 12.

17. Ibid., Apr. 1712, 16.

18. "Foster's Instructions," in Saunders, *CRNC*, 1:898–901.

19. Minutes of Council Meeting, July 31, 1712, in Cain, *CRNC*, 22.

20. Edward Hyde to Palin, Aug. 3, 1712, in *NCHGR*, 1:438.

21. Pollock to Lords Proprietors, Sept. 20, 1712, in Saunders, *CRNC*, 1:873.

22. Council Journal, Sept. 12, 1712, in ibid., 869–70.

23. Pollock to Lords Proprietors, Sept. 20, 1712, in ibid., 873–74. One Quaker, Edmund Chauncey, who paid the five pounds had to answer to the monthly meeting and was threatened with expulsion by the Friends until he admitted publicly that "he [wa]s sorry that he should be overtaken in such a weakness and that he should give way to the Enemy" (Minutes of Symons Creek [Pasquotank] Monthly Meetings, Sept. 1714, Reel 1, 1699–1785, Friends Historical Collection, Guilford College, Greensboro, North Carolina).

24. Pollock to Lords Proprietors, Sept. 20, 1712, in Saunders, *CRNC*, 1:876.

25. Pollock to Lord Carteret, Sept. 20, 1712, in ibid., 877–78.

26. Ibid.

27. Urmston to Society for the Propagation of the Gospel, Oct. 22, 1712, in ibid., 884–85.

28. Gallay, *Indian Slave Trade*, 277–83, discusses South Carolina's decision.

29. Pollock's Letter Book, Jan. 1713, Spotswood to Lords Proprietors, Feb. 11, 1713, both in Saunders, *CRNC*, 2:7, 14–16.

30. Pollock to Craven, Feb. 20, 1713, in ibid., 19.

31. "Items Relating to the Indian War," n.d., in *NCHGR*, 1:438–39.

32. Spotswood to Lords of Trade, Feb. 11, 1713, in Saunders, *CRNC*, 2:13.

33. Pollock to Spotswood, Jan. 15, 1713, in ibid., 4.

34. Pollock to Craven, Feb. 20, 1713, Pollock to Moore, Feb. 24, 1713, in ibid., 19, 21–22.

35. Pollock's Letter Book, Mar. 6, 1713, in ibid., 23–25.

36. Report from James Moore, Mar. 27, 1713, Pollock to Moore, Mar. 31, 1713, both in ibid., 27–29; Gallay, *Indian Slave Trade*, 283–85.

37. Pollock's Letter Book, Mar. 1713, Saunders, *CRNC*, 2:31–32.

38. Pollock to Craven, June 25, 1713, in ibid., 52.

39. Council Meeting, Apr. 1714, Urmston to Secretary, Aug. 7, 1714, Pollock to Lords Proprietors, Oct. 20, 1714, Council Meeting, Feb. 11, 1715, all in ibid., 2:124–25, 138, 144, 168.

40. Pollock to Craven, May 25, 1713, Pollock's Letter Book, Sept. 1, 1713, both in ibid., 46, 61.

41. Council Meetings, Aug. 7, 1713, Aug. 19, 1713, Apr. 7, 1714, all in ibid., 56, 59, 125.

42. Pollock to Lords Proprietors, Oct. 20, 1714, in ibid., 145.

43. Ibid., 207–16.

44. St. Paul's Parish Vestry to Society for the Propagation of the Gospel, Mar. 2, 1714, in ibid., 119.

45. Urmston to Secretary, Apr. 13, 1715, in ibid., 176.

46. Urmston to Secretary, June 12, 1714, Urmston to Nicholson, Apr. 12, 1714, both in ibid., 131, 126.

47. Urmston to Secretary, June 21, 1715, in ibid., 187. Urmston's constant and vivid criticisms of North Carolina drew the ire of the proprietors, who, he claimed, told him he "had better let alone except I had written more like a Missionary: they may and ought to be ashamed of their famous Country, they would have all men do as Lawson did[;] write whole Volumes in praise of such a worthless place: he has had his reward: all I can say to it is; there is not the like to it under the sun" (Urmston to Secretary, in Saunders, *CRNC*, 2:186).

48. Lefler and Powell, *Colonial North Carolina*, 84–86; Rediker, *Villains*, 82. The members of Virginia's ruling elite were very concerned in these years that piracy would attract and accommodate runaway slaves (Rediker, *Villains*, 55).

49. Grimes, *Abstract*, 292–93; Wolf, "Proud and the Poor," 151. One of Pollock's plantations alone encompassed forty thousand acres (Powell, *Dictionary*, 5:117).

50. Wolf, "Proud and the Poor," 26.

51. Bradford J. Wood, *This Remote Part of The World*, 17–18.

52. "The Remonstrance of the Inhabitants off Paspatancke to All the Rest of the County of Albemarle," Dec. 3, 1677, in Saunders, *CRNC*, 1:249.

## Afterword

1. Peter H. Wood, "Slave Labor Camps in Early America: Overcoming Denial and Discovering the Gulag," in *Inequality in Early America*, edited by Pestana and Salinger.

2. Henry Laurens quoted in Olwell, *Masters, Slaves and Subjects*, 192–93.

3. Ekirch, *"Poor Carolina,"* 38–44.

4. Petition from Orange County Inhabitants, 1770, in Saunders, *CRNC*, 8:234.

5. Kars, *Breaking Loose Together*.

6. Saunders, *CRNC*, 10:870.

# BIBLIOGRAPHY

## Manuscript Sources

Friends Historical Collection, Guilford College, Greensboro, North Carolina
    Minutes of Perquimans Monthly Meetings, Microfilm Reel 1, 1680–1762
    Minutes of Symons Creek (Pasquotank) Monthly Meetings, Microfilm Reel 1,
        1699–1785
    Minutes of Virginia Yearly Meeting, 1702–13
North Carolina State Archives, Raleigh
    Nathaniel Batts Papers
    Joshua Lamb Papers
    Miller v. Riscoe Papers
    Palatine Papers
    Thomas Pollock Papers
    Thomas Story Papers
Southern Historical Collection, University of North Carolina, Chapel Hill
    Blount Family Papers

## Published Primary Sources

Andrews, Charles M., ed. *Narratives of the Insurrections, 1675–1690*. New York:
    Scribner's, 1915.
Barnwell, John. "Journal." *Virginia Magazine of History and Biography* 5 (Jan. 1898):
    391–402; 6 (June 1899): 42–55.
Beverley, Robert. *The History and Present State of Virginia*. Edited and introduction
    by Louis B. Wright. 1705; Chapel Hill: University of North Carolina Press for
    the Institute of Early American Culture, 1947.
Billings, Warren, ed., with the assistance of Maria Kimberley. *The Papers of Sir
    William Berkeley, 1605–1677*. Richmond: Library of Virginia, 2007.
Cain, Robert J., ed. *Colonial Records of North Carolina*. Vol. 7, *Records of the Executive*

*Council, 1664–1734.* Raleigh: Department of Cultural Resources, North Carolina Division of Archives and History, 1984.

Cheves, Langdon, ed. *The Shaftesbury Papers and Other Records Relating to Carolina and the First Settlement on Ashley River prior to the Year 1676.* Charleston: South Carolina Historical Society, 1897.

Clark, Walter, ed. *Laws, 1715–1776.* Vol. 23 of *The State Records of North Carolina.* Wilmington, N.C.: Broadfoot, 1994.

*Collections of the South Carolina Historical Society.* Vol. 5. Charleston: South Carolina Historical Society, 1897.

Edmondson, William. *The Journal (Abridged) of William Edmondson: Quaker Apostle to Ireland and the Americas, 1627–1712.* Edited by Caroline M. Jacob. Philadelphia: Religious Society of Friends, 1968.

Fox, George. *A Collection of Many Select and Christian Epistles, Letters, and Testimonies.* Vol. 2. New York: AMS, 1975.

——. *The Journal of George Fox.* Edited by John L. Nickalls. London: Religious Society of Friends, 1975.

——. *The Journal of George Fox.* Edited by Norman Penney. Cambridge: Cambridge University Press, 1911.

Grimes, J. Bryan, ed. *Abstract of North Carolina Wills.* Raleigh: Uzzell, 1910.

Hall, Michael G., Lawrence H. Leder, and Michael G. Kammen, eds. *The Glorious Revolution in America: Documents on the Colonial Crisis of 1689.* Chapel Hill: University of North Carolina Press, 1964.

Hathaway, J. R. B., ed. *North Carolina Historical and Genealogical Register.* Vols. 1–3. Edenton, N.C., 1900–1903.

Haun, Weynette P., ed. *Old Albemarle County North Carolina Book of Land Warrants and Surveys, 1681–1706.* Durham: Self-published, 1984.

——, ed. *Old Albemarle County, North Carolina: Perquimans Precinct Court Minutes, 1688–1738.* Durham: Self-published, 1980.

Hening, William W., ed. *The Statutes at Large of Virginia.* Vols. 1–2. Richmond: Franklin, 1820.

Hofmann, Margaret M., ed. *Province of North Carolina, 1663–1729, Abstracts of Land Patents.* Weldon, N.C.: Roanoke News, 1979.

James, Edward W., ed. *The Lower Norfolk County Virginia Antiquary.* Vols. 3–4. Richmond: Whittet and Shepperson, 1901–4.

Lawson, John. *A New Voyage to Carolina.* Edited and introduction by Hugh Talmage Lefler. Chapel Hill: University of North Carolina Press, 1967.

Lerner, Gerda, ed. *The Female Experience: An American Documentary.* Oxford: Oxford University Press, 1977.

Ludwell, Philip, and Nathaniel Harrison. "Boundary Line Proceedings, 1710."
   *Virginia Magazine of History and Biography* 5 (July 1897): 1–21.
McIlwaine, H. R., ed. *Executive Journals of the Council of Colonial Virginia.* Vol. 2,
   *August 3, 1669–April 27, 1705.* Richmond: Virginia State Library, 1927.
———, ed. *Executive Journals of the Council of Colonial Virginia.* Vol. 3, *May 1, 1705–*
   *October 23, 1721.* Richmond: Virginia State Library, 1928.
———, ed. *Journals of the House of Burgesses of Virginia, 1702/3–1705, 1705–1706, 1710–*
   *1712.* Richmond: Virginia State Library, 1912.
Parker, Mattie E. E., ed. *Colonial Records of North Carolina.* Vol. 2, *North Carolina*
   *Higher-Court Records, 1670–1696.* Raleigh: North Carolina Department of
   Archives and History, 1968.
———, ed. *Colonial Records of North Carolina.* Vol. 3, *North Carolina Higher-Court*
   *Records, 1697–1701.* Raleigh: North Carolina Department of Archives and
   History, 1971.
Powell, William S., ed. *Ye Countie of Albemarle in Carolina: A Collection of Documents,*
   *1664–1675.* Raleigh: North Carolina Department of Archives and History, 1958.
Price, William S., Jr., ed. *Colonial Records of North Carolina.* Vol. 4, *North Carolina*
   *Higher-Court Records, 1702–1708.* Raleigh: Department of Cultural Resources,
   North Carolina Division of Archives and History, 1974.
Salley, A. S., Jr., ed. *Narratives of Early Carolina, 1605–1708.* New York: Scribner's, 1911.
———, ed. *Commissions and Instructions from the Lords Proprietors of Carolina to Public*
   *Officials of South Carolina, 1685–1715.* Columbia, S.C.: Historical Commission of
   South Carolina, 1916.
Saunders, William L., ed. *Colonial Records of North Carolina.* Vol. 1, *1662–1712.*
   Raleigh: Hale, 1886.
———, ed. *Colonial Records of North Carolina.* Vol. 2, *1713–1728.* Raleigh: Hale, 1886.
———, ed. *Colonial Records of North Carolina.* Vol. 8, *1769–1771.* Raleigh: Hale, 1886.
———, ed. *Colonial Records of North Carolina.* Vol. 10, *1775–1776.* Raleigh: Hale, 1886.
Veale, Francis. "The Manner of Living of the North Carolinians," Dec. 19, 1730.
   Edited by Edmund and Dorothy Berkeley. *North Carolina Historical Review* 41
   (April 1964): 239–45

## Secondary Sources

### Books

Albertson, Catherine. *In Ancient Albemarle.* Raleigh: North Carolina Society,
   Daughters of the American Revolution, 1914.

Aylmer, G. E. *Rebellion or Revolution?: England, 1640–1660*. New York: Oxford University Press, 1986.

——, ed. *The Levellers in the English Revolution*. Ithaca: Cornell University Press, 1975.

Ashe, Samuel A'Court. *History of North Carolina*. Vol. 1, *From 1584 to 1783*. Greensboro, N.C.: Van Noppen, 1908.

Bailyn, Bernard. *The New England Merchants in the Seventeenth Century*. Cambridge: Harvard University Press, 1979.

Barck, Oscar T., and Hugh T. Lefler. *Colonial America*. New York: Macmillan, 1968.

Billings, Warren M. *Sir William Berkeley and the Forging of Colonial Virginia*. Baton Rouge: Louisiana State University Press, 2004.

Blanton, Dennis B., and Julia A. King, eds. *Indian and European Contact in Context: The Mid-Atlantic Region*. Gainesville: University Press of Florida, 2004.

Bond, B. W., Jr. *The Quitrent System in the American Colonies*. New Haven: Yale University Press, 1919.

Bowden, James. *The History of the Society of Friends in America*. London: Gilpin, 1850.

Brown, Kathleen M. *Good Wives, Nasty Wenches, and Anxious Patriarchs: Gender, Race, and Power in Colonial Virginia*. Chapel Hill: University of North Carolina Press, 1996.

Burnard, Trevor. *Creole Gentlemen: The Maryland Elite, 1691–1776*. New York: Routledge, 2002.

Burns, Alan. *History of the British West Indies*. London: Allan and Unwin, 1954.

Byrd, John E. *Tuscarora Subsistence Practices in the Late Woodland Period: The Zooarchaeology of the Jordan's Landing Site*. Raleigh: North Carolina Archaeological Council, 1997.

Churchill, Edwin, Emerson W. Baker, and Richard D'Abate, eds. *American Beginnings: Exploration, Culture, and Cartography in the Land of Norumbega*. Lincoln: University of Nebraska Press, 1995.

Clark, J. C. D. *Revolution and Rebellion: State and Society in England in the Seventeenth and Eighteenth Centuries*. New York: Cambridge University Press, 1986.

Craton, Michael, and Gail Saunders. *Islanders in the Stream: A History of the Bahamian People*. Vol. 1, *From Aboriginal Times to the End of Slavery*. Athens: University of Georgia Press, 1992.

Craven, Wesley F. *The Southern Colonies in the Seventeenth Century, 1607–1689*. Baton Rouge: Louisiana State University Press, 1949.

Cressy, David. *England on Edge: Crisis and Revolution, 1640–1642*. New York: Oxford University Press, 2006.

Cumming, William P. *The Southeast in Early Maps*. Princeton: Princeton University Press, 1958.

Deetz, James. *Flowerdew Hundred: The Archaeology of a Virginia Plantation, 1619–1864*. Charlottesville: University Press of Virginia, 1993.

Dickerson, Oliver M. *American Colonial Government, 1669–1765: A Study of the British Board of Trade in Relation to the American Colonies*. New York: Russell and Russell, 1962.

Ekirch, A. Roger. *"Poor Carolina": Politics and Society in Colonial North Carolina, 1729–1776*. Chapel Hill: University of North Carolina Press, 1981.

Fenn, Elizabeth, and Peter Wood. *Natives and Newcomers: The Way We Lived in North Carolina before 1770*. Chapel Hill: University of North Carolina Press, 1983.

Fischer, Kirsten. *Suspect Relations: Sex, Race, and Resistance in Colonial North Carolina*. Ithaca: Cornell University Press, 2002.

Gallay, Alan. *The Indian Slave Trade: The Rise of the English Empire in the American South, 1670–1717*. New Haven: Yale University Press, 2002.

Gallivan, Martin D. *James River Chiefdoms: The Rise of Social Inequality in the Chesapeake*. Lincoln: University of Nebraska Press, 2003.

Games, Alison. *Migration and the Origins of the English Atlantic World*. Cambridge: Harvard University Press, 1999.

George, Margaret. *Women in the First Capitalist Society: Experiences in Seventeenth-Century England*. Urbana: University of Illinois Press, 1988.

Greene, Jack P. *The Quest for Power: The Lower Houses of Assembly in the Southern Royal Colonies, 1689–1776*. Chapel Hill: University of North Carolina Press, 1963.

Greene, Jack P., Rosemary Brana-Shute, and Randy J. Sparks, eds. *Money, Trade, and Power: The Evolution of Colonial South Carolina's Plantation Society*. Columbia: University of South Carolina Press, 2001.

Gura, Philip F. *A Glimpse of Sion's Glory: Puritan Radicalism in New England, 1620–1660*. Middletown, Conn.: Wesleyan University Press, 1984.

Haley, Kenneth H. D. *The First Earl of Shaftesbury*. Oxford: Clarendon, 1968.

Hall, Michael G. *Edward Randolph and the American Colonies, 1676–1703*. Chapel Hill: University of North Carolina Press, 1960.

Hatfield, April. *Atlantic Virginia: Intercolonial Relations in the Seventeenth Century*. Philadelphia: University of Pennsylvania Press, 2004.

Hawks, Francis L. *Embracing the Period of the Proprietary Government, from 1663–1729*. Vol. 2 of *History of North Carolina, with Maps and Illustrations*. Fayetteville, N.C.: Hale, 1858.

Hill, Christopher. *The Century of Revolution, 1603–1714*. London: Routledge, 1961.

———. *The Experience of Defeat: Milton and Some Contemporaries*. London: Bookmarks, 1994.

——. *A Nation of Change and Novelty: Radical Politics, Religion, and Literature in Seventeenth-Century England*. London: Routledge, 1990.

——. *Some Intellectual Consequences of the English Revolution*. Madison: University of Wisconsin Press, 1980.

——. *The World Turned Upside Down: Radical Ideas during the English Revolution*. London: Penguin, 1975.

Holmes, Geoffrey. *The Making of a Great Power: Late Stuart and Early Georgian Britain, 1660–1722*. London: Longman, 1993.

Holton, Woody. *Forced Founders: Indians, Debtors, Slaves, and the Making of the American Revolution in Virginia*. Chapel Hill: University of North Carolina Press, 1999.

Hornsby, Stephen J. *British Atlantic, American Frontier: Spaces of Power in Early Modern British America*. Lebanon, N.H.: University Press of New England, 2005.

Hughes, Ann. *The Causes of the English Civil War*. New York: St. Martin's, 1991.

Hutton, Ronald, *The Restoration: A Political and Religious History of England and Wales, 1658–1667*. Oxford: Clarendon, 1985.

Karras, Alan L., and J. R. McNeill, eds. *Atlantic American Societies: From Columbus through Abolition*. New York: Routledge, 1992.

Kars, Marjoleine. *Breaking Loose Together: The Regulator Rebellion in Pre-Revolutionary North Carolina*. Chapel Hill: University of North Carolina Press, 2002.

Kirk, Paul W., ed. *The Great Dismal Swamp*. Charlottesville: University Press of Virginia, 1979.

Kulikoff, Allan. *From British Peasants to Colonial American Farmers*. Chapel Hill: University of North Carolina Press, 2000.

——. *Tobacco and Slaves: The Development of Southern Cultures in the Chesapeake, 1680–1800*. Chapel Hill: University of North Carolina Press, 1986.

Landsman, Ned C. *Scotland and Its First American Colony, 1683–1765*. Princeton: Princeton University Press, 1985.

Leaming, Hugo Prosper. *Hidden Americans: Maroons of Virginia and the Carolinas*. New York: Garland, 1995.

Lee, E. Lawrence. *The Lower Cape Fear in Colonial Days*. Chapel Hill: University of North Carolina Press, 1965.

Lefler, Hugh T., and William S. Powell. *Colonial North Carolina: A History*. New York: Scribner's, 1973.

Linebaugh, Peter, and Marcus Rediker, *The Many-Headed Hydra: Sailors, Slaves, Commoners, and the Hidden History of the Revolutionary Atlantic*. Boston: Beacon, 2000.

Lovejoy, David S. *The Glorious Revolution in America*. New York: Harper and Row, 1972.

Mack, Phyllis. *Visionary Women: Ecstatic Prophesy in Seventeenth-Century England*. Berkeley: University of California Press, 1992.

MacPherson, C. B. *The Political Theory of Possessive Individualism: Hobbes to Locke*. Oxford: Clarendon, 1962.

Manning, Brian. *The English People and the English Revolution*. London: Heineman, 1976.

McConville, Brendan. *These Daring Disturbers of the Public Peace: The Struggle for Property and Power in Early New Jersey*. Ithaca: Cornell University Press, 1999.

McCusker, John J., and Russell R. Menard. *The Economy of British America, 1607–1789*. Chapel Hill: University of North Carolina Press for the Institute of Early American History and Culture, 1985.

Meanley, Brooke. *The Great Dismal Swamp*. Washington, D.C.: Audubon Naturalist Society, 1973.

Merrell, James. *Into the American Woods: Negotiators on the Pennsylvania Frontier*. New York: Norton, 1999.

Merrens, Harry Roy. *Colonial North Carolina in the Eighteenth Century: A Study in Historical Geography*. Chapel Hill: University of North Carolina Press, 1964.

Moore, Rosemary. *The Light in Their Consciences: The Early Quakers in Britain, 1646–1666*. University Park: Pennsylvania State University Press, 2000.

Morgan, Edmund S. *American Slavery, American Freedom: The Ordeal of Colonial Virginia*. New York: Norton, 1975.

Mulcahy, Matthew. *Hurricanes and Society in the British Greater Caribbean, 1624–1783*. Baltimore: Johns Hopkins University Press, 2006.

Olwell, Robert. *Masters, Slaves, and Subjects: The Culture of Power in the South Carolina Low Country, 1740–1790*. Ithaca: Cornell University Press, 1998.

Olwell, Robert, and Alan Tully, eds. *Cultures and Identities in Colonial British America*. Baltimore: Johns Hopkins University Press, 2006.

Osgood, Herbert L. *The Chartered Colonies: Beginnings of Self-Government*. Vol. 2 of *The American Colonies in the Seventeenth Century*. New York: Macmillan, 1904.

Parent, Anthony S., Jr. *Foul Means: The Formation of a Slave Society in Virginia, 1660–1740*. Chapel Hill: University of North Carolina Press, 2003.

Paschal, Herbert R., Jr. *A History of Colonial Bath*. Raleigh: Edwards and Broughton, 1955.

Pestana, Carla G. *The English Atlantic in an Age of Revolution, 1640–1661*. Cambridge: Harvard University Press, 2004.

Pestana, Carla G., and Sharon V. Salinger, eds. *Inequality in Early America*. Hanover, N.H.: University Press of New England, 1999.

Pluckhahn, Thomas J., and Robbie Ethridge, eds. *Light on the Path: The Anthropology and History of the Southeastern Indians*. Tuscaloosa: University of Alabama Press, 2006.

Pocock, J. G. A., ed. *Three British Revolutions, 1641, 1688, 1776*. Princeton: Princeton University Press, 1980.

Pomfret, John. *The Province of East New Jersey: The Rebellious Proprietary, 1609–1702*. Princeton: Princeton University Press, 1962.

Powell, William S. *The Carolina Charter of 1663: How It Came to North Carolina and Its Place in History, with Biographical Sketches of the Proprietors*. Raleigh: North Carolina Department of Archives and History, 1954.

——. *North Carolina: A History*. Chapel Hill: University of North Carolina Press, 1977.

——, ed. *Dictionary of North Carolina Biography*. Vols. 1–6. Chapel Hill: University of North Carolina Press, 1979.

Price, Edward. *Dividing the Land: Early American Beginnings of Our Private Property Mosaic*. Chicago: University of Chicago Press, 1995.

Rankin, Hugh F. *The Pirates of Colonial North Carolina*. Raleigh: North Carolina Department of Archives and History, 1960.

——. *Upheaval in Albemarle: The Story of Culpeper's Rebellion, 1675–1689*. Raleigh: Carolina Charter Tercentenary Commission, 1962.

Raper, Charles Lee. *North Carolina: A Study in English Colonial Government*. New York: Macmillan, 1904.

Rediker, Marcus. *Between the Devil and the Deep Blue Sea: Merchant Seamen, Pirates, and the Anglo-American Maritime World, 1700–1750*. Cambridge: Cambridge University Press, 1987.

——. *Villains of All Nations: Atlantic Pirates in the Golden Age*. Boston: Beacon, 2004.

Richardson, R. C. *The Debate on the English Revolution Revisited*. New York: Routledge, 1988.

Roper, L. H. *Conceiving Carolina: Proprietors, Planters, and Plots, 1662–1729*. New York: Palgrave Macmillan, 2004.

Russell, Conrad, ed. *The Origins of the English Civil War*. New York: Barnes and Noble, 1973.

Sensbach, Jon F. *A Separate Canaan: The Making of an Afro-Moravian World in North Carolina, 1763–1840*. Chapel Hill: University of North Carolina Press, 1998.

Silver, Timothy. *A New Face on the Countryside: Indians, Colonists, and Slaves in South Atlantic Forests, 1500–1800*. Cambridge: Cambridge University Press, 1990.

Sirmans, M. Eugene. *Colonial South Carolina: A Political History, 1663–1763*. Chapel Hill: University of North Carolina Press, 1966.

Smith, Margaret Supplee, and Emily Herring Wilson. *North Carolina Women: Making History*. Chapel Hill: University of North Carolina Press, 1999.

Steele, Ian K. *The English Atlantic, 1675–1740: An Exploration of Communication and Community*. New York: Oxford University Press, 1986.

Stone, Lawrence. *The Causes of the English Revolution, 1529–1642*. New York: Harper and Row, 1972.

Thirsk, Joan, ed. *Chapters from the Agrarian History of England and Wales*. Vol. 2. Cambridge: Cambridge University Press, 1990.

Thomas, Hugh. *The Slave Trade: The Story of the Atlantic Slave Trade: 1440–1870*. New York: Simon and Schuster, 1997.

Underdown, David. *A Freeborn People: Politics and the Nation in Seventeenth-Century England*. New York: Clarendon, 1996.

——. *Revel, Riot, and Rebellion*. Oxford: Clarendon, 1985.

Watson, Alan D. *Perquimans County: A Brief History*. Raleigh: Department of Cultural Resources, North Carolina Division of Archives and History, 1987.

——. *Society in Colonial North Carolina*. Raleigh: Department of Cultural Resources, North Carolina Division of Archives and History, 1996.

Webb, Stephen Saunders. *1676: The End of American Independence*. New York: Knopf, 1984.

——. *Lord Churchill's Coup: The Anglo-American Empire and the Glorious Revolution Reconsidered*. New York: Knopf, 1995.

Weeks, Stephen B. *Southern Quakers and Slavery: A Study in Institutional History*. Baltimore: Johns Hopkins University Press, 1896.

——. *William Drummond, the Governor of North Carolina, 1664–1667*. New York: National History, 1892.

Weir, Robert. *Colonial South Carolina: A History*. New York: KTO, 1983.

Winslow, Ellen G. *History of Perquimans County: As Compiled from Records Found There and Elsewhere*. Raleigh: Edwards and Broughton, 1931.

Wood, Bradford J. *This Remote Part of The World: Regional Formation in Lower Cape Fear, North Carolina, 1725–1775*. Columbia: University of South Carolina Press, 2004.

Wood, Peter H. *Black Majority: Negroes in Colonial South Carolina from 1670 through the Stono Rebellion*. New York: Norton, 1974.

## Articles

Bassett, John S. "Landholding in the Colony of North Carolina." *Trinity College Historical Society Papers* (1898), series 2, 44–61.

Beiler, Rosalind J. "German-Speaking Immigrants in the British Atlantic World,

1680–1730." *Organization of American Historians Magazine of History* 18, no. 3 (Apr. 2004): 19–22.

Billings, Warren M. "Sir William Berkeley and the Carolina Proprietary." *North Carolina Historical Review* 72, no. 3 (July 1995): 329–42.

Butler, Lindley S. "The Governors of Albemarle County, 1663–1689." *North Carolina Historical Review* 46 (July 1969): 281–99.

Clonts, F. W. "Travel and Transportation in Colonial North Carolina." *North Carolina Historical Review* 3, no. 1 (Jan. 1926): 16–35.

Cumming, William P. "The Earliest Permanent Settlement in Carolina: Nathaniel Batts and the Cumberford Map." *American Historical Review* 45, no. 1 (Oct. 1939): 82–89.

Dawdy, Shannon Lee. "The Meherrin's Secret History of the Dividing Line." *North Carolina Historical Review* 72, no. 4 (Oct. 1995): 387–415.

Gallman, James M. "Determinants of Age at Marriage in Colonial Perquimans County, North Carolina." *William and Mary Quarterly*, 3rd ser., 39, no. 1 (Jan. 1982): 176–91.

Gallman, Robert E. "Changes in the Level of Literacy in a New Community of Early America." *Journal of Economic History* 48, no. 3 (Sept. 1988): 567–82.

———. "Influences on the Distribution of Landholdings in Early Colonial North Carolina." *Journal of Economic History* 42, no. 3 (Sept. 1982): 549–75.

Garrow, Patrick H. "The Mattamuskeet Documents: A Study in Social History." *Carolina Comments*, Mar. 1977.

Hall, Michael G. "The House of Lords, Edward Randolph, and the Navigation Act of 1696." *William and Mary Quarterly*, 3rd ser., 14, no. 4 (Oct. 1957): 494–515.

Laslet, Peter. "John Locke, the Great Recoinage, and the Origins of the Board of Trade, 1695–1698." *William and Mary Quarterly*, 3rd ser., 14, no. 3 (July 1957): 370–402.

Lee, Wayne. "Fortify, Fight, or Flee: Tuscarora and Cherokee Defensive Warfare and Military Culture Adaptation." *Journal of Military History* 68, no. 3 (July 2004): 713–70.

Margolin, Samuel G. " 'Contrary to All Law and Justice': The Unauthorized Salvage of Stranded and Sunken Vessels in the Greater Chesapeake, 1698–1750." *North Carolina Historical Review* 72, no. 1 (Jan. 1995): 1–29.

Mook, Maurice A. "Algonkian Ethnohistory of Carolina Sound." *Journal of the Washington Academy of Sciences* 34, no. 6 (June 1944): 181–96.

Morgan, L. N. "Land Tenure in Proprietary North Carolina." *James Sprunt Historical Publications* 12, no. 1 (1913): 43–63.

Parramore, Thomas C. "The Tuscarora Ascendancy." *North Carolina Historical Review* 59, no. 4 (Oct. 1982): 307–26.

——. "With Tuscarora Jack on the Back Path to Bath." *North Carolina Historical Review* 64, no. 2 (Apr. 1987): 115–38.

Perkin, H. J. "The Social Causes of the British Industrial Revolution." *Transactions of the Royal Historical Society* 18 (1968): 127–35.

Spindel, Donna J. "Women's Civil Actions in the North Carolina Higher Courts, 1670–1730." *North Carolina Historical Review* 71, no. 2 (Apr. 1994): 151–73.

Spindel, Donna J., and Stuart W. Thomas Jr. "Crime and Society in North Carolina, 1663–1740." *Journal of Southern History* 49, no. 2 (May 1983): 223–44.

Steele, Ian K. "The Board of Trade, the Quakers, and Resumption of Colonial Charters, 1699–1702." *William and Mary Quarterly*, 3rd ser., 23, no. 4 (Oct. 1966): 596–619.

Watson, Alan D. "The Quitrent System in Royal South Carolina." *William and Mary Quarterly*, 3rd ser., 33, no. 2 (Apr. 1976): 183–211.

Webb, Stephen Saunders. "The Data and Theory of Restoration Empire." *William and Mary Quarterly*, 3rd ser., 43, no. 3 (July 1986): 431–59.

Williams, Justin. "English Mercantilism and Carolina Naval Stores, 1705–1776." *Journal of Southern History* 1, no. 2 (May 1935): 169–85.

## *Theses and Dissertations*

Beeth, Howard. "Outside Agitators in Southern History: The Society of Friends, 1656–1800." Ph.D. diss., University of Houston, 1984.

Chaffin, Nora C. "The Colonial Land System in North Carolina, 1578–1754." Master's thesis, Duke University, 1930.

Fagg, Daniel W. "Carolina 1663–1683: The Founding of a Proprietary." Ph.D. diss., Emory University, 1970.

Lowry, Charles B. "Class, Politics, Rebellion, and Regional Development in Proprietary North Carolina (1697–1720)." Ph.D. diss., University of Florida, 1979.

Paschal, Herbert R., Jr. "Proprietary North Carolina: A Study in Colonial Government." Ph.D. diss., University of North Carolina, Chapel Hill, 1961.

Suttlemyre, Charles Greer, Jr. "Proprietary Policy and the Development of North Carolina, 1663–1729." Ph.D. diss., Oxford University, 1991.

Wolf, Jacquelyn H. "The Proud and the Poor: The Social Organization of Leadership in Proprietary North Carolina, 1663–1729." Ph.D. diss., University of Pennsylvania, 1977.

# INDEX